Teach Your VISUALLY

Excel 365

by Paul McFedries

Visual
A Wiley Brand

Teach Yourself VISUALLY™ Excel 365

Copyright © 2023 by John Wiley & Sons, Inc. All rights reserved.

Published by John Wiley & Sons, Inc., Hoboken, New Jersey.

Published simultaneously in Canada.

ISBN: 978-1-119-93362-5

ISBN: 978-1-119-93363-2 (ebk.)

ISBN: 978-1-119-93364-9 (ebk.)

SKY10035763_081822

For general information on our other products and services or for technical support, please contact our Customer Care Department within the United States at (800) 762-2974, outside the United States at (317) 572-3993 or fax (317) 572-4002.

If you believe you've found a mistake in this book, please bring it to our attention by emailing our Reader Support team at wileysupport@ wiley.com with the subject line "Possible Book Errata Submission."

Wiley also publishes its books in a variety of electronic formats. Some content that appears in print may not be available in electronic formats. For more information about Wiley products, visit our web site at www. wiley.com.

Library of Congress Control Number: 2022939049

Cover images: © 200degrees/Getty Images; Screenshot Courtesy of Paul McFedries

Cover design: Wiley

About the Author

Paul McFedries is a full-time technical writer. He has been authoring computer books since 1991 and has more than 100 books to his credit. Paul's books have sold more than 4 million copies worldwide. These books include the Wiley titles *Teach Yourself VISUALLY Microsoft 365*, *Teach Yourself VISUALLY Microsoft Windows 11*, *Microsoft Excel All-in-One For Dummies*, and *Microsoft Excel Data Analysis For Dummies, Fifth Edition*. Paul invites you to drop by his personal website at www.paulmcfedries.com or follow him on Twitter @paulmcf or on Facebook at www.facebook.com/PaulMcFedries.

Author's Acknowledgments

It goes without saying that writers focus on text, and I certainly enjoyed focusing on the text that you will read in this book. However, this book is more than just the usual collection of words and phrases designed to educate and stimulate the mind. A quick thumb through the pages will show you that this book is also chock-full of treats for the eye, including copious screenshots, beautiful colors, and sharp fonts. Those sure make for a beautiful book, and that beauty comes from a lot of hard work by the production team at Straive. Of course, what you read in this book must also be accurate, logically presented, and free of errors. Ensuring all of this was an excellent group of editors that I got to work with directly, including project manager Lynn Northrup, technical editor Joyce Nielsen, content refinement specialist Archana Pragash, copyeditor Elizabeth Welch, and managing editor Christine O'Connor. Thanks to all of you for your exceptional competence and hard work. Thanks, as well, to associate publisher Jim Minatel for asking me to write this book.

How to Use This Book

Who This Book Is For

This book is for the reader who has never used this particular technology or software application. It is also for readers who want to expand their knowledge.

The Conventions in This Book

① Steps

This book uses a step-by-step format to guide you easily through each task. **Numbered steps** are actions you must do; **bulleted steps** clarify a point, step, or optional feature; and **indented steps** give you the result.

② Notes

Notes give additional information — special conditions that may occur during an operation, a situation that you want to avoid, or a cross-reference to a related area of the book.

③ Icons and Buttons

Icons and buttons show you exactly what you need to click to perform a step.

④ Tips

Tips offer additional information, including warnings and shortcuts.

⑤ Bold

Bold type shows command names, options, and text or numbers you must type.

⑥ Italics

Italic type introduces and defines a new term.

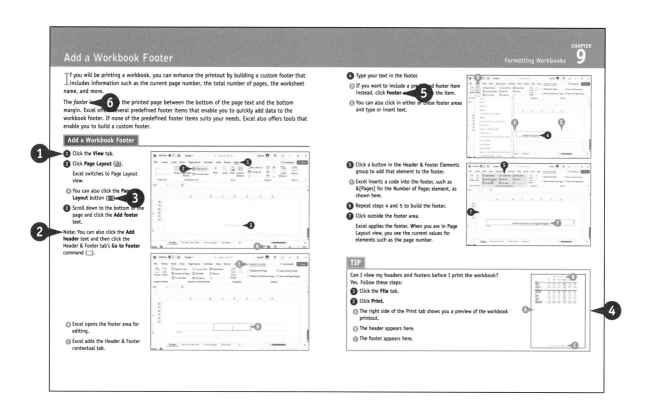

Table of Contents

Chapter 1 Getting Started with Excel

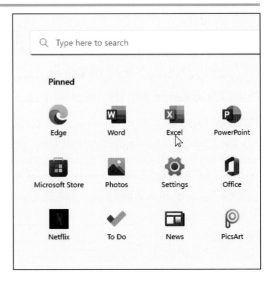

Chapter 2 Entering Data

Chapter 3   Working with Ranges

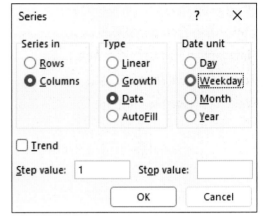

Chapter 4   Working with Range Names

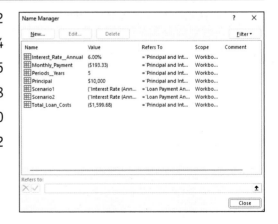

Table of Contents

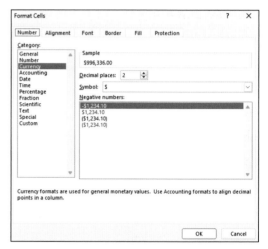

Chapter 7   Manipulating Worksheets

Chapter 8   Dealing with Workbooks

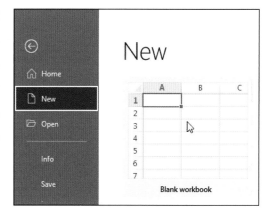

Table of Contents

Chapter 9 Formatting Workbooks

Chapter 10 Importing Data into Excel

Chapter 11 Working with Tables

Chapter 12 Analyzing with PivotTables

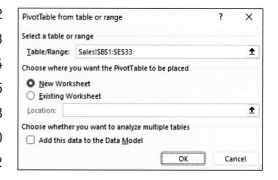

Table of Contents

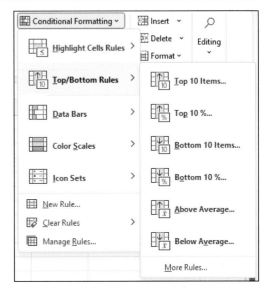

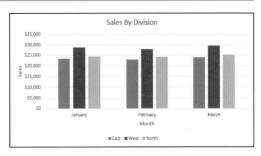

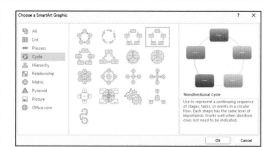

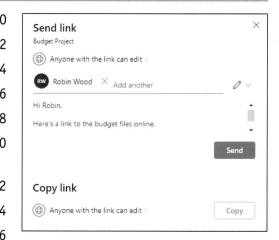

CHAPTER 1

Getting Started with Excel

You use Microsoft Excel to create *spreadsheets,* which are documents that enable you to manipulate numbers and formulas to quickly create powerful mathematical, financial, and statistical models. In this chapter you get some background about Excel, learn how to access the desktop and online versions of the program, and take a tour of the program's features.

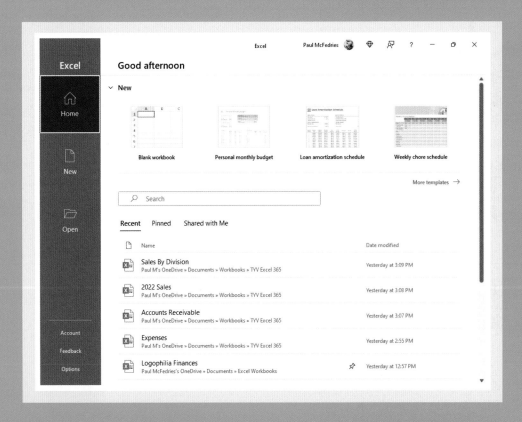

Getting to Know Excel

Working with Excel involves two basic tasks: building a spreadsheet and then manipulating the data on the spreadsheet. Building a spreadsheet involves adding data such as numbers and text, creating formulas that run calculations, and adding functions that perform specific tasks. Manipulating spreadsheet data involves calculating totals, adding data series, organizing data into tables, and visualizing data with charts.

This section gives you an overview of these tasks. You learn about each task in greater detail as you work through the book.

Build a Spreadsheet

Add Data

You can insert numbers, text, and other characters into any cell in the spreadsheet. Click the cell that you want to work with and then type your data. Your typing appears in the cell that you selected, as well as in the formula bar, which is the large text box above the column letters. When you are done, press Enter. To edit existing cell data, click the cell and then edit the text in the formula bar.

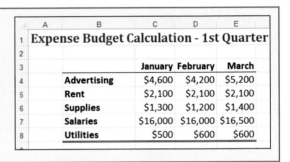

Add a Formula

A *formula* is a collection of numbers, cell addresses, and mathematical operators that performs a calculation. In Excel, you enter a formula in a cell by typing an equal sign (=) and then the formula text. For example, the formula =B1 – B2 subtracts the value in cell B2 from the value in cell B1.

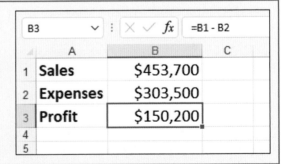

Add a Function

A *function* is a predefined formula that performs a specific task. For example, the AVERAGE function calculates the average of a list of numbers, and the PMT function calculates a loan or mortgage payment. You can use functions on their own, preceded by =, or as part of a larger formula. Click **Insert Function** (*fx*) to see a list of the available functions.

Manipulate Data

Calculate Totals Quickly

If you just need a quick sum of a list of numbers, click a cell below the numbers and then click the **Sum** button ($\sum$), which is available in the Home tab of the Excel Ribbon. You can also select the cells that you want to sum, and their total appears in the status bar.

	A	B	C	D	E	F
1	Expense Budget Calculation - 1st Quarter					
2						
3			January	February	March	
4		Advertising	$4,600	$4,200	$5,200	
5		Rent	$2,100	$2,100	$2,100	
6		Supplies	$1,300	$1,200	$1,400	
7		Salaries	$16,000	$16,000	$16,500	
8		Utilities	$500	$600	$600	
9		TOTAL	=SUM(C4:C8)			
10						

Fill a Series

Excel enables you to save time by completing a series of values automatically. For example, if you need to enter the numbers 1 to 100 in consecutive cells, you can enter just the first few numbers, select the cells, and then click and drag the lower-right corner to fill in the rest of the numbers. With Excel you can also fill in dates, as well as the names for weekdays and months.

	A	B	C
1	January		
2	February		
3	March		
4	April		
5	May		
6	June		
7	July		
8	August		
9	September	October	
10	October		
11			

Manage Tables

The row-and-column format of a spreadsheet makes Excel suitable for simple databases called *tables*. Each column becomes a field in the table, and each row is a record. You can sort the records, filter the records to show only certain values, and add subtotals.

Account Name	Account Number	Invoice Number	Invoice Amount	Due Date
Door Stoppers Ltd.	01-0045	117328	$58.50	2/2/2023
Door Stoppers Ltd.	01-0045	117319	$78.85	1/16/2023
Door Stoppers Ltd.	01-0045	117324	$101.01	1/26/2023
Door Stoppers Ltd.	01-0045	117333	$1,685.74	2/11/2023
Chimera Illusions	02-0200	117334	$303.65	2/12/2023
Chimera Illusions	02-0200	117350	$456.21	3/15/2023
Chimera Illusions	02-0200	117345	$588.88	3/6/2023

Add a Chart

A *chart* is a graphic representation of spreadsheet data. As the data in the spreadsheet changes, the chart automatically changes to reflect the new numbers. Excel offers a wide variety of charts, including bar charts, line charts, and pie charts.

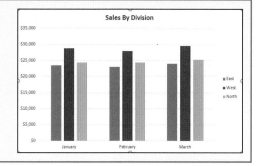

5

Start Excel on the Desktop

Before you can perform tasks such as adding data and building formulas, you must first start the desktop version of Excel. This brings the Excel window onto the Windows desktop, and you can then begin using the program. In this section, you learn how to start Excel in Windows 11, but the steps are similar if you are using Windows 10.

This task assumes that you have already installed Excel 365 on your computer. If you prefer to use Excel on the web, see the next section, "Navigate to Excel for the Web."

Start Excel on the Desktop

1 Click **Start** (![icon]).

The Start menu appears.

2 Click **Excel.**

The Microsoft Excel window appears on the desktop.

Note: Click **Blank workbook** to open a new Excel file.

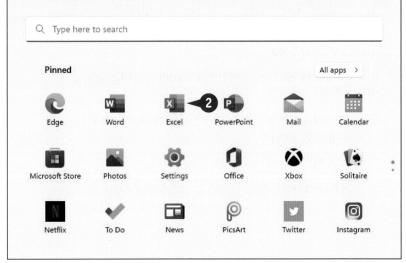

6

Navigate to Excel for the Web

Ｉf you want to work with Excel online instead of on the desktop, you need to know how to use your web browser to navigate to the Excel for the web version of the program.

With your Microsoft 365 subscription, you get access to both the desktop and online versions of each app, including Excel. This book uses the desktop version of Excel for its example screens. Fortunately, Excel for the web uses the same layout as the desktop version and offers mostly the same features, so everything you learn in this book applies to Excel for the web.

Navigate to Excel for the Web

1 Click **Start**.

The Start menu appears.

2 Click **Edge**.

Ⓐ If you have Edge pinned to the Windows taskbar, click the **Edge** icon (🔵) instead of following steps **1** and **2**.

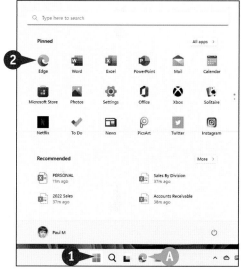

The Microsoft Edge web browser window appears.

Note: If you prefer to use a different web browser, start that browser instead of Edge.

3 In the address bar, type www.office.com/launch/excel and press Enter.

4 If prompted, enter your Microsoft 365 username and password (not shown).

The Excel for the web app appears.

Note: Click **New blank workbook** to open a new Excel file.

Tour the Excel Window

To get up to speed quickly with Excel, it helps to understand the various elements of the Excel window. These include standard window elements such as the title bar, window controls, and status bar; Office-specific elements such as the Ribbon and File tab; and Excel-specific elements such as the worksheet.

If you are using Excel for the web, note that the window you see is nearly identical to the Excel desktop window. The main exception is that, by default, Excel for the web displays a simplified version of the Ribbon.

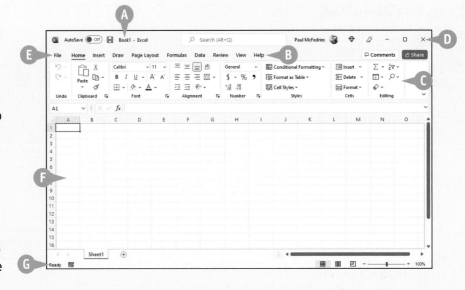

Ⓐ Title Bar

The title bar displays the name of the current workbook.

Ⓑ Ribbon Tabs

You use these controls to display different sets of Ribbon commands.

Ⓒ Ribbon

This area gives you access to all the Excel commands, options, and features. To learn how to use this element, see the following section, "Work with the Excel Ribbon."

Ⓓ Workbook Window Controls

You use these controls to minimize, maximize, restore, and close the current workbook window.

Ⓔ File Tab

Click this tab to access file-related commands, such as Save and Open.

Ⓕ Worksheet

This area displays the current worksheet, and it is where you will do most of your Excel work.

Ⓖ Status Bar

This area displays messages about the current status of Excel, the results of certain operations, and other information.

Work with the Excel Ribbon

You use the Ribbon to access all the features, commands, and options in Excel. The Ribbon is organized into tabs, such as Home, Insert, and Page Layout, and each tab contains a collection of related controls. For example, the Insert tab contains controls related to inserting objects into a worksheet, while the Formulas tab contains controls related to building formulas. Each tab usually includes buttons, lists, and check boxes.

The File tab is a bit different because it displays the Backstage view, which contains controls related to working with Excel files, such as opening, saving, and printing them.

Work with the Excel Ribbon

1 Click the tab that contains the Excel feature you want to work with.

Excel displays the controls in the tab.

Ⓐ Each tab is organized into groups of related controls.

Ⓑ In many groups you can click the dialog box launcher button (🖾) to display a dialog box that contains group settings.

2 Click the control for the feature.

Ⓒ If the control displays a list of options, click the option you want.

Excel runs the command or sets the option.

Note: By default, Excel for the web displays a simplified Ribbon. To see the full Ribbon, click the **Switch Ribbon** icon (∨) on the far right of the simplified Ribbon.

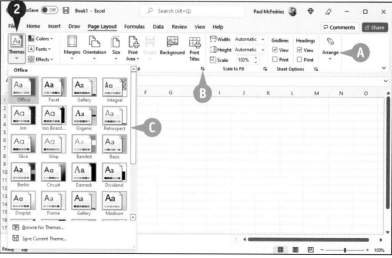

CHAPTER 2

Entering Data

Are you ready to start building a spreadsheet? To create a spreadsheet in Excel, you must know how to enter data into the worksheet cells, and how to edit that data to fix typos, adjust information, and remove data you no longer need.

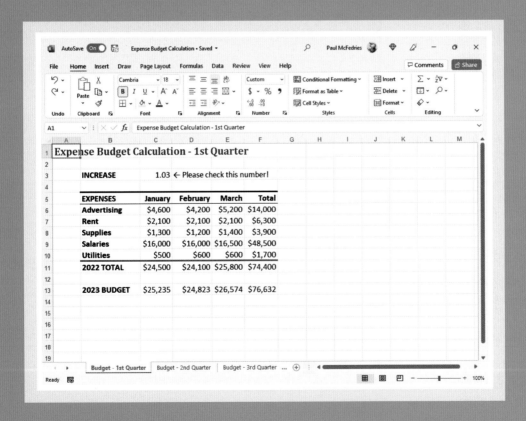

Learning the Layout of a Worksheet

In Excel, a spreadsheet file is called a *workbook*, and each workbook consists of one or more *worksheets*. These worksheets are where you enter your data and formulas, so you need to know the layout of a typical worksheet.

In particular, you need to know that worksheets are laid out in *rows* and *columns*, that a *cell* is the intersection of a row and column that has its own unique address, and that a *range* is a collection of cells. You also need to be familiar with *worksheet tabs* and the Excel *mouse pointer*.

A Cell

A *cell* is a box in which you enter your spreadsheet data.

B Column

A *column* is a vertical line of cells. Each column has a unique letter that identifies it. For example, the leftmost column is A, and the next column is B.

C Row

A *row* is a horizontal line of cells. Each row has a unique number that identifies it. For example, the topmost row is 1, and the next row is 2.

D Cell Address

Each cell has its own *address,* which is determined by the letter and number of the intersecting column and row. For example, the cell at the intersection of column C and row 10 has the address C10.

E Range

A *range* is a rectangular grouping of two or more cells. The range is indicated by the address of the top-left cell and the address of the bottom-right cell. H11:K15 is an example of a range of cells, and it refers to all the cells within the rectangle from column H, row 11 to column K, row 15.

F Worksheet Tab

The *worksheet tab* displays the worksheet name. Most workbooks contain multiple worksheets, and you use the tabs to navigate between the worksheets.

G Mouse Pointer

Use the Excel mouse pointer (⬥) to select cells.

Understanding the Types of Data You Can Use

Y ou might think that Excel would accept only numeric input, but it is actually much more flexible than that. So, to build a spreadsheet in Excel, you should understand the different types of data that Excel accepts. There are three main types of data that you can enter into a cell: text, numbers, and dates and times. Excel places no restrictions on where or how often you can enter these types of data on a worksheet.

Text

Text entries can include any combination of letters, symbols, and numbers. You will mostly use text to describe the contents of your worksheets. This is very important because even a modest-sized spreadsheet can become a confusing jumble of numbers without some kind of text guidelines to keep things straight. Most text entries are usually labels such as *Sales* or *Territory* that make a worksheet easier to read. However, text entries can also be text or number combinations for items such as phone numbers and account codes.

Account Name	Account Number
Door Stoppers Ltd.	01-0045
Door Stoppers Ltd.	01-0045
Door Stoppers Ltd.	01-0045
Door Stoppers Ltd.	01-0045
Chimera Illusions	02-0200
Chimera Illusions	02-0200
Chimera Illusions	02-0200
Chimera Illusions	02-0200
Renaud & Son	07-0025
Renaud & Son	07-0025
Renaud & Son	07-0025
Rooter Office Solvents	07-4441
Reston Solicitor Offices	07-4441

Numbers

Numbers are the most common type of Excel data. The numbers you enter into a cell can be dollar values, weights, interest rates, temperatures, or any other numerical quantity. In most cases you just type the number that you want to appear in the cell. However, you can also precede a number with a dollar sign ($) or other currency symbol to indicate a monetary value, or follow a number with a percent sign (%) to indicate a percentage value.

Loan Amortization

Period	Payment	Interest	Principal
1	(299.71)	(41.67)	(258.04)
2	(299.71)	(40.59)	(259.12)
3	(299.71)	(39.51)	(260.20)
4	(299.71)	(38.43)	(261.28)
5	(299.71)	(37.34)	(262.37)
6	(299.71)	(36.25)	(263.46)
7	(299.71)	(35.15)	(264.56)
8	(299.71)	(34.05)	(265.66)
9	(299.71)	(32.94)	(266.77)
10	(299.71)	(31.83)	(267.88)
11	(299.71)	(30.71)	(269.00)

Dates and Times

Date entries appear in spreadsheets that include dated information, such as invoices and sales. You can either type out the full date (such as August 23, 2023) or use either the forward slash (/) or the hyphen (-) as a date separator (such as 8/23/2023 or 8-23-2023). Note that the order in which you enter the date values depends on your regional settings. For example, in the United States the format is month/day/year. For time values, you use a colon (:) as a time separator, followed by either a.m. or p.m., such as 9:15 a.m.

	Current Date	20-Mar-23

Due Date	Date Paid	Days Overdue
2/2/2023		
1/16/2023	1/16/2023	
1/26/2023		
2/11/2023		37
2/12/2023	2/16/2023	
3/15/2023		5
3/6/2023	3/6/2023	
1/14/2023		65
2/8/2023		40
4/9/2023		
2/13/2023		35
2/15/2023	3/2/2023	

Enter Text into a Cell

Your first step when building a spreadsheet is usually to enter the text data that defines the spreadsheet's labels or headings. Most labels appear in the cell to the right or above where the data will appear, whereas most headings appear above a column of data or to the left of a row of data.

Note, however, that you do not have to use text for just labels and headings. You can also enter text as data, such as a database of book or movie names. You can also write short notes that explain sections of the worksheet, and add reminders to yourself or others about missing data or other worksheet to-do items.

Enter Text into a Cell

1 Click the cell in which you want to enter the text.

A Excel marks the current cell by surrounding it with a thick, green border.

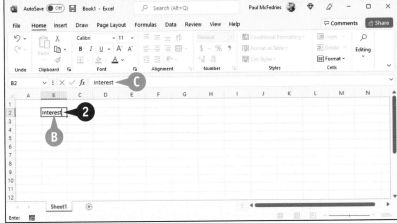

2 Start typing your text.

B Excel opens the cell for editing and displays the text as you type.

C Your typing also appears in the formula bar.

Note: Rather than typing the text directly into the cell, you can also type the text into the formula bar.

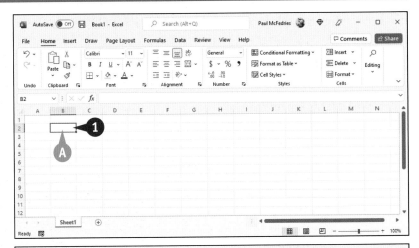

③ When your text entry is complete, press **Enter**.

Ⓓ If you do not want Excel to move the selection, you can instead either click **Enter** (✓) or press **Ctrl** + **Enter**.

Ⓔ Excel closes the cell for editing.

Ⓕ If you pressed **Enter**, Excel moves the selection to the cell below.

Ⓖ If your text is longer than the cell width, Excel either extends the text into the cell to the right (if that cell is empty, as shown here) or temporarily truncates the display of the text (if the cell to the right is not empty). To learn how to widen a column, see Chapter 5.

TIPS

When I press Enter, the selection moves to the next cell down. Can I make the selection move to the right instead?
Yes. When you have finished adding the data to the cell, press ⮕. This tells Excel to close the current cell for editing and move the selection to the next cell on the right. If you prefer to move left instead, press ⬅; if you prefer to move up, press ⬆.

When I start typing text into a cell, why does Excel sometimes display the text from another cell?
This is part of an Excel feature called AutoComplete. If the letters you type at the start of a cell match the contents of another cell in the same column, Excel fills in the full text from the other cell under the assumption that you are repeating the text in the new cell. If you want to use the text, click ✓ or press **Enter**; otherwise, just keep typing your text.

Enter a Number into a Cell

Excel's forte is crunching numbers, so most of your worksheets will include numeric values. Although you will often use numbers by themselves as part of a database or table, many of the numbers you enter will be used as the inputs for the formulas you build, as described in Chapter 6.

You can enter whole numbers (such as 5 or 1,024), decimals (such as 0.25 or 3.14), negative numbers (such as –10 or –6.2), percentages (such as 6% or 25.9%), and currency values (such as $0.25 or $24.99). To get the most out of Excel, you need to know how to enter these numeric values.

Enter a Number into a Cell

1 Click the cell in which you want to enter the number.

A Excel marks the current cell by surrounding it with a thick, green border.

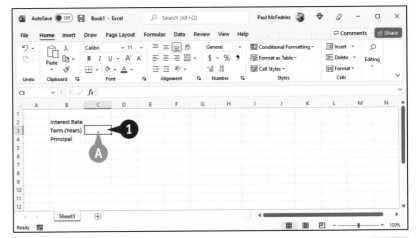

2 Start typing your number.

B Excel opens the cell for editing and displays the number as you type.

C Your typing also appears in the formula bar.

Note: Rather than typing the number directly into the cell, you can also type the number into the formula bar.

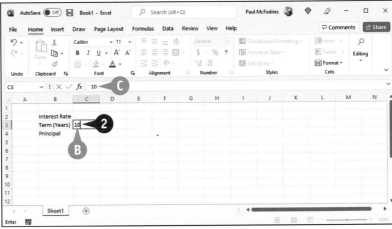

3 When your number is complete, press **Enter**.

D If you do not want Excel to move the selection, you can instead either click **Enter** (✓) or press **Ctrl**+**Enter**.

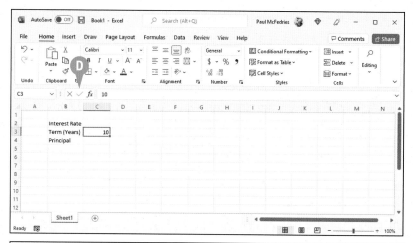

E Excel closes the cell for editing.

F To enter a percentage value, type the number followed by a percent sign (%).

G To enter a currency value, type the dollar sign ($) followed by the number.

TIPS

Can I use symbols such as a comma, decimal point, or minus sign when I enter a numeric value?

Yes. If your numeric value is in the thousands, you can include the thousands separator (,) within the number. For example, if you enter **10000**, Excel displays the value as 10000; however, if you enter **10,000**, Excel displays the value as 10,000, which is easier to read. If your numeric value includes one or more decimals, you can include the decimal point when you type the value. If your numeric value is negative, precede the value with a minus sign.

Is there a quick way to repeat a number rather than entering the entire number all over again?

Yes. Excel offers a few methods for doing this. The easiest method is to select the cell directly below the value you want to repeat and then press **Ctrl**+'. Excel adds the value to the cell. For another method, see "Fill a Range with the Same Data" in Chapter 3.

Enter a Date or Time into a Cell

Many Excel worksheets use dates and times either as part of the sheet data or for use in calculations, such as the number of days an invoice is overdue. For these and similar uses, you need to know how to enter date and time values into a cell.

The date format you use depends on your location. In the United States, for example, you can use the month/day/year format (such as 8/23/2023). The time format also depends on your location, but the general format for entering a time is hour:minute:second followed by am or pm (such as 3:15:30 pm).

Enter a Date or Time into a Cell

Enter a Date

1 Click the cell in which you want to enter the date.

A Excel marks the current cell by surrounding it with a thick, green border.

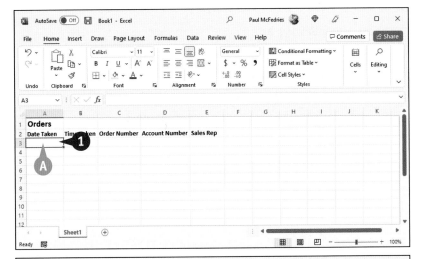

2 Type the date.

Note: See the following tip to learn which date formats your version of Excel accepts.

3 When your date is complete, press **Enter**.

B If you do not want Excel to move the selection, you can instead either click **Enter** (✓) or press **Ctrl** + **Enter**.

Excel closes the cell for editing.

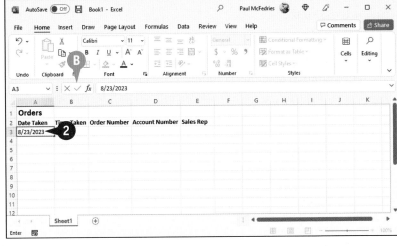

Enter a Time

1 Click the cell in which you want to enter the time.

C Excel marks the current cell by surrounding it with a thick, green border.

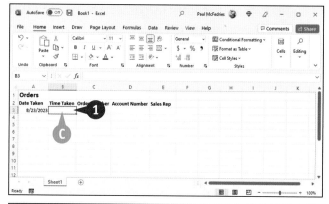

2 Type the time.

Note: See the following tip to learn which time formats your version of Excel accepts.

3 When your time is complete, press Enter.

D If you do not want Excel to move the selection, you can instead either click **Enter** (✓) or press Ctrl + Enter.

Excel closes the cell for editing.

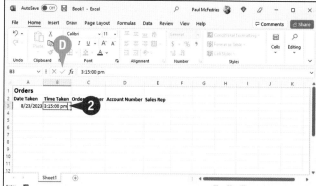

TIP

How can I tell which date and time formats my version of Excel accepts?

Follow these steps:

1 Click the **Home** tab.

2 Click the dialog box launcher (⌄) in the bottom-right corner of the **Number** group.

3 Click the **Number** tab.

4 Click **Date**.

5 Click the **Locale (location)** drop-down arrow (⌄) and then click your location.

6 Examine the **Type** list to see the formats you can use to enter dates.

7 Click **Time**.

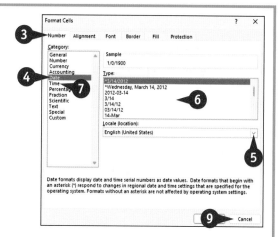

8 Examine the **Type** list to see the formats you can use to enter times.

9 Click **Cancel**.

Edit Cell Data

The data that you enter into a worksheet cell is not set in stone after you press Enter or click ✓. Whether you entered text, numbers, dates, or times, if the data you typed into a cell has changed or is incorrect, you can edit the data to update or fix the information. You can edit cell data either directly in the cell or by using the formula bar.

Edit Cell Data

1 Click the cell in which you want to edit the text.

Note: If you want to replace the entire entry, you can skip to step **3** and just start typing the new entry.

2 Press **F2**.

You can also double-click the cell you want to edit.

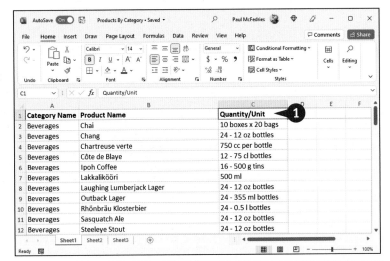

A Excel opens the cell for editing and moves the cursor to the end of the existing data.

B Excel displays Edit in the status bar.

C You can also click inside the formula bar and edit the cell data there.

3 Make your changes to the cell data.

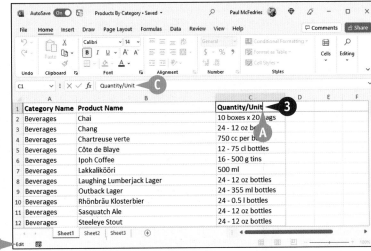

④ When you finish editing the data, press **Enter**.

Ⓓ If you do not want Excel to move the selection, you can instead either click **Enter** (✓) or press **Ctrl**+**Enter**.

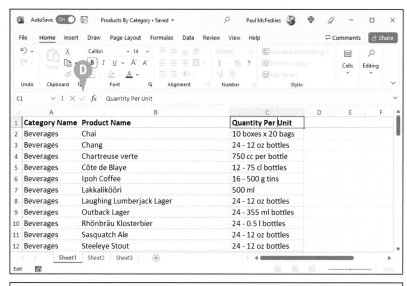

Ⓔ Excel closes the cell for editing.

Ⓕ If you pressed **Enter**, Excel moves the selection to the cell below.

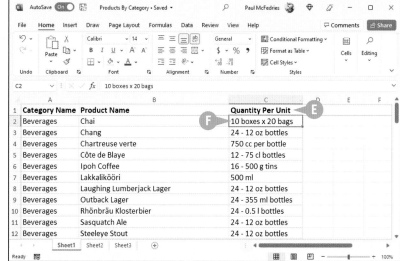

TIPS

Is there a faster way to open a cell for editing?

Yes. Move the mouse (✛) over the cell you want to edit and center the ✛ over the character where you want to start editing. Double-click the mouse. Excel opens the cell for editing and positions the cursor at the spot where you double-clicked.

I made a mistake when I edited a cell. Do I have to fix the text manually?

Most likely not. If the cell edit was the last action you performed in Excel, press **Ctrl**+**Z** or click the Home tab's **Undo** button (↶). If you have performed other actions in the meantime, click **Undo** (↶) and then click the edit in the list that appears. Note, however, that doing this also undoes the other actions you performed after the edit.

Delete Data from a Cell

If your worksheet has a cell that contains data you no longer need, you can delete that data. This helps to reduce worksheet clutter, ensures that your worksheet does not contain erroneous or unnecessary data, and makes your worksheet easier to read.

If you want to delete data from multiple cells, you must first select those cells; see "Select a Range" in Chapter 3. To delete cells and not just the data, see "Delete a Range" in Chapter 3.

Delete Data from a Cell

Delete Cell Data

1 Select the cell that contains the data you want to delete.

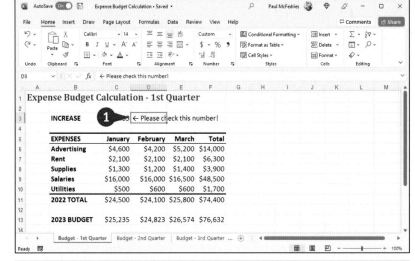

2 Click the **Home** tab.

3 Click **Clear** (◇ ˅).

4 Click **Clear Contents**.

Note: You can also delete cell data by pressing Delete .

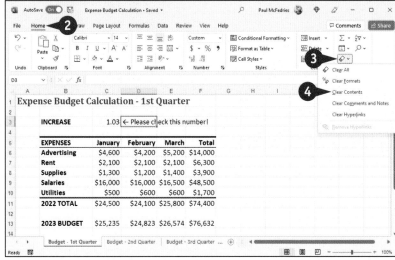

Ⓐ Excel removes the cell data.

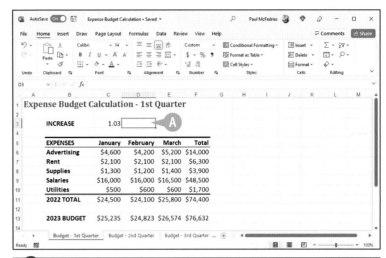

Undo Cell Data Deletion

❶ Click the **Home** tab.

❷ Click the **Undo** drop-down arrow (∨).

❸ Click **Clear**.

Note: If the data deletion was the most recent action you performed, you can undo it by pressing Ctrl + Z or by clicking **Undo** (↺).

Excel restores the data to the cell.

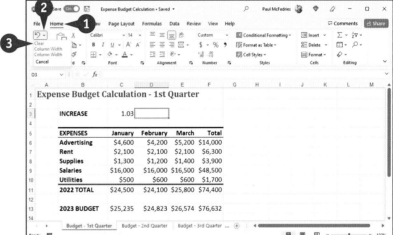

When I delete cell data, Excel keeps the cell formatting intact. Is it possible to delete the data and the formatting?

Yes. Excel offers a command that deletes everything from a cell. First, select the cell with the data and formatting that you want to delete. Click **Home**, click **Clear** (✦ ∨), and then click **Clear All**. Excel removes both the data and the formatting from the selected cell.

Is it possible to delete just a cell's formatting?

Yes. Excel offers a command that deletes just the cell formatting while leaving the cell data intact. Select the cell with the formatting that you want to delete. Click **Home**, click **Clear** (✦ ∨), and then click **Clear Formats**. Excel removes just the formatting from the selected cell.

CHAPTER 3

Working with Ranges

In Excel, a *range* is a collection of two or more cells that you work with as a group rather than separately. This enables you to fill the range with values, move or copy the range, merge the range cells, and insert and delete ranges. You learn these and other range techniques in this chapter.

Select a Range

To work with a range in Excel, you must first select the cells that you want to include in the range. After you select the range, you can fill it with data, move or copy it to another part of the worksheet, format the cells, and perform the other range-related tasks that you learn about in this chapter.

You can select a range as a rectangular group of cells, as a collection of individual cells, or as an entire row or column.

Select a Range

Select a Rectangular Range

1 Position the mouse (✛) over the first cell you want to include in the range.

2 Click and drag the ✛ over the cells that you want to include in the range.

A Excel selects the cells.

3 Release the mouse button.

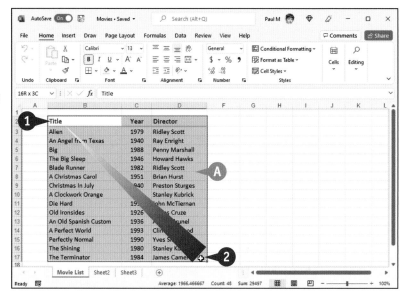

Select a Range of Individual Cells

1 Click in the first cell that you want to include in the range.

2 Hold down Ctrl and click in each of the other cells that you want to include in the range.

B Each time you click in a cell, Excel adds it to the range.

3 Release Ctrl.

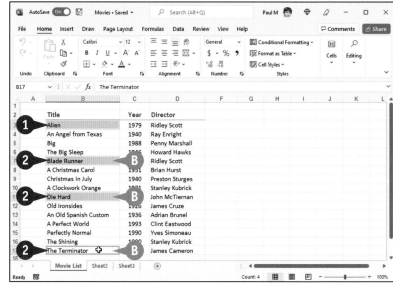

Select an Entire Row

1 Position the mouse (⊕) over the header of the row you want to select (⊕ changes to ➡).

2 Click the row header.

C Excel selects the entire row.

To select multiple rows, click and drag across the row headers or hold down Ctrl and click each row header.

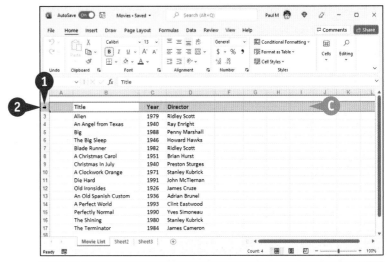

Select an Entire Column

1 Position the mouse (⊕) over the header of the column you want to select (⊕ changes to ⬇).

2 Click the column header.

D Excel selects the entire column.

To select multiple columns, click and drag across the column headers, or hold down Ctrl and click each column header.

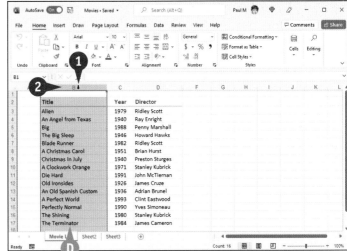

TIPS

Are there keyboard techniques I can use to select a range?

Yes. To select a rectangular range, navigate to the first cell that you want to include in the range, hold down Shift, and then press ➡ or ⬇ to extend the selection. To select an entire row, navigate to any cell in the row and press Shift + Spacebar. To select an entire column, navigate to any cell in the column and then press Ctrl + Spacebar.

Is there an easy way to select every cell in the worksheet?

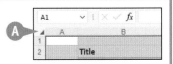

Yes. There are two methods you can use. The easiest is to click the **Select All** button (◢) in the upper-left corner of the worksheet (**A**). Alternatively, select an empty cell outside of any range that contains data, then press Ctrl + A.

Fill a Range with the Same Data

If you need to fill a range with the same data, you can save time by getting Excel to fill the range for you. The AutoFill feature makes it easy to fill a vertical or horizontal range with the same value, but you can also fill any selected range. This method is much faster than manually entering the same data in each cell.

See the previous section, "Select a Range," to learn how to select a range of cells.

Fill a Range with the Same Data

Fill a Vertical or Horizontal Range

1 In the first cell of the range you want to work with, enter the data you want to fill.

2 Position the mouse (✛) over the bottom-right corner of the cell (✛ changes to ✚).

3 Click and drag ✚ down to fill a vertical range or across to fill a horizontal range.

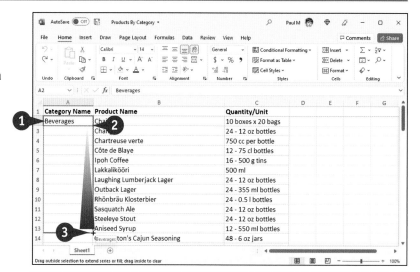

4 Release the mouse button.

Ⓐ Excel fills the range with the initial cell value.

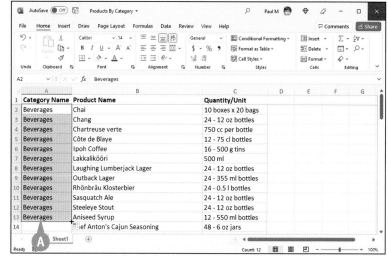

Fill a Selected Range

1 Select the range you want to fill.

2 Type the text, number, or other data.

3 Press Ctrl + Enter.

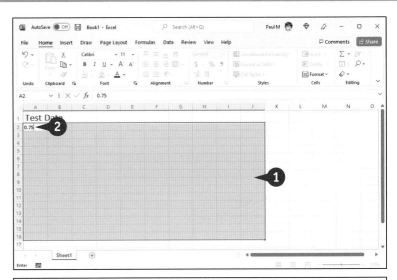

B Excel fills the range with the value you typed.

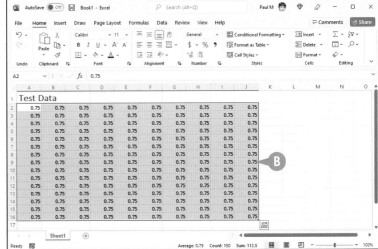

How do I fill a vertical or horizontal range without also copying the formatting of the original cell?

Follow these steps:

1 Perform steps 1 to 4 to fill the data.

A Excel displays the AutoFill Options button (⊞).

2 Click **AutoFill Options** (⊞).

3 Click **Fill Without Formatting**.

Excel removes the original cell's formatting from the copied cells.

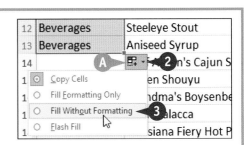

Fill a Range with a Series of Values

I f you need to fill a range with a series of values, you can save time by using the AutoFill feature to create the series for you. AutoFill can fill a series of numeric values such as 5, 10, 15, 20, and so on; a series of date values such as January 1, 2023, January 2, 2023, and so on; or a series of alphanumeric values such as Chapter 1, Chapter 2, Chapter 3, and so on.

You can also create your own series with a custom *step value*, which determines the numeric difference between each item in the series.

Fill a Range with a Series of Values

AutoFill a Series of Numeric, Date, or Alphanumeric Values

1 Click in the first cell and type the first value in the series.

2 Click in an adjacent cell and type the second value in the series.

3 Select the two cells.

4 Position the mouse (✛) over the bottom-right corner of the second cell (✛ changes to ✚).

5 Click and drag ✚ down to fill a vertical range or across to fill a horizontal range.

A As you drag through each cell, Excel displays the series value that it will add to the cell.

6 Release the mouse button.

B Excel fills the range with a series that continues the pattern of the initial two cell values.

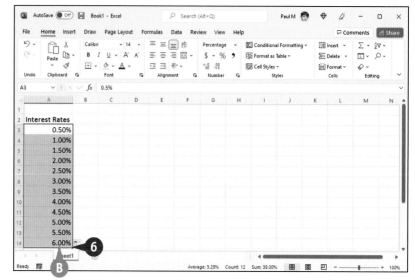

Fill a Custom Series of Values

1. Click in the first cell and type the first value in the series.

2. Select the range you want to fill, including the initial value.

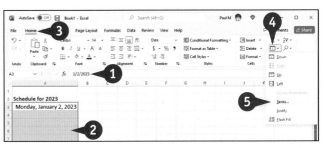

3. Click the **Home** tab.

4. Click **Fill** (⬛).

5. Click **Series**.

The Series dialog box appears.

6. In the Type group, select the type of series you want to fill (○ changes to ⦿).

7. If you selected Date in step **6**, select an option in the Date unit group (○ changes to ⦿).

8. In the Step Value text box, type the value you want to use.

9. Click **OK**.

C Excel fills the range with the series you created.

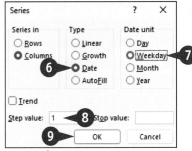

Can I create my own AutoFill series?

Yes. You can create a *custom list*, which is a series of text values. When you add the first value in your custom list, you can then use AutoFill to fill a range with the rest of the series. Follow these steps:

1. Click the **File** tab.

2. Click **Options**.

The Excel Options dialog box appears.

3. Click **Advanced**.

4. Scroll down to the General section and then click **Edit Custom Lists**.

The Custom Lists dialog box appears.

5. Click **NEW LIST**.

6. In the List entries box, type each item in your list, and press Enter after each item.

7. Click **Add**.

8. Click **OK** to return to the Excel Options dialog box.

9. Click **OK**.

Flash Fill a Range

Y ou can save time and effort by using the Flash Fill feature in Excel to automatically fill a range of data based on a sample pattern that you provide.

Although there are many ways to use Flash Fill, the two most common are flash filling a range with extracted data and flash filling a range with formatted data. For example, if you have a column of full names, you might want to create a new column that includes just the first names extracted from the original column. Similarly, if you have a column of phone numbers in the form 1234567890, you might want a new column that formats the numbers as (123) 456-7890.

Flash Fill a Range

Flash Fill a Range with Extracted Data

1 Make sure the column of original data has a heading.

2 Type a heading for the column of extracted data.

3 Type the first value you want in the new column.

4 Begin typing the second value.

A Excel recognizes the pattern and displays suggestions for the rest of the column.

5 Press Enter.

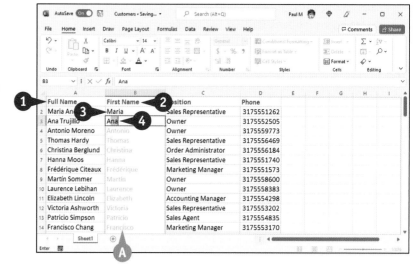

B Excel flash fills the column with the extracted data.

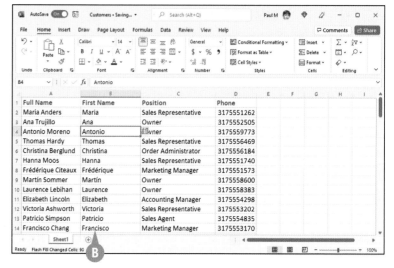

Flash Fill a Range with Formatted Data

1 Make sure the column of original data has a heading.

2 Type a heading for the new column of formatted data.

3 Type the first value you want in the new column.

4 Begin typing the second value.

C Excel recognizes the pattern and displays suggestions for the rest of the column.

5 Press Enter.

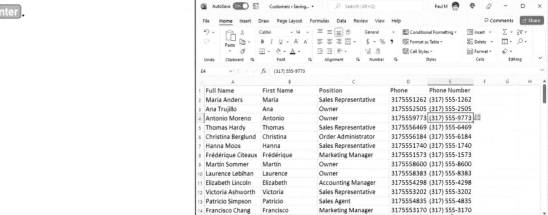

D Excel flash fills the column with the formatted data.

Why do I not see the automatic Flash Fill suggestions when I type the sample data?

For Flash Fill's automatic suggestions to appear, you must have headings at the top of both the column of original data and the column you are using for the filled data. Also, the flash fill column must be adjacent to the original column and the sample entries you make in the fill column must occur one after the other. Finally, note that Flash Fill's automatic suggestions usually only work with text data (including phone numbers), not numeric data.

Can I still use Flash Fill even though I do not see the automatic suggestions?

Yes, you can still invoke Flash Fill on any range by running the Ribbon command. In the fill range, type the first value, then select that value and the rest of the fill range. Click the **Data** tab and then click **Flash Fill** (⊞). Excel flash fills the selected range.

Move or Copy a Range

I f your worksheet is not set up the way you want, you can restructure or reorganize the worksheet by moving an existing range to a different part of the sheet.

You can also make a copy of a range, which is a useful technique if you require a duplicate of the range elsewhere, or if you require a range that is similar to an existing range. In the latter case, after you copy the range, you can then edit the copied version of the data as needed.

Move or Copy a Range

Move a Range

1 Select the range you want to move.

2 Position the mouse (✛) over any outside border of the range (✛ changes to ⬚).

3 Click and drag the range to the new location (⬚ changes to ⬚).

A Excel displays an outline of the range.

B Excel displays the address of the new location.

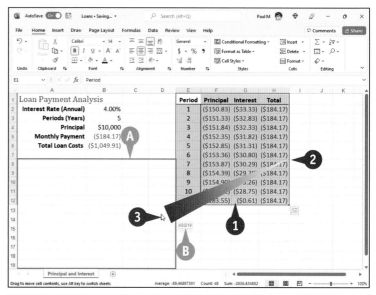

4 Release the mouse button.

C Excel moves the range to the new location.

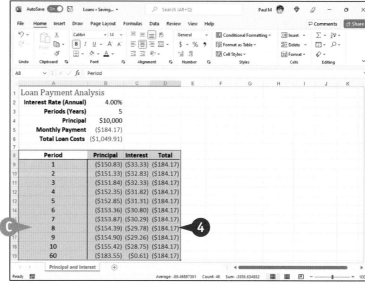

Copy a Range

① Select the range you want to copy.

② Press and hold **Ctrl**.

③ Position the mouse (✛) over any outside border of the range (✛ changes to ⇖).

④ Click and drag the range to the location where you want the copy to appear.

Ⓓ Excel displays an outline of the range.

Ⓔ Excel displays the address of the new location.

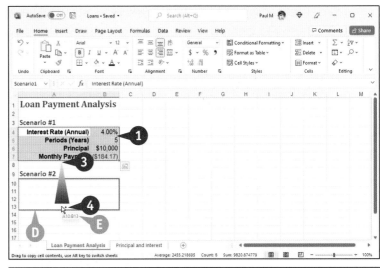

⑤ Release the mouse button.

⑥ Release **Ctrl**.

Ⓕ Excel creates a copy of the range in the new location.

TIPS

Can I move or copy a range to another worksheet?

Yes. Click and drag the range as described in this section. Remember to hold down **Ctrl** if you are copying the range. Press and hold **Alt** and then drag the mouse pointer over the tab of the sheet you want to use as the destination. Excel displays the worksheet. Release **Alt** and then drop the range on the worksheet.

Can I move or copy a range to another workbook?

Yes. If you can see the other workbook on-screen, click and drag the range as described in this section, and then drop it on the other workbook. Remember to hold down **Ctrl** if you are copying the range. Otherwise, select the range, click the **Home** tab, click **Cut** (✂) to move the range or **Copy** (▣) to copy it, switch to the other workbook, select the cell where you want the range to appear, click **Home**, and then click **Paste** (▣).

Insert a Row or Column

You can insert a row or column into your existing worksheet data to accommodate more information. The easiest way to add more information to a worksheet is to add it to the right or at the bottom of your existing data. However, you will often find that the new information you need to add fits naturally within the existing data. In such cases, you first need to insert a new row or column in your worksheet at the place where you want the new data to appear, and then add the new information in the blank row or column.

Insert a Row or Column

Insert a Row

1. Click any cell in the row below where you want to insert the new row.

2. Click the **Home** tab.

3. Click the **Insert** ∨.

4. Click **Insert Sheet Rows**.

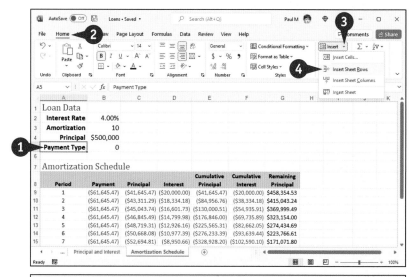

Ⓐ Excel inserts the new row.

Ⓑ The rows below the new row are shifted down.

5. Click the **Insert Options** button (🖉).

6. Select a formatting option for the new row (○ changes to ●).

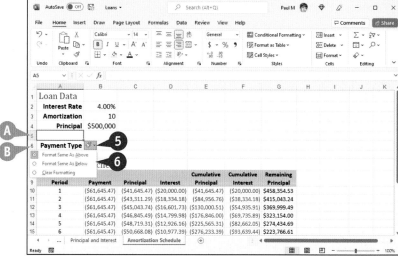

Insert a Column

1 Click any cell in the column to the right of where you want to insert the new column.

2 Click the **Home** tab.

3 Click the **Insert** ∨.

4 Click **Insert Sheet Columns**.

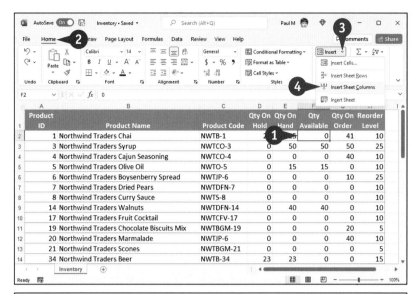

C Excel inserts the new column.

D The columns to the right of the new column are shifted to the right.

5 Click the **Insert Options** button (🖌).

6 Select a formatting option for the new column (○ changes to ●).

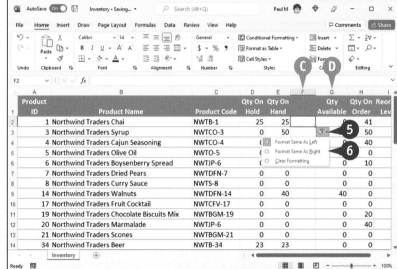

TIP

Can I insert more than one row or column at a time?

Yes. You can insert as many new rows or columns as you need. First, select the same number of rows or columns that you want to insert. (See the "Select a Range" section earlier in this chapter to learn how to select rows and columns.) For example, if you want to insert four rows, select four existing rows. For rows, be sure to select existing rows below where you want the new rows inserted and then follow steps **2** to **4** in the "Insert a Row" subsection. For columns, be sure to select existing columns to the right of where you want to insert the new columns and then follow steps **2** to **4** in the "Insert a Column" subsection.

Insert a Cell or Range

If you need to add data to an existing range, you can insert a single cell or a range of cells within that range. When you insert a cell or range, Excel shifts the existing data to accommodate the new cells.

Although it is often easiest to create room for new data within a range by inserting an entire row or column, as explained in the previous section, "Insert a Row or Column," this causes problems for some types of worksheet layouts. (See the first tip in this section to learn more.) You can work around such problems by inserting just a cell or range.

Insert a Cell or Range

1 Select the cell or range where you want the inserted cell or range to appear.

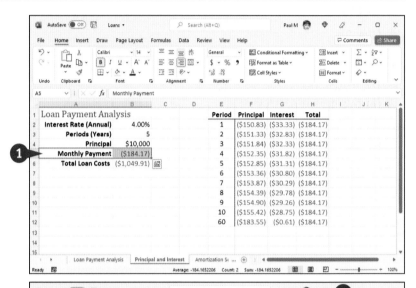

2 Click the **Home** tab.

3 Click the **Insert** ∨.

4 Click **Insert Cells**.

Note: You can also press Ctrl + Shift + =.

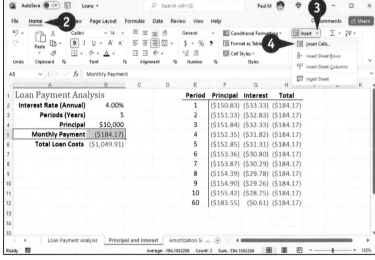

The Insert dialog box appears.

5 Select the option that corresponds to how you want Excel to shift the existing cells to accommodate your new cells (○ changes to ●).

Note: In most cases, if you selected a horizontal range, you should click the **Shift cells down** option; if you selected a vertical range, you should click the **Shift cells right** option.

6 Click **OK**.

Ⓐ Excel inserts the cell or range.

Ⓑ The existing data is shifted down (in this case) or to the right.

7 Click the **Insert Options** button (🖌).

8 Select a formatting option for the new cell or range (○ changes to ●).

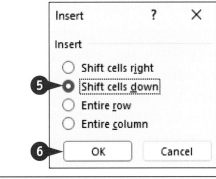

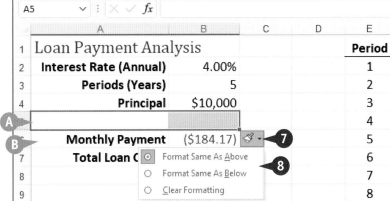

Under what circumstances would I insert a cell or range instead of inserting an entire row or column?
In most cases, it is better to insert a cell or range when you have other data either to the left or right of the existing range, or above or below the range. For example, if you have data to the left or right of the existing range, inserting an entire row would create a gap in the other data.

How do I know which cells to select to get my inserted cell or range in the correct position?
The easiest way to do this is to select the existing cell or range that is exactly where you want the new cell or range to appear. For example, if you want the new range to be A5:B5 as shown in this section's example, you first select the existing A5:B5 range. When you insert the new range, Excel shifts the existing cells (down in this case) to accommodate it.

Delete Data from a Range

If your worksheet has a range that contains data you no longer need, you can delete that data. This helps to reduce worksheet clutter and makes your worksheet easier to read.

Note that deleting cell data does not adjust the structure of your worksheet in any way. That is, after you delete the cell data, the rest of your worksheet data remains intact and in the same place that it was before the data deletion. If you want to delete cells and not just the data within the cells, see the following section, "Delete a Range."

Delete Data from a Range

Delete Range Data

1 Select the range that contains the data you want to delete.

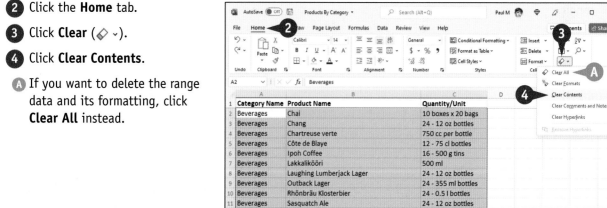

2 Click the **Home** tab.

3 Click **Clear** (◇ ˅).

4 Click **Clear Contents**.

Ⓐ If you want to delete the range data and its formatting, click **Clear All** instead.

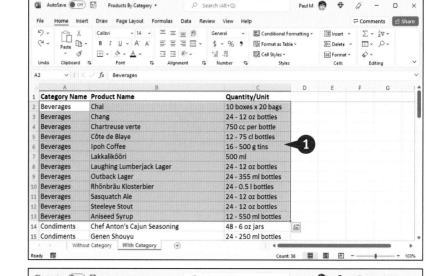

Ⓑ Excel removes the range data.

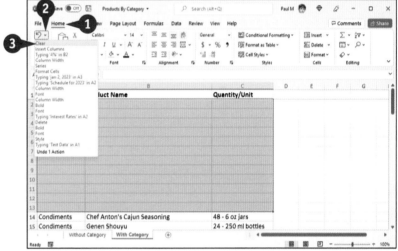

Undo Range Data Deletion

① Click the **Home** tab.

② Click the **Undo** ∨.

③ Click **Clear**.

Note: If the data deletion was the most recent action you performed, you can undo it by pressing Ctrl + Z or by clicking **Undo** (↺).

Excel restores the data to the range.

TIPS

Are there faster ways to delete the data from a range?
Yes. Probably the fastest method is to select the range and then press Delete. You can also select the range, right-click any part of the range, and then click **Clear Contents**.

Is it possible to delete a cell's numeric formatting?
Yes. Select the range with the formatting that you want to remove, click **Home**, click ◇ ∨, and then click **Clear Formats**. Excel removes all the formatting from the selected range. If you prefer to delete only the numeric formatting, click **Home**, click the **Number Format** ∨, and then click **General**.

Delete a Range

If your worksheet contains a range that you no longer need, you can delete that range. Note that this is not the same as deleting the data within a cell or range, as described in the previous section, "Delete Data from a Range." When you delete a range, Excel deletes not just the data within the range, but also the range of cells. Excel then shifts the remaining worksheet data to replace the deleted range. Excel displays a dialog box that enables you to choose whether the data is shifted up or to the left.

Delete a Range

1 Select the range that you want to delete.

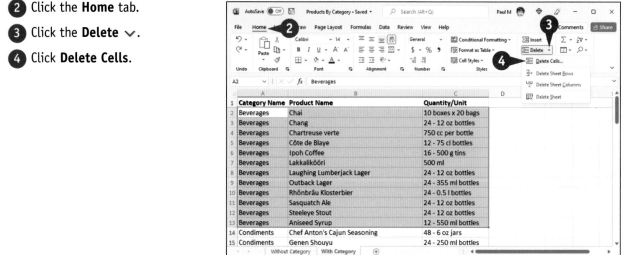

2 Click the **Home** tab.

3 Click the **Delete** ⌄.

4 Click **Delete Cells**.

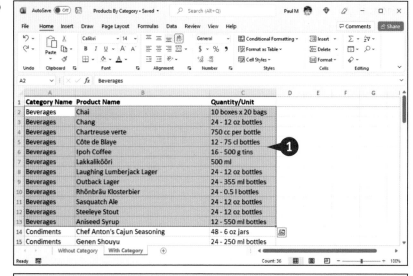

The Delete dialog box appears.

5 Select the option that corresponds to how you want Excel to shift the remaining cells after it deletes the range (○ changes to ◉).

Note: In most cases, if you have data below the selected range, you should click the **Shift cells up** option; if you have data to the right of the selected range, you should click the **Shift cells left** option.

6 Click **OK**.

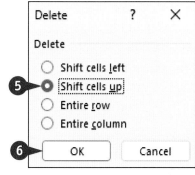

A Excel deletes the range and shifts the remaining data.

	A	B	C	D
1	Category Name	Product Name	Quantity/Unit	
2	Condiments	Chef Anton's Cajun Seasoning	48 - 6 oz jars	
3	Condiments	Genen Shouyu	24 - 250 ml bottles	
4	Condiments	Grandma's Boysenberry Spread	12 - 8 oz jars	
5	Condiments	Gula Malacca	20 - 2 kg bags	
6	Condiments	Louisiana Fiery Hot Pepper Sauce	32 - 8 oz bottles	
7	Condiments	Louisiana Hot Spiced Okra	24 - 8 oz jars	
8	Condiments	Northwoods Cranberry Sauce	12 - 12 oz jars	
9	Condiments	Original Frankfurter grüne Soße	12 boxes	
10	Condiments	Sirop d'érable	24 - 500 ml bottles	
11	Condiments	Vegie-spread	15 - 625 g jars	
12	Confections	Chocolade	10 pkgs.	
13	Confections	Gumbär Gummibärchen	100 - 250 g bags	
14	Confections	Maxilaku	24 - 50 g pkgs.	
15	Confections	NuNuCa Nuß-Nougat-Creme	20 - 450 g glasses	

Without Category | **With Category** | ⊕

TIPS

Are there faster ways to delete a range?
Yes. Probably the fastest method is to select the range and then press Ctrl + ⊟. You can also select the range, right-click any part of the range, and then click **Delete**. Both methods display the Delete dialog box.

How do I delete a row or column?
To delete a row, select any cell in the row, click the **Home** tab, click the **Delete** ⌄, and then click **Delete Sheet Rows**. To delete a column, select any cell in the column, click the **Home** tab, click the **Delete** ⌄, and then click **Delete Sheet Columns**. Note, too, that you can delete multiple rows or columns by selecting at least one cell in each row or column.

Hide a Row or Column

If you do not need to see or work with a row or column temporarily, you can make your worksheet easier to read and navigate by hiding the row or column. Hiding a row or column is also useful if you are showing someone a worksheet that contains private or sensitive data that you do not want the person to see.

Hiding a row or column does not affect other parts of your worksheet. In particular, formulas that use or rely on data in the hidden rows and columns still display the same results.

Hide a Row or Column

Hide a Row

1 Click in any cell in the row you want to hide.

2 Click the **Home** tab.

3 Click **Format**.

4 Click **Hide & Unhide**.

5 Click **Hide Rows**.

Note: You can also hide a row by pressing Ctrl + 9.

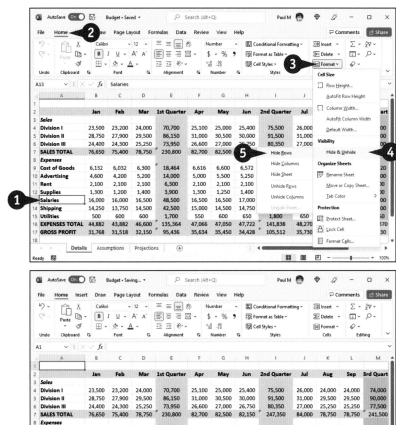

Ⓐ Excel removes the row from the worksheet display.

Ⓑ Excel displays a double-line border between the surrounding row headers to indicate that a hidden row lies between them.

Another way to hide a row is to move the mouse (✛) over the bottom edge of the row heading (✛ changes to ✚), and then click and drag the edge up until the height displays 0.

Hide a Column

① Click in any cell in the column you want to hide.

② Click the **Home** tab.

③ Click **Format**.

④ Click **Hide & Unhide**.

⑤ Click **Hide Columns**.

Note: You can also hide a column by pressing Ctrl + 0.

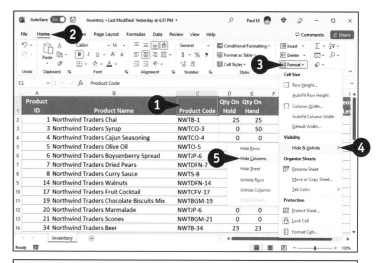

Ⓒ Excel removes the column from the worksheet display.

Ⓓ Excel displays a slightly thicker heading border between the surrounding columns to indicate that a hidden column lies between them.

Another way to hide a column is to move the mouse (✥) over the right edge of the column heading (✥ changes to ↔), and then click and drag the edge left until the width displays 0.

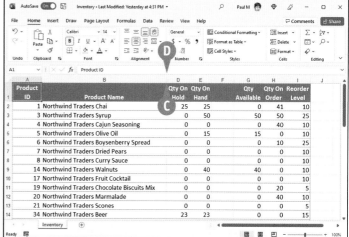

TIP

How do I display a hidden row or column?

To display a hidden row, select the row above and the row below the hidden row, click **Home**, click **Format**, click **Hide & Unhide**, and then click **Unhide Rows**. Alternatively, move the mouse (✥) between the headings of the selected rows (✥ changes to ╪) and then double-click. To unhide row 1, right-click the top edge of the row 2 header and then click **Unhide**.

To display a hidden column, select the column to the left and the column to the right of the hidden column, click **Home**, click **Format**, click **Hide & Unhide**, and then click **Unhide Columns**. Alternatively, move the ✥ between the headings of the selected columns (✥ changes to ↔) and then double-click. To unhide column A, right-click the left edge of the column B header and then click **Unhide**.

Freeze Rows or Columns

You can keep your column labels in view as you vertically scroll the worksheet by freezing the row or rows that contain the labels. This makes it easier to review and add data to the worksheet because you can always see the column labels.

If your worksheet also includes row labels, you can keep those labels in view as you horizontally scroll the worksheet by freezing the column or columns that contain the labels.

Freeze Rows or Columns

Freeze Rows

① Scroll the worksheet so that the row or rows that you want to freeze are visible.

② Select the cell in column A that is one row below the last row you want to freeze.

For example, if you want to freeze row 1, select cell A2.

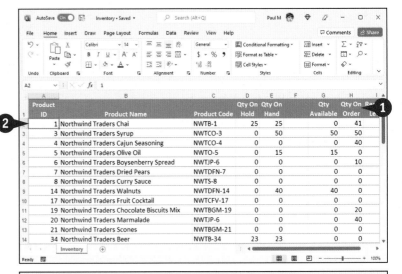

③ Click the **View** tab.

④ Click **Freeze Panes**.

⑤ Click **Freeze Panes**.

Excel freezes the rows.

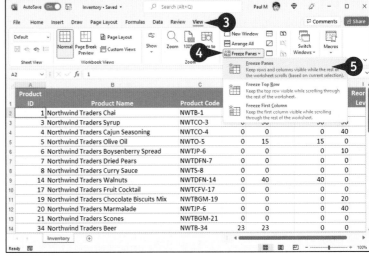

Freeze Columns

① Scroll the worksheet so that the column or columns that you want to freeze are visible.

② Select the cell in row 1 that is one column to the right of the last column you want to freeze.

For example, if you want to freeze column A, select cell B1.

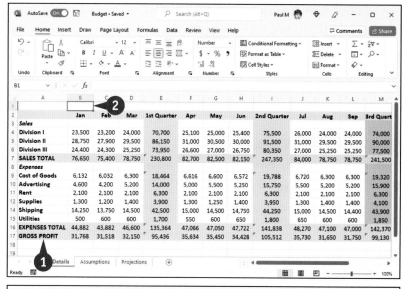

③ Click the **View** tab.

④ Click **Freeze Panes**.

⑤ Click **Freeze Panes**.

Excel freezes the columns.

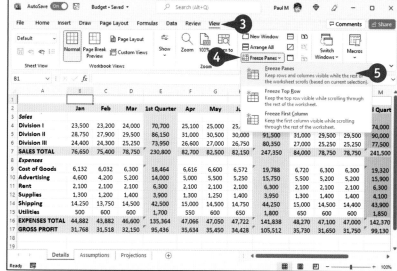

TIPS

Are there easier methods I can use to freeze just the top row or the first column?

Yes. To freeze just the top row, click **View**, click **Freeze Panes**, and then click **Freeze Top Row**. To freeze just the first column, click **View**, click **Freeze Panes**, and then click **Freeze First Column**. Note that in both cases you do not need to select a cell in advance.

How do I unfreeze a row or column?

If you no longer require a row or column to be frozen, you can unfreeze it by clicking **View**, clicking **Freeze Panes**, and then clicking **Unfreeze Panes**.

Merge Two or More Cells

You can create a single large cell by merging two or more cells. For example, it is common to merge several cells in the top row to use as a worksheet title.

Another common reason for merging cells is to create a label that applies to multiple columns of data. For example, if you have three columns labeled *January*, *February*, and *March*, you could select the three cells in the row above these labels, merge them, and then use the merged cell to add the label *First Quarter*.

Merge Two or More Cells

1 Select the cells that you want to merge.

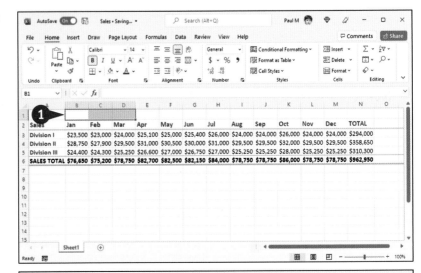

2 Click the **Home** tab.

3 Click the **Merge & Center** ∨.

4 Click **Merge Cells**.

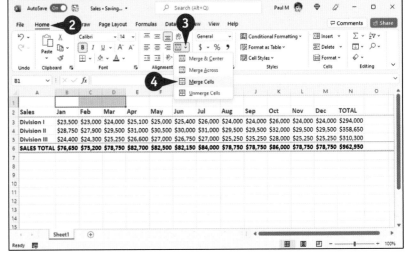

Ⓐ Excel merges the selected cells into a single cell.

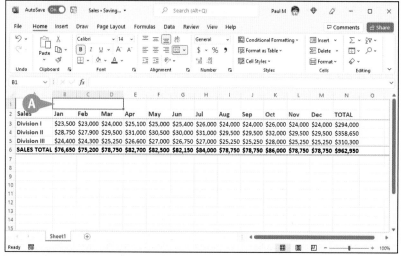

5 Type your text in the merged cell.

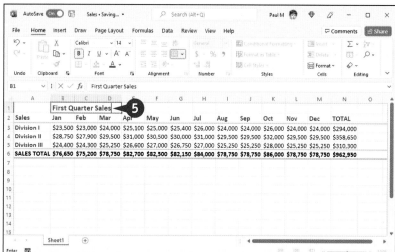

How do I center text across multiple columns?

This is a useful technique for your worksheet titles or headings. You can center a title across the entire worksheet, or you can center a heading across the columns that it refers to. Follow steps **1** to **3** and then click **Merge & Center**. Excel creates the merged cell and formats the cell with the Center alignment option. Any text you enter into the merged cell appears centered within the cell.

CHAPTER 4

Working with Range Names

You can make it easier to navigate Excel worksheets and build Excel formulas by applying names to your ranges. This chapter explains range names and shows you how to define, edit, and use range names.

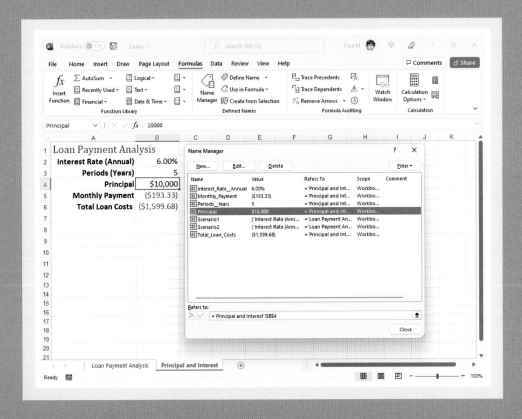

Understanding the Benefits of Using Range Names

A *range name* is a text label that you apply to a single cell or to a range of cells. Once you have defined a name for a range, you can use that name in place of the range coordinates, which has several benefits. These benefits include making your worksheets more intuitive and making your work more accurate. In addition, a range name is easier to remember than range coordinates, it does not change when you move the underlying range, and it makes navigating your worksheets easier than using range coordinates does.

More Intuitive

Range names are more intuitive than range coordinates, particularly in formulas. For example, if you see the range A13:D13 in a formula, the only way to know what the range refers to is to look at the data. However, if you see the name Quarterly_Sales in the formula, then you already know what the range refers to.

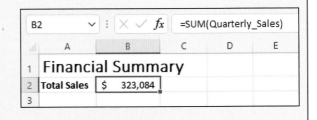

More Accurate

Range names are more accurate than range coordinates. For example, consider the range address A1:B3, which consists of four different pieces of information: the column (A) and row (1) of the cell in the upper-left corner of the

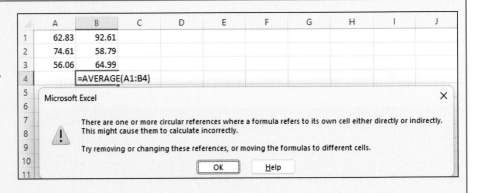

range, and the column (B) and row (3) of the cell in the lower-right corner. If you get even one of these values wrong, it can cause errors throughout a spreadsheet. By contrast, with a range name you need only reference the actual name.

Easier to Remember

Range names are easier to remember than range coordinates. For example, if you want to use a particular range in a formula but that range is not currently visible, to get the coordinates you must scroll until you can see the range and then determine the range's coordinates. However, if you have already assigned the range an intuitive name such as Project_Expenses, you can add that name directly without having to view the range.

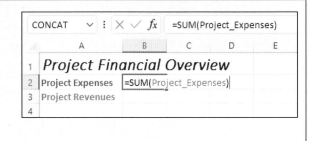

Names Do Not Change

Range names do not change when you adjust the position of a range, as they do with range coordinates. For example, if you move the range A1:B5 to the right by five columns, the range coordinates change to F1:G5. If you have a formula that references that range, Excel updates the formula with the new range coordinates, which could confuse someone examining the worksheet. By contrast, a range name does not change when you move the range.

Easier Navigation

Range names make it easier to navigate a worksheet. For example, Excel has a Go To command that enables you to choose a range name, and Excel takes you directly to the range. You can also use the Name box to select a range name and navigate to that range. You can also use Go To and the Name box to specify range coordinates, but range coordinates are much more difficult to work with.

Define a Range Name

Before you can use a range name in your formulas or to navigate a worksheet, you must first define the range name. You can define as many names as you need, and you can even define multiple names for the same range.

You can create range names manually, or you can get Excel to create the names for you automatically based on the existing text labels in a worksheet. To do the latter, see the following section, "Using Worksheet Text to Define a Range Name."

Define a Range Name

1 Select the range you want to name.

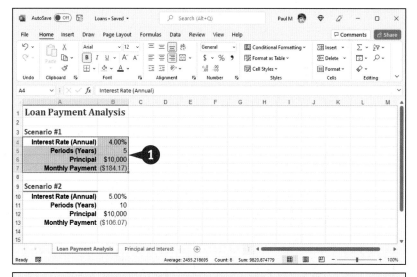

2 Click the **Formulas** tab.

3 Click **Define Name**.

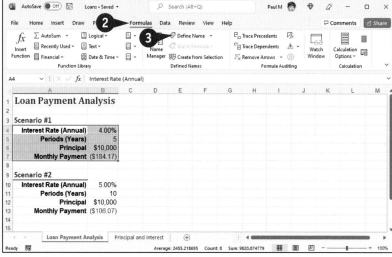

The New Name dialog box appears.

4 Type the name you want to use in the **Name** text box.

Note: The first character of the name must be a letter or an underscore (_). The name cannot include spaces or cell references, and it cannot be any longer than 255 characters.

Note: You can use a particular range name only once in a workbook.

5 Click **OK**.

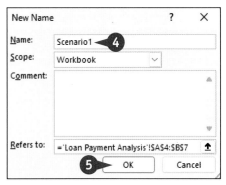

Excel assigns the name to the range.

A The new name appears in the Name box whenever you select the range.

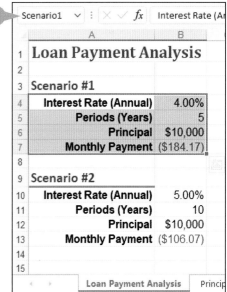

TIP

Is there an easier way to define a range name?
Yes, you can follow these steps to bypass the New Name dialog box:

1 Select the range you want to name.

2 Click inside the **Name** box.

3 Type the name you want to use.

4 Press Enter.

Excel assigns the name to the range.

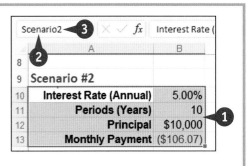

Using Worksheet Text to Define a Range Name

If you have several ranges to name, you can speed up the process by getting Excel to create the names for you automatically based on each range's text labels.

You can create range names from worksheet text when the labels are in the top or bottom row of the range, or in the left or right column of the range. For example, if you have a column named Company, using the technique in this section results in that column's data being assigned the range name "Company."

Using Worksheet Text to Define a Range Name

1 Select the range or ranges you want to name.

A Be sure to include the text labels you want to use for the range names.

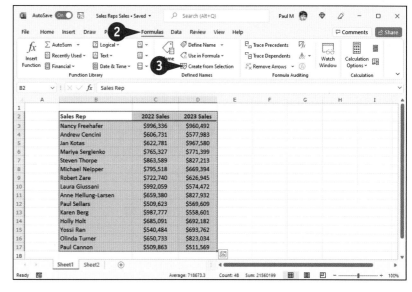

2 Click the **Formulas** tab.

3 Click **Create from Selection**.

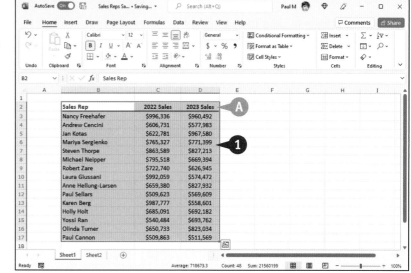

The Create Names from Selection dialog box appears.

④ Select the setting or settings that correspond to where the text labels are located in the selected range (☐ changes to ☑).

If Excel has activated a check box that does not apply to your data, click it (☑ changes to ☐).

⑤ Click **OK**.

Excel assigns the text labels as range names.

Ⓑ When you select one of the ranges, the range name assigned by Excel appears in the Name box.

Note: If the label text contains any illegal characters, such as a space, Excel replaces each of those characters with an underscore (_).

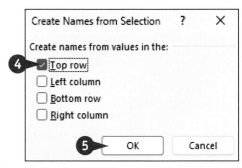

	Sales Rep	2022 Sales	2023 Sales
3	Nancy Freehafer	$996,336	$960,492
4	Andrew Cencini	$606,731	$577,983
5	Jan Kotas	$622,781	$967,580
6	Mariya Sergienko	$765,327	$771,399
7	Steven Thorpe	$863,589	$827,213
8	Michael Neipper	$795,518	$669,394
9	Robert Zare	$722,740	$626,945
10	Laura Giussani	$992,059	$574,472
11	Anne Hellung-Larsen	$659,380	$827,932
12	Paul Sellars	$509,623	$569,609
13	Karen Berg	$987,777	$558,601
14	Holly Holt	$685,091	$692,182
15	Yossi Ran	$540,484	$693,762
16	Olinda Turner	$650,733	$823,034
17	Paul Cannon	$509,863	$511,569

TIPS

Is there a faster way to run the Create from Selection command?

Yes, Excel offers a keyboard shortcut for the command. Select the range or ranges you want to work with and then press `Ctrl`+`Shift`+`F3`. Excel displays the Create Names from Selection dialog box. Follow steps 4 and 5 to create the range names.

	A	B	C	D
1	*Sales*	Team 1	Team 2	Team 3
2	**Division I**	294,000	323,400	279,300
3	**Division II**	358,550	394,405	340,623
4	**Division III**	310,000	341,000	294,500

Is there a way to automatically assign a name to just a table's data?

Yes. The table data refers to the range of cells that does not include the table headings in the top row and left column. To assign a name to the data range, type a label in the top-left corner of the table. When you run the Create from Selection command on the entire table, Excel assigns the top-left label to the data range, as shown here.

Navigate a Workbook Using Range Names

One of the big advantages of defining range names is that they make it easier to navigate a workbook. You can choose a range name from a list and Excel automatically selects the associated range. This works even if the named range exists in a different worksheet of the same workbook.

Excel offers two methods for navigating a workbook using range names: the Name box and the Go To command.

Navigate a Workbook Using Range Names

Using the Name Box

1 Open the workbook that contains the range you want to work with.

2 Click the **Name** box ∨.

3 Click the name of the range you want to select.

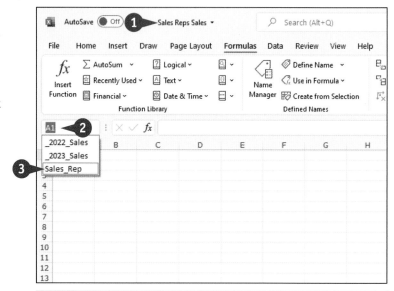

A Excel selects the range.

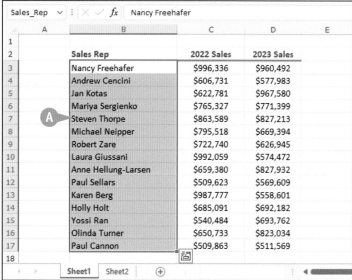

Using the Go To Command

1 Open the workbook that contains the range you want to work with.

2 Click the **Home** tab.

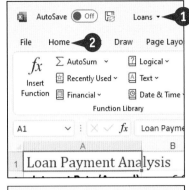

3 Click **Find & Select** (🔍).

4 Click **Go To**.

Note: You can also select the Go To command by pressing Ctrl+G.

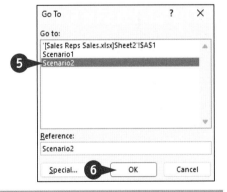

The Go To dialog box appears.

5 Click the name of the range you want to select.

6 Click **OK**.

Excel selects the range.

TIP

Is it possible to navigate to a named range in a different workbook?

Yes, but it is not easy or straightforward:

1 Follow steps 1 to 4 in the "Using the Go To Command" subsection to display the Go To dialog box.

2 In the **Reference** text box, type the following:

'[*workbook*]*worksheet*'!*name*

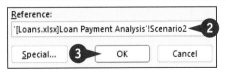

Replace *workbook* with the filename of the workbook, replace *worksheet* with the name of the worksheet that contains the range, and replace *name* with the range name.

3 Click **OK**.

Change a Range Name

Y ou can change any range name to a more suitable or accurate name. Changing a range name is
useful if you are no longer satisfied with the original name you applied to a range or if the existing
name no longer accurately reflects the contents of the range. You might also want to change a range
name if you do not like the name that Excel generated automatically from the worksheet labels.

If you want to change the range coordinates associated with a range name, see the second tip.

Change a Range Name

1 Open the workbook that contains the
   range name you want to change.

2 Click the **Formulas** tab.

3 Click **Name Manager**.

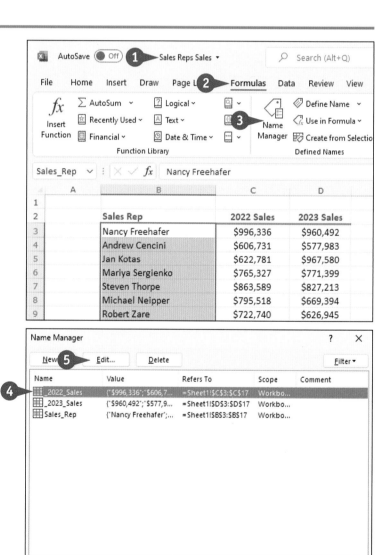

The Name Manager dialog box
appears.

4 Click the name you want to change.

5 Click **Edit**.

The Edit Name dialog box appears.

6 Use the **Name** text box to edit the name.

7 Click **OK**.

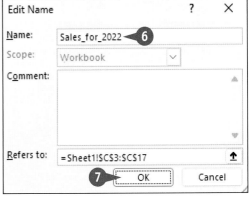

A The new name appears in the Name Manager dialog box.

8 Click **Close**.

Excel closes the dialog box and returns you to the worksheet.

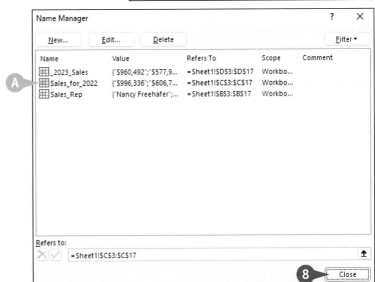

Is there a faster method I can use to open the Name Manager dialog box?

Yes, Excel offers a shortcut key that enables you to bypass steps **2** and **3**. Open the workbook that contains the range name you want to change, and then press Ctrl + F3. Excel opens the Name Manager dialog box.

Can I assign a name to a different range?

Yes. If you add another range to your workbook and you feel that an existing name would be more suited to that range, you can modify the name to refer to the new range. Follow steps **1** to **5** to open the Edit Name dialog box. Click inside the **Refers to** reference box, click and drag the mouse (⊕) on the worksheet to select the new range, and then press Enter. Click **Close**.

Delete a Range Name

If you have a range name that you no longer need, you should delete it. This reduces clutter in the Name Manager dialog box and makes the Name box easier to navigate.

Note, however, that deleting a range name will generate an error in any formula that uses the name. This occurs because when you delete a range name, Excel does not convert the name to its range coordinates in formulas that use the name. Therefore, before deleting a range name, you should convert that name to its range coordinates in every formula that uses the name.

Delete a Range Name

1 Open the workbook that contains the range name you want to delete.

2 Click the **Formulas** tab.

3 Click **Name Manager**.

Note: You can also open the Name Manager dialog box by pressing `Ctrl` + `F3`.

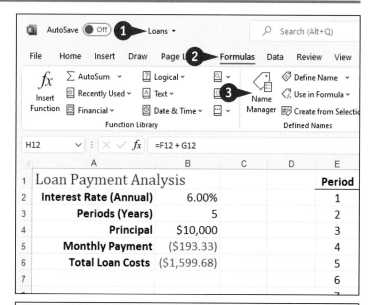

The Name Manager dialog box appears.

4 Click the name you want to delete.

5 Click **Delete**.

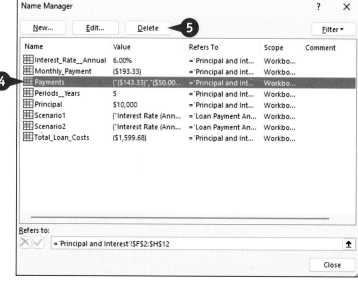

Excel asks you to confirm the deletion.

6 Click **OK**.

A Excel deletes the range name.

7 Click **Close**.

Excel closes the dialog box and returns you to the worksheet.

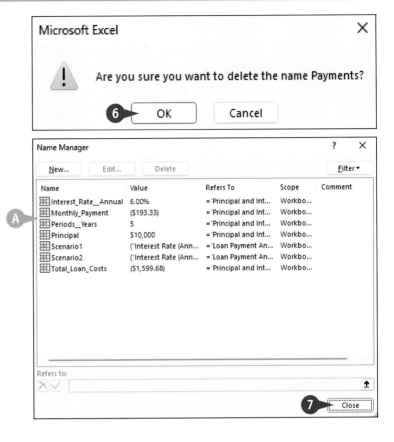

Is there a faster way to delete multiple range names?

Yes, you can delete two or more range names at once. First, follow steps **1** to **3** to display the Name Manager dialog box. Next, select the range names you want to delete. To select consecutive names, click the first name you want to delete, hold down Shift, and then click the last name you want to delete; to select nonconsecutive names, click the first name you want to delete, hold down Ctrl, and then click each name you want to delete. When you have selected the names you want to remove, click **Delete** and then click **OK** when Excel asks you to confirm the deletion. Click **Close** to return to the worksheet.

CHAPTER 5

Formatting Excel Ranges

Microsoft Excel offers many commands and options for formatting ranges, including the font, text color, text alignment, background color, number format, column width, row height, and more.

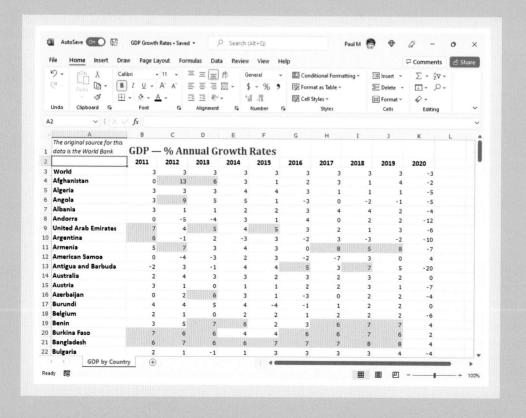

Change the Font and Font Size

Whenyou work in an Excel worksheet, you can add visual appeal to a cell or range by changing the font. In this section and throughout this book, the term *font* is synonymous with *typeface*, and both terms refer to the overall look of each character.

You can also make labels and other text stand out from the rest of the worksheet by changing the font size. The font size is measured in *points*, where there are roughly 72 points in an inch.

Change the Font and Font Size

Change the Font

1 Select the range you want to format.

2 Click the **Home** tab.

3 Click ∨ in the **Font** list.

Note: When you hover the mouse ▷ over a typeface, Excel temporarily changes the selected text to that typeface.

4 Click the typeface you want to apply.

Ⓐ Excel applies the font to the text in the selected range.

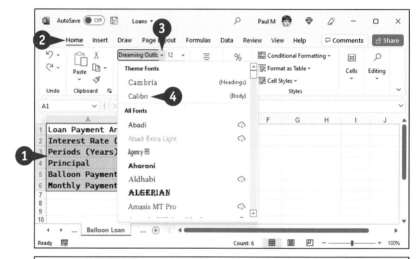

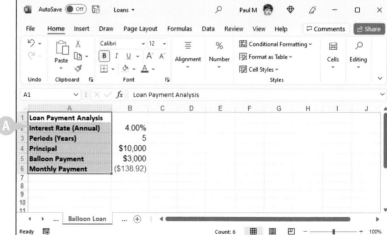

Change the Font Size

1 Select the range you want to format.

2 Click the **Home** tab.

3 Click ∨ in the **Font Size** list.

Note: When you hover the mouse ⟩ over a font size, Excel temporarily changes the selected text to that size.

4 Click the size you want to apply.

Ⓑ You can also type the size you want in the Size text box.

Ⓒ Excel applies the font size to the text in the selected range.

TIPS

In the Theme Fonts section of the Font list, what do the designations Body and Headings mean?

When you create a workbook, Excel automatically applies a document theme to the workbook, and that theme includes predefined fonts. The theme's default font is referred to as Body, and it is the font used for regular worksheet text. Each theme also defines a Headings font, which Excel uses for cells formatted with a heading or title style.

Can I change the default font and font size?

Yes. Click the **File** tab and then click **Options** to open the Excel Options dialog box. Click the **General** tab, click the **Use this as the default font** ∨, and then click the typeface you want to use as the default. Click the **Font size** ∨ and then click the size you prefer to use as the default. Click **OK**.

Apply Font Effects

Y ou can improve the look and impact of text in an Excel worksheet by applying font effects to a cell or to a range.

Font effects include common formatting such as **bold**, which is often used to make labels stand out from regular text; *italic*, which is often used to add emphasis to text; and <u>underline</u>, which is often used for worksheet titles and headings. You can also apply special effects such as ~~strikethrough~~, superscripts (for example, x^2+y^2), and subscripts (for example, H_2O).

Apply Font Effects

1 Select the range you want to format.

2 Click the **Home** tab.

3 To format the text as bold, click the **Bold** button (**B**).

A Excel applies the bold effect to the selected range.

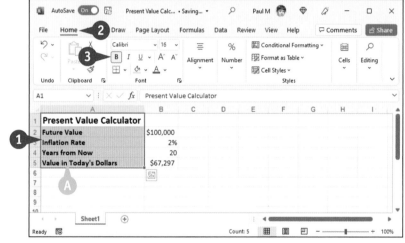

B Before applying more formatting, adjust the selected range, if required.

4 To format the text as italic, click the **Italic** button (*I*).

5 To format the text as underline, click the **Underline** button (U).

C Excel applies the effects to the selected range.

6 Click the **Font** dialog box launcher (⤢).

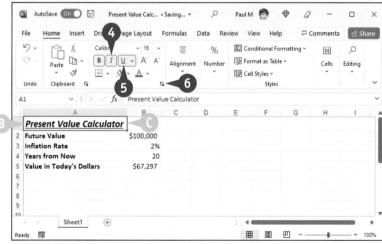

68

The Format Cells dialog box appears with the Font tab displayed.

7 To format the text as strikethrough, click **Strikethrough** (☐ changes to ☑).

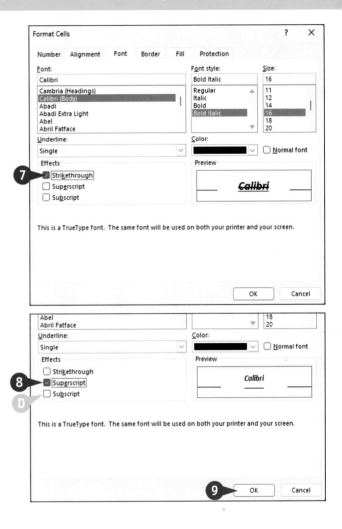

8 To format the text as a superscript, click **Superscript** (☐ changes to ☑).

Ⓓ To format the text as a subscript instead, click **Subscript** (☐ changes to ☑).

9 Click **OK**.

Excel applies the font effects.

TIPS

Are there any font-related keyboard shortcuts I can use?
Yes. Excel supports the following font shortcuts:

Press	To
Ctrl + B	Toggle the selected range as bold
Ctrl + I	Toggle the selected range as italic
Ctrl + U	Toggle the selected range as underline
Ctrl + 5	Toggle the selected range as strikethrough
Ctrl + 1	Display the Format Cells dialog box

Are there other underline types I can use?
Yes, you can click the **Underline** ⌄ and then click **Double** to get a double underline. If you only want the underline under the numbers (and not under, say, the currency sign), display the **Font** tab of the Format Cells dialog box and use the **Underline** list to select either **Single Accounting** or **Double Accounting**.

Change the Font Color

Whenever you work in an Excel worksheet, you can add visual interest by changing the font color. Most worksheets are meant to convey specific information, but that does not mean the sheet has to be plain. By adding a bit of color to your text, you make your worksheets more appealing. Adding color can also make the worksheet easier to read by, for example, differentiating titles, headings, and labels from regular text.

You can change the font color by applying a color from the workbook's theme, from the Excel palette of standard colors, or from a custom color that you create.

Change the Font Color

Select a Theme or Standard Color

1. Select the range you want to format.

2. Click the **Home** tab.

3. Click ∨ in the **Font Color** list (**A**).

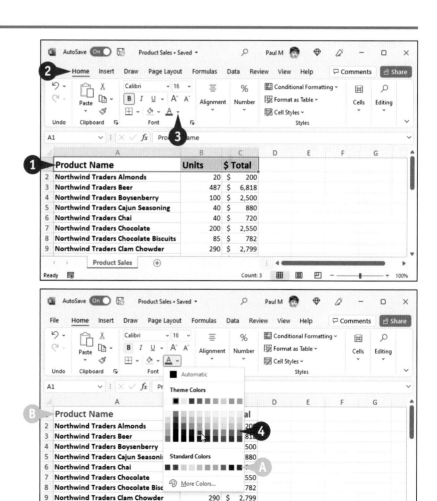

4. Click a theme color.

Ⓐ Alternatively, click one of the Excel standard colors.

Ⓑ Excel applies the color to the selected range.

Select a Custom Color

1 Select the range you want to format.

2 Click the **Home** tab.

3 Click ﹀ in the **Font Color** list (A̲).

4 Click **More Colors**.

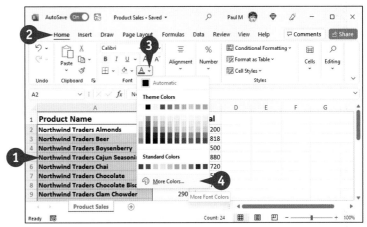

The Colors dialog box appears.

5 Click the color you want to use.

C You can also click the **Custom** tab and then either click the color you want or enter the values for the Red, Green, and Blue components of the color.

6 Click **OK**.

Excel applies the color to the selected range.

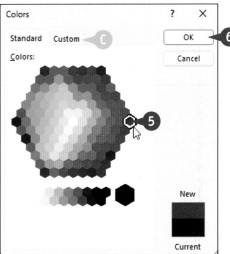

How can I make the best use of fonts in my documents?

• Do not use many different typefaces in a single document. Stick to one, or at most two, typefaces to avoid the ransom note look.

• Avoid overly decorative typefaces because they are often difficult to read.

• Use bold only for document titles, subtitles, and headings.

• Use italics only to emphasize words and phrases, or for the titles of books and magazines.

• Use larger type sizes only for document titles, subtitles, and, possibly, the headings.

• If you change the text color, be sure to leave enough contrast between the text and the background. In general, dark text on a light background is the easiest to read.

Align Text Within a Cell

You can make your worksheets easier to read by aligning text and numbers within each cell. By default, Excel aligns numbers with the right side of the cell, and it aligns text with the left side of the cell. You can also align numbers or text with the center of each cell.

Excel also allows you to align your data vertically within each cell. By default, Excel aligns all data with the bottom of each cell, but you can also align text with the top or middle.

Align Text Within a Cell

Align Text Horizontally

1. Select the range you want to format.

2. Click the **Home** tab.

3. In the Alignment group, click the horizontal alignment option you want to use:

   Click **Align Text Left** (≡) to align data with the left side of each cell.

   Click **Center** (≡) to align data with the center of each cell.

   Click **Align Text Right** (≡) to align data with the right side of each cell.

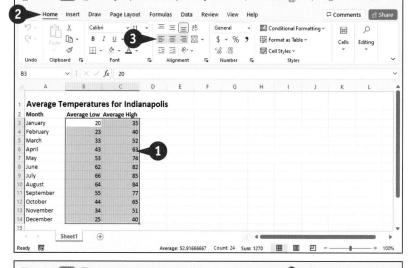

Excel aligns the data horizontally within each selected cell.

A. In this example, the data in the cells is centered.

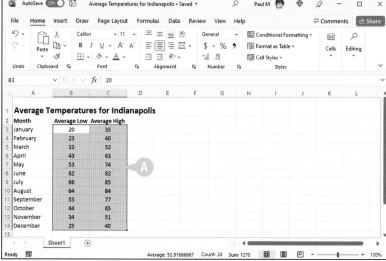

Align Text Vertically

1 Select the range you want to format.

2 Click the **Home** tab.

3 In the Alignment group, click the vertical alignment option you want to use:

Click **Top Align** (≡) to align data with the top of each cell.

Click **Middle Align** (≡) to align data with the middle of each cell.

Click **Bottom Align** (≡) to align data with the bottom of each cell.

Excel aligns the data vertically within each selected cell.

B In this example, the text is aligned with the middle of the cell.

How do I format text so that it aligns with both the left and right sides of the cell?

This is called *justified* text, and it is useful if you have a lot of text in one or more cells. Select the range, click the **Home** tab, and then click the dialog box launcher (⬛) in the Alignment group. The Format Cells dialog box appears with the Alignment tab displayed. In the **Horizontal** list, click ⌄ and then click **Justify**. Click **OK** to justify the cells.

How do I indent cell text?

Select the range you want to indent, click the **Home** tab, and then click the Alignment group's dialog box launcher (⬛). In the Alignment tab, click the **Horizontal** list ⌄ and then click **Left (Indent)**. Use the **Indent** text box to type the indent, in characters, and then click **OK**. You can also click the **Increase Indent** (≡) or **Decrease Indent** (≡) button in the Home tab's Alignment group.

Center Text Across Multiple Columns

You can make a worksheet more visually appealing and easier to read by centering text across multiple columns. This feature is most useful when you have text in a cell that you use as a label or title for a range. Centering the text across the range makes it easier to see that the label or title applies to the entire range.

Center Text Across Multiple Columns

1 Select a range that consists of the text you want to work with and the cells across which you want to center the text.

Note: Make sure that the text you want to center resides in the leftmost cell of the selected range.

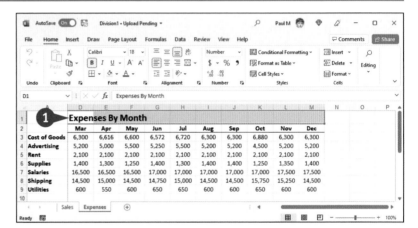

2 Click the **Home** tab.

3 In the **Alignment** group, click the dialog box launcher (⌐⌐).

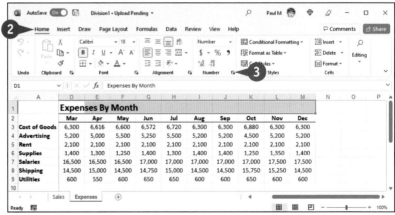

Excel opens the Format Cells dialog box with the Alignment tab displayed.

4 Click the **Horizontal** ⌄ and then click **Center Across Selection**.

5 Click **OK**.

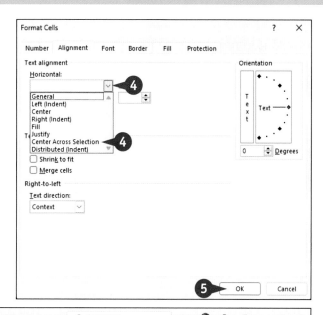

A Excel centers the text across the selected cells.

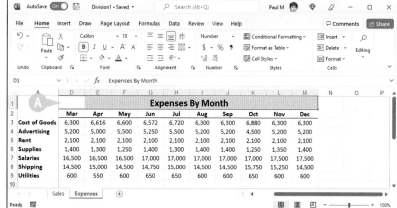

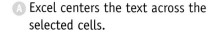

TIP

Is there an easier way to center text across multiple columns?
Yes, although this technique also merges the selected cells into a single cell. (See "Merge Two or More Cells" in Chapter 3 to learn more about merging cells.) Follow these steps:

1 Repeat steps **1** and **2**.

2 In the Alignment group, click the **Merge & Center** button (⊞).

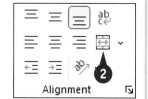

Excel merges the selected cells into a single cell and centers the text within that cell.

Rotate Text Within a Cell

Y ou can add visual interest to your text by slanting the text upward or downward in the cell. You can also use this technique to make a long column heading take up less horizontal space on the worksheet.

You can choose a predefined rotation, or you can make cell text angle upward or downward by specifying the degrees of rotation.

Rotate Text Within a Cell

1 Select the range containing the text you want to angle.

2 Click the **Home** tab.

3 Click **Orientation** (✎).

Ⓐ If you want to use a predefined orientation, click one of the menu items and skip the rest of the steps.

4 Click **Format Cell Alignment**.

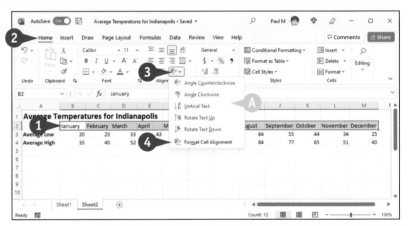

The Format Cells dialog box appears with the Alignment tab displayed.

5 Click an orientation marker.

Ⓑ You can also use the Degrees spin box to type or click a degree of rotation. (See the tip at the end of this section.)

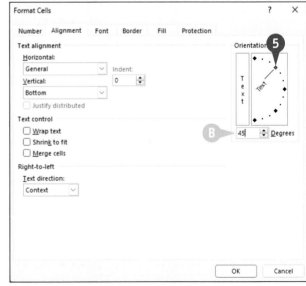

C You can click the vertical text area to display your text vertically instead of horizontally in the cell.

6 Click **OK**.

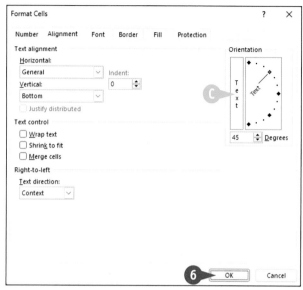

D Excel rotates the cell text.

E The row height automatically increases to contain the slanted text.

F You can reduce one or more of the column widths to free up space and make your cells more presentable.

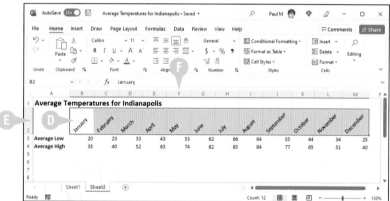

How does the Degrees spin box work?

If you use the Degrees spin box to set the text orientation, you can set the orientation to a positive number, such as 25, and Excel angles the text in an upward (counterclockwise) direction. If you set the text orientation to a negative number, such as −40, Excel angles the text in a downward (clockwise) direction.

You can specify values in the range from 90 degrees (which is the same as clicking the Rotate Text Up command in the Orientation menu) to −90 degrees (which is the same as clicking the Rotate Text Down command).

Add a Background Color to a Range

You can make a range stand out from the rest of the worksheet by applying a background color to the range. Note, however, that if you want to apply a background color to a range based on the values in that range — for example, red for negative values and green for positive — it is easier to apply a conditional format, as described in the "Apply a Conditional Format to a Range" section, later in this chapter.

You can change the background color by applying a color from the workbook's theme, from the Excel palette of standard colors, or from a custom color that you create.

Add a Background Color to a Range

Select a Theme or Standard Color

1 Select the range you want to format.

2 Click the **Home** tab.

3 Click ⌄ in the **Fill Color** list (🖌).

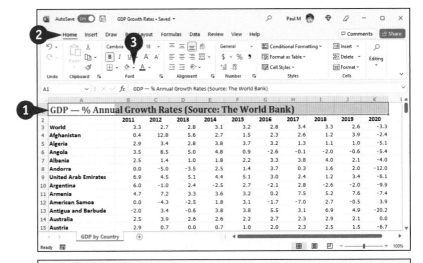

4 Click a theme color.

Ⓐ Alternatively, click one of the standard Excel colors.

Ⓑ Excel applies the color to the selected range.

Ⓒ To remove the background color from the range, click **No Fill**.

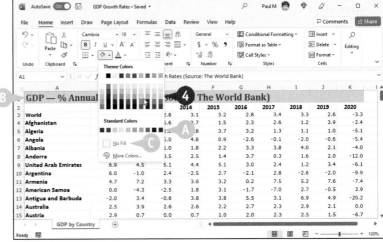

Select a Custom Color

1 Select the range you want to format.

2 Click the **Home** tab.

3 Click ⌄ in the **Fill Color** list (◇).

4 Click **More Colors**.

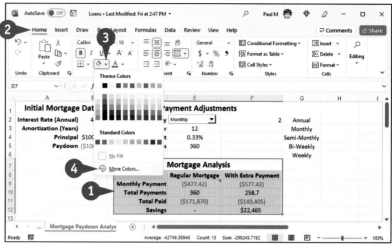

The Colors dialog box appears.

5 Click the color you want to use.

Ⓓ You can also click the **Custom** tab and then either click the color you want or enter the values for the Red, Green, and Blue components of the color.

6 Click **OK**.

Excel applies the color to the selected range.

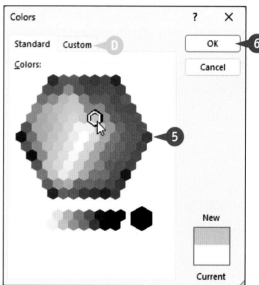

Are there any pitfalls to watch out for when I apply background colors?

Yes. The biggest pitfall is applying a background color that clashes with the range text. For example, the default text color is black, so if you apply any dark background color, the text will be very difficult to read. Always use either a light background color with dark-colored text, or a dark background color with light-colored text.

Can I apply a background that fades from one color to another?

Yes. This is called a *gradient* effect. Select the range, click the **Home** tab, and then click the Font group's dialog box launcher (⬛). Click the **Fill** tab and then click **Fill Effects**. In the Fill Effects dialog box, use the **Color 1** ⌄ and the **Color 2** ⌄ to choose your colors. Click an option in the **Shading styles** section (○ changes to ◉), and then click **OK**.

Apply a Number Format

Y ou can make your worksheet easier to read by applying a number format to your data. For
example, if your worksheet includes monetary data, you can apply the Currency format to display
each value with a dollar sign and two decimal places.

Excel offers 10 number formats, most of which apply to numeric data. However, you can also apply
the Date format to date data, the Time format to time data, and the Text format to text data.

Apply a Number Format

1 Select the range you want to
format.

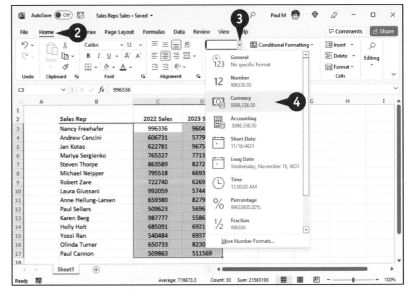

2 Click the **Home** tab.

3 Click the **Number Format** ∨.

4 Click the number format you want
to use.

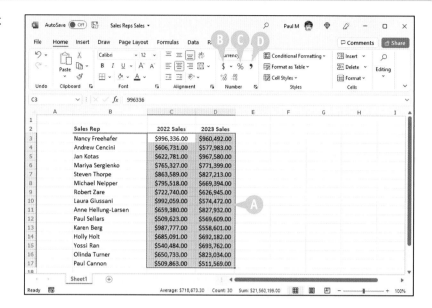

A Excel applies the number format to the selected range.

B For monetary values, you can also click **Accounting Number Format** ($).

C For percentages, you can also click **Percent Style** (%).

D For large numbers, you can also click **Comma Style** (,).

TIP

Is there a way to get more control over the number formats?

Yes. You can use the Format Cells dialog box to control properties such as the display of negative numbers, the currency symbol used, and how dates and times appear. Follow these steps:

1 Select the range you want to format.

2 Click the **Home** tab.

3 Click the **Number** group's dialog box launcher (⌄).

The Format Cells dialog box appears with the Number tab displayed.

4 In the **Category** list, click the type of number format you want to apply.

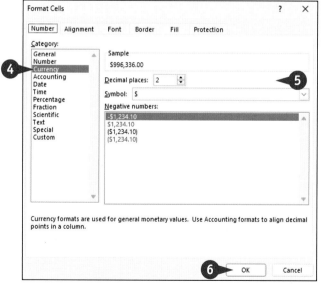

5 Use the controls that Excel displays to customize the number format.

The controls you see vary, depending on the number format you chose in step **4**.

6 Click **OK**.

Excel applies the number format.

Change the Number of Decimal Places Displayed

Y ou can make your numeric values easier to read and interpret by adjusting the number of decimal places that Excel displays. For example, you might want to ensure that all dollar-and-cent values show two decimal places, while dollar-only values show no decimal places. Similarly, you can adjust the display of percentage values to suit your audience by showing more decimals (greater accuracy but more difficult to read) or fewer decimals (less accuracy but easier to read).

You can either decrease or increase the number of decimal places that Excel displays.

Change the Number of Decimal Places Displayed

Decrease the Number of Decimal Places

1 Select the range you want to format.

2 Click the **Home** tab.

3 Click the **Decrease Decimal** button (.00→.0).

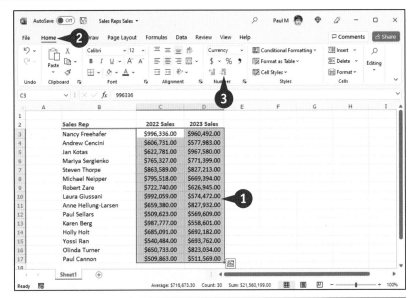

Ⓐ Excel decreases the number of decimal places by one.

4 Repeat step **3** until you get the number of decimal places you want.

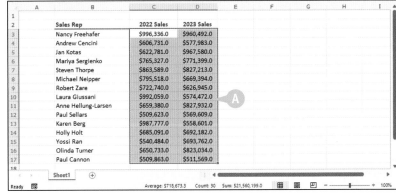

Increase the Number of Decimal Places

1 Select the range you want to format.

2 Click the **Home** tab.

3 Click the **Increase Decimal** button ($\leftarrow^0_{.00}$).

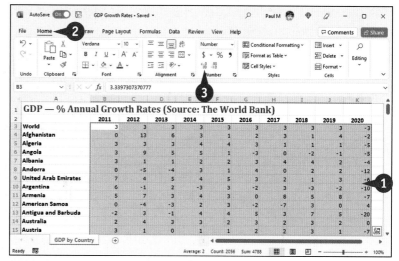

B Excel increases the number of decimal places by one.

4 Repeat step **3** until you get the number of decimal places you want.

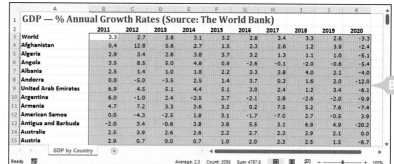

My range currently has values that display different numbers of decimal places. What happens when I change the number of decimal places?

In this situation, Excel uses the value that has the most displayed decimal places as the basis for formatting all the values. For example, if the selected range has values that display no, one, two, or four decimal places, Excel uses the value with four decimals as the basis. If you click **Decrease Decimal** ($\overset{.00}{\rightarrow}$), Excel displays every value with three decimal places; if you click **Increase Decimal** ($\leftarrow^0_{.00}$), Excel displays every value with five decimal places.

Apply a Conditional Format to a Range

You can make a worksheet easier to analyze by applying a conditional format to a range. A *conditional format* is formatting that Excel applies only to cells that meet the condition you specify. For example, you can tell Excel to apply the formatting only if a cell's value is greater than some specified amount.

When you set up your conditional format, you can specify the font, border, and background pattern, which helps to ensure that the cells that meet your criteria stand out from the other cells in the range.

Apply a Conditional Format to a Range

1 Select the range you want to work with.

2 Click the **Home** tab.

3 Click **Conditional Formatting**.

4 Click **Highlight Cells Rules**.

5 Click the operator you want to use for your condition.

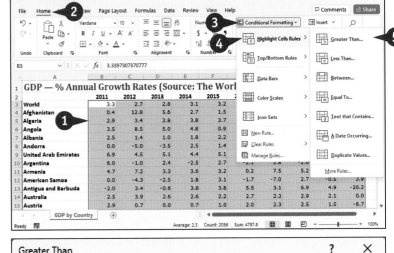

An operator dialog box appears, such as the Greater Than dialog box shown here.

6 Type the value you want to use for your condition.

A You can also click the **Collapse Dialog** button (↕) and then click a worksheet cell.

Depending on the operator, you may need to specify two values.

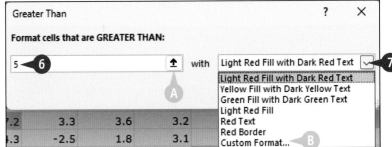

7 Click the **with** ⌄ and then click the formatting you want to use.

B To create your own format, click **Custom Format**.

8 Click **OK**.

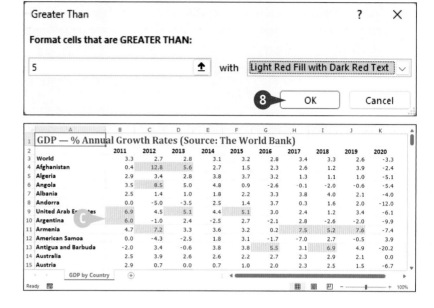

Greater Than
? ✕

Format cells that are GREATER THAN:

5 ⬆ with [Light Red Fill with Dark Red Text] ⌄

8 OK Cancel

C Excel applies the formatting to cells that meet your condition.

	A	B	C	D	E	F	G	H	I	J	K
1	GDP — % Annual Growth Rates (Source: The World Bank)										
2		2011	2012	2013	2014	2015	2016	2017	2018	2019	2020
3	World	3.3	2.7	2.8	3.1	3.2	2.8	3.4	3.3	2.6	-3.3
4	Afghanistan	0.4	12.8	5.6	2.7	1.5	2.3	2.6	1.2	3.9	-2.4
5	Algeria	2.9	3.4	2.8	3.8	3.7	3.2	1.3	1.1	1.0	-5.1
6	Angola	3.5	8.5	5.0	4.8	0.9	-2.6	-0.1	-2.0	-0.6	-5.4
7	Albania	2.5	1.4	1.0	1.8	2.2	3.3	3.8	4.0	2.1	-4.0
8	Andorra	0.0	-5.0	-3.5	2.5	1.4	3.7	0.3	1.6	2.0	-12.0
9	United Arab Er ✦es	6.9	4.5	5.1	4.4	5.1	3.0	2.4	1.2	3.4	-6.1
10	Argentina	6.0	-1.0	2.4	-2.5	2.7	-2.1	2.8	-2.6	-2.0	-9.9
11	Armenia	4.7	7.2	3.3	3.6	3.2	0.2	7.5	5.2	7.6	-7.4
12	American Samoa	0.0	-4.3	-2.5	1.8	3.1	-1.7	-7.0	2.7	-0.5	3.9
13	Antigua and Barbuda	-2.0	3.4	-0.6	3.8	3.8	5.5	3.1	6.9	4.9	-20.2
14	Australia	2.5	3.9	2.6	2.6	2.2	2.7	2.3	2.9	2.1	0.0
15	Austria	2.9	0.7	0.0	0.7	1.0	2.0	2.3	2.5	1.5	-6.7

GDP by Country ⊕

Ready 🔲 ▦ ▣ 🔲 — ▬ + 100%

TIPS

Can I set up more than one condition for a single range?

Yes. Excel enables you to specify multiple conditional formats. For example, you could set up one condition for cells that are greater than some value, and a separate condition for cells that are less than some other value. You can apply unique formats to each condition. Follow steps **1** to **8** to configure the new condition.

How do I remove a conditional format from a range?

If you no longer require a conditional format, you can delete it. Follow steps **1** to **3** to select the range and display the Conditional Formatting menu, and then click **Manage Rules**. Excel displays the Conditional Formatting Rules Manager dialog box. Click the **Show formatting rules for** ⌄ and then click **This Worksheet**. Click the conditional format you want to remove and then click **Delete Rule**. Click **OK** to return to the worksheet.

Apply a Style to a Range

You can reduce the time it takes to format your worksheets by applying the predefined Excel styles to your ranges. Excel comes with more than 20 predefined styles for different worksheet elements such as headings, numbers, calculations, and special range types such as explanatory text, worksheet notes, and warnings. Excel also offers two dozen styles associated with the current document theme.

Each style includes the number format, cell alignment, font typeface and size, border, and fill color.

Apply a Style to a Range

1 Select the range you want to format.

2 Click the **Home** tab.

3 Click **Cell Styles**.

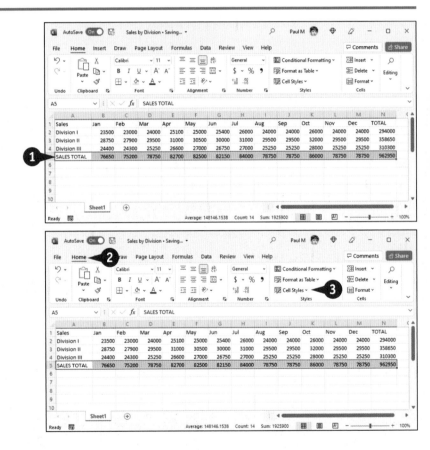

Excel displays the Cell Styles gallery.

4 Click the style you want to apply.

Note: If the style is not exactly the way you want, you can right-click the style, click **Modify**, and then click **Format** to customize the style.

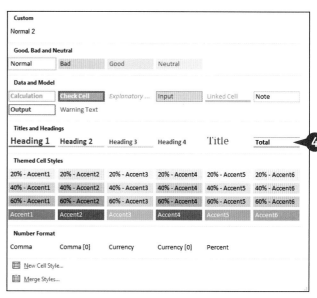

Ⓐ Excel applies the style to the range.

Are there styles I can use to format tabular data?

Yes. Excel comes with a gallery of table styles that offer formatting options that highlight the first row, apply different formats to alternating rows, and so on. Select the range that includes your data, click the **Home** tab, and then click **Format as Table**. In the gallery that appears, click the table format you want to apply.

Can I create my own style?

Yes. This is useful if you find yourself applying the same set of formatting options over and over. By saving those options as a custom style, you can apply it by following steps **1** to **4**. Apply your formatting to a cell or range, and then select that cell or range. Click **Home**, click **Cell Styles**, and then click **New Cell Style**. In the Style dialog box, type a name for your style, and then click **OK**.

Change the Column Width

You can make your worksheets neater and more readable by adjusting the column widths to suit the data contained in each column.

For example, if you have a large number or a long line of text in a cell, Excel may display only part of the cell value. To avoid this, you can increase the width of the column. Similarly, if a column only contains a few characters in each cell, you can decrease the width to fit more columns on the screen.

Change the Column Width

1 Click in any cell in the column you want to resize.

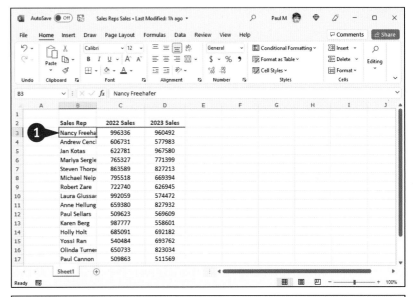

2 Click the **Home** tab.

3 Click **Format**.

4 Click **Column Width**.

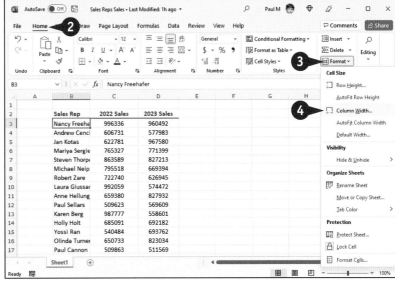

The Column Width dialog box appears.

5 In the Column width text box, type the width you want to use.

6 Click **OK**.

Column Width   ?   ✕

Column width: 20 ◂ **5**

6   OK   Cancel

	A	B	C	D	E
1					
2		Sales Rep	2022 Sales	2023 Sales	
3		Nancy Freehafer	996336	960492	
4		Andrew Cencini	606731	577983	
5		Jan Kotas	622781	967580	
6		Mariya Sergienko	765327	771399	
7		Steven Thorpe	863589	827213	
8		Michael Neipper	795518	669394	
9		Robert Zare	722740	626945	
10		Laura Giussani	992059	574472	
11		Anne Hellung-Larsen	659380	827932	
12		Paul Sellars	509623	569609	
13		Karen Berg	987777	558601	
14		Holly Holt	685091	692182	
15		Yossi Ran	540484	693762	
16		Olinda Turner	650733	823034	
17		Paul Cannon	509863	511569	

A Excel adjusts the column width.

B You can also move ✛ over the right edge of the column heading (✛ changes to ↔) and then click and drag the edge to set the width.

TIPS

Is there an easier way to adjust the column width to fit the contents of a column?

Yes. You can use the Excel AutoFit feature, which automatically adjusts the column width to fit the widest item in a column. Click any cell in the column, click **Home**, click **Format**, and then click **AutoFit Column Width**. Alternatively, move ✛ over the right edge of the column heading (✛ changes to ↔) and then double-click.

Is there a way to change all the column widths at once?

Yes. Click ◢ to select the entire worksheet, and then follow the steps in this section to set the width you prefer. If you have already adjusted some column widths and you want to change all the other widths, click **Home**, click **Format**, and then click **Default Width** to open the Standard Width dialog box. Type the new standard column width, and then click **OK**.

Change the Row Height

You can make your worksheet more visually appealing by increasing the row heights to create more space. This is particularly useful in worksheets that are crowded with text. Changing the row height is also useful if the current height is too small and your cell text is cut off at the top.

If you want to change the row height to display multiline text within a cell, you must also turn on text wrapping within the cell. See the following section, "Wrap Text Within a Cell."

Change the Row Height

1. Select a range that includes at least one cell in every row you want to resize.

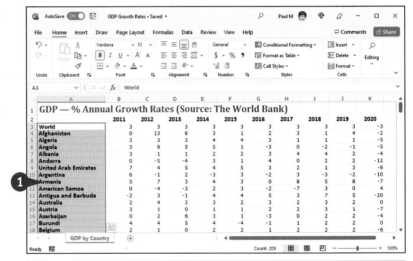

2. Click the **Home** tab.
3. Click **Format**.
4. Click **Row Height**.

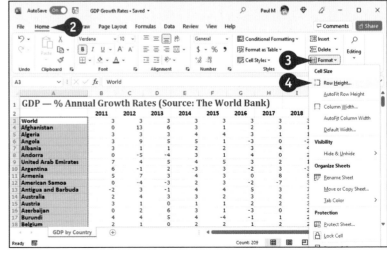

The Row Height dialog box appears.

5 In the Row height text box, type the height you want to use.

6 Click **OK**.

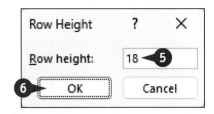

Ⓐ Excel adjusts the row heights.

Ⓑ You can also move ✛ over the bottom edge of a row heading (✛ changes to ✤) and then click and drag the bottom edge to set the height.

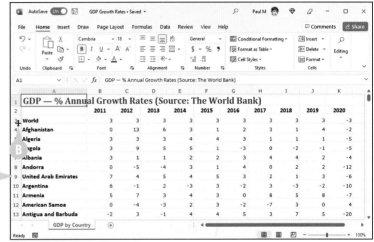

TIPS

Is there an easier way to adjust the row height to fit the contents of a row?
Yes. You can use the Excel AutoFit feature, which automatically adjusts the row height to fit the tallest item in a row. Click in any cell in the row, click **Home**, click **Format**, and then click **AutoFit Row Height**. Alternatively, move ✛ over the bottom edge of the row heading (✛ changes to ✤) and then double-click.

Is there a way to change all the row heights at once?
Yes. Click ◢ to select the entire worksheet. You can then either follow the steps

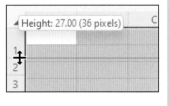

in this section to set the height manually, or move ✛ over the bottom edge of any row heading (✛ changes to ✤) and then click and drag the edge to set the height of all the rows.

Wrap Text Within a Cell

Y ou can make a long text entry in a cell more readable by formatting the cell to wrap the text. *Wrapping* cell text means that the text is displayed on multiple lines within the cell instead of just a single line.

If you type more text in a cell than can fit horizontally, Excel either displays the text over the next cell if it is empty or displays only part of the text if the next cell contains data. To prevent Excel from showing only truncated cell data, you can format the cell to wrap text within the cell.

Wrap Text Within a Cell

1 Select the cell that you want to format.

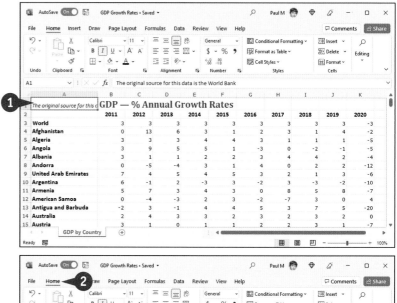

2 Click the **Home** tab.

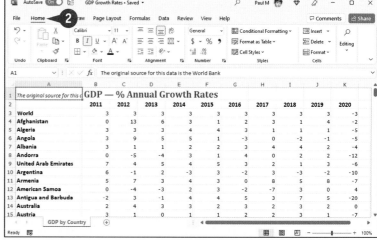

3 Click **Wrap Text** (ab).

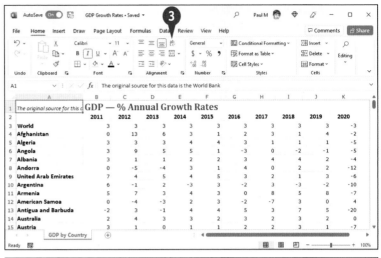

Excel turns on text wrapping for the selected cell.

A If the cell has more text than can fit horizontally, Excel wraps the text onto multiple lines and increases the row height to compensate.

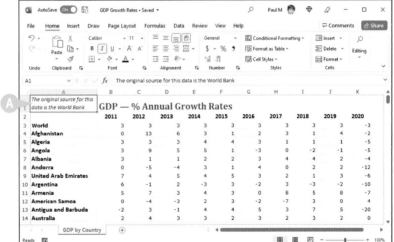

My text is only slightly bigger than the cell. Is there a way to view all the text without turning on text wrapping?

Yes. There are several things you can try. For example, you can widen the column until you see all your text; see the "Change the Column Width" section, earlier in this chapter.

Alternatively, you can try reducing the cell font size. One way to do this is to choose a smaller value in the **Font Size** list of the Home tab's Font group. However, an easier way is to click the Alignment group's dialog box launcher (⤢) to open the Format Cells dialog box with the Alignment tab displayed. Click the **Shrink to fit** check box (☐ changes to ☑) and then click **OK**.

Add Borders to a Range

You can make a range stand out from the rest of your worksheet data by adding a border around the range. For example, if you have a range of cells that are used as the input values for one or more formulas, you could add a border around the input cells to make it clear the cells in that range are related to each other.

You can also use borders to make a range easier to read. For example, if your range has totals on the bottom row, you can add a double border above the totals.

Add Borders to a Range

1 Select the range that you want to format.

2 Click the **Home** tab.

3 Click the **Borders** ⌄.

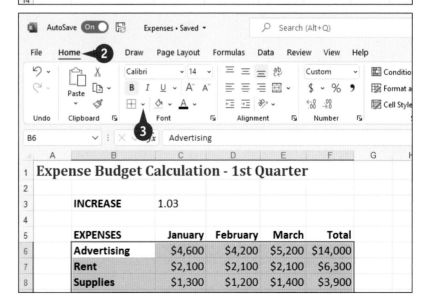

④ Click the type of border you want to use.

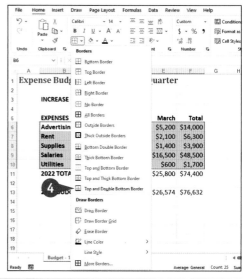

Ⓐ Excel applies the border to the range.

A	B	C	D	E	F	G	H
1 Expense Budget Calculation - 1st Quarter							
2							
3	INCREASE	1.03					
4							
5	EXPENSES	January	February	March	Total		
6	Advertising	$4,600	$4,200	$5,200	$14,000		
7	Rent	$2,100	$2,100	$2,100	$6,300		
8	Supplies	$1,300	$1,200	$1,400	$3,900		
9	Salaries	$16,000	$16,000	$16,500	$48,500		
10	Utilities	$500	$600	$600	$1,700		
11	2022 TOTAL	$24,500	$24,100	$25,800	$74,400		
12							
13	2023 BUDGET	$25,235	$24,823	$26,574	$76,632		
14							

TIPS

How do I get my borders to stand out from the worksheet gridlines?

One way to make your borders stand out is to click the **Borders** ⌄, click **Line Style**, and then click a thicker border style. You can also click **Line Color** and then click a color that is not a shade of gray. However, perhaps the most effective method is to turn off the worksheet gridlines. Click the **View** tab, and then in the Show group, click the **Gridlines** check box (☑ changes to ☐).

None of the border types is quite right for my worksheet. Can I create a custom border?

Yes. You can draw the border manually. Click the **Borders** ⌄ and then click **Draw Border**. Use the **Line Style** and **Line Color** lists to configure your border. Click a cell edge to add a border to that edge; click and drag a range to add a border around that range. If you prefer to create a grid where the border surrounds every cell, click the **Draw Border Grid** command instead.

Copy Formatting from One Cell to Another

Ymuch of time by copying existing formatting to other areas of a
worksheet.

As you have seen in this chapter, although formatting cells is not difficult, it can be time-consuming to apply the font, color, alignment, number format, and other options. After you spend time formatting text or data, rather than spending time repeating the steps for other data, you can use the Format Painter tool to copy the formatting with a couple of mouse clicks.

Copy Formatting from One Cell to Another

1 Select the cell that has the formatting you want to copy.

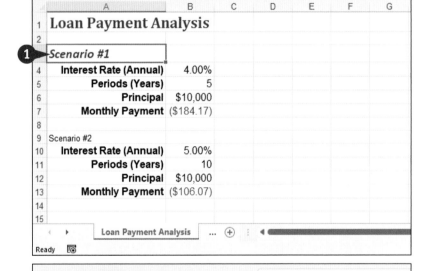

2 Click the **Home** tab.

3 Click **Format Painter** (🖌).

⊹ changes to ⊹🖌.

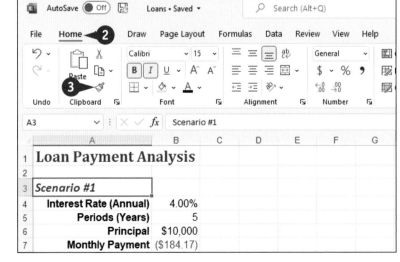

④ Click the cell to which you want to copy the formatting.

Note: If you want to apply the formatting to multiple cells, click and drag 🖑🖌 over the cells.

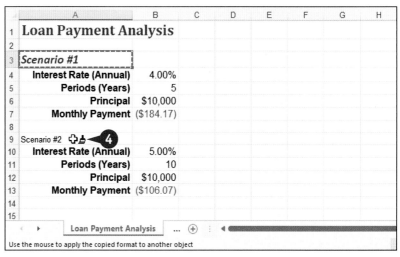

A Excel copies the formatting to the cell.

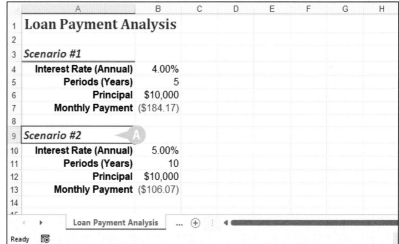

Is there an easy way to copy formatting to multiple cells or ranges?
Yes. If the cells are together, you can click and drag over the cells to apply the copied formatting. If the cells or ranges are not together, Excel offers a shortcut that means you do not have to select the Format Painter multiple times to copy formatting to multiple ranges.

Click the cell that contains the formatting you want to copy, click the **Home** tab, and then double-click 🖌. Click each cell to which you want to copy the formatting or click and drag over each range that you want to format. When you are done, click 🖌 to cancel the Format Painter command.

CHAPTER 6

Building Formulas

Are you ready to start creating powerful and useful worksheets by build
your own formulas? This chapter explains formulas, shows you how to b
them, and shows you how to incorporate the versatile worksheet functic
Excel into your formulas.

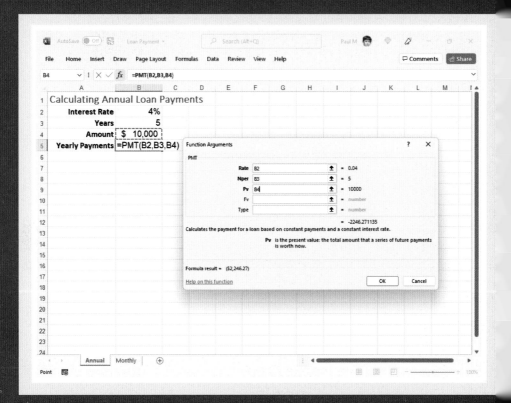

Understanding Excel Formulas

Although you can use Excel to create simple databases to store text, numbers, dates, and other data, the spreadsheets you create are also designed to analyze data and make calculations. Therefore, to get the most out of Excel, you need to understand formulas so that you can use them to analyze and perform calculations on your worksheet data.

To build accurate and useful formulas, you need to know the components of a formula, including operators and operands. You also need to understand arithmetic and comparison formulas as well as the importance of precedence when building a formula.

Formulas

A *formula* is a set of symbols and values that perform some kind of calculation and produce a result. All Excel formulas have the same general structure: an equal sign (=) followed by one or more operands and operators. The equal sign tells Excel to interpret everything that follows in the cell as a formula. For example, if you type =7 + 8 into a cell, Excel interprets the 7+8 text as a formula, and displays the result (15) in the cell.

Operands

Every Excel formula includes one or more *operands*, which are the data that Excel uses in the calculation. The simplest type of operand is a constant value, which is usually a number. However, most Excel formulas include references to worksheet data, which can be a cell address (such as A1), a range address (such as B1:B5), or a range name. Finally, you can also use any of the built-in Excel functions as an operand.

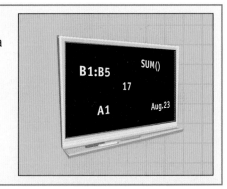

Operators

In an Excel formula that contains two or more operands, each operand is separated by an *operator*, which is a symbol that combines the operands in some way, usually mathematically. Example operators include the plus sign (+) and the multiplication sign (*). For example, the formula =B1 + B2 + B3 adds the values in cells B1, B2, and B3. Similarly, the formula =C3 * F10 multiplies the values in cells C3 and F10.

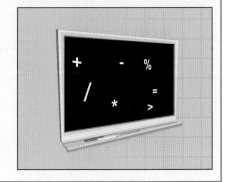

Arithmetic Formulas

An arithmetic formula combines numeric operands — numeric constants, functions that return numeric results, and fields or items that contain numeric values — with mathematical operators to perform a calculation. Because Excel worksheets primarily deal with numeric data, arithmetic formulas are by far the most common formulas used in worksheet calculations.

The following table lists the seven arithmetic operators that you can use to construct arithmetic formulas:

Operator	Name	Example	Result
+	Addition	=10 + 5	15
−	Subtraction	=10 − 5	5
−	Negation	=−10	−10
*	Multiplication	=10 * 5	50
/	Division	=10 / 5	2
%	Percentage	=10%	0.1
^	Exponentiation	=10 ^ 5	100000

Comparison Formulas

A comparison formula combines numeric operands — numeric constants, functions that return numeric results, and fields or items that contain numeric values — with special operators to compare one operand with another. A comparison formula always returns a logical result. This means that if the comparison is true, then the formula returns the value TRUE, which is equivalent to the numeric value 1; if the comparison is false, then the formula returns the value FALSE, which is equivalent to the numeric value 0.

The following table lists the six operators that you can use to construct comparison formulas:

Operator	Name	Example	Result
=	Equal to	=10 = 5	FALSE
<	Less than	=10 < 5	FALSE
<=	Less than or equal to	=10 <= 5	FALSE
>	Greater than	=10 > 5	TRUE
>=	Greater than or equal to	=10 >= 5	TRUE
<>	Not equal to	=10 <> 5	TRUE

Operator Precedence

Most of your formulas include multiple operands and operators. In many cases, the order in which Excel performs the calculations is crucial. For example, consider the formula =3 + 5 ^ 2. If you calculate from left to right, the answer you get is 64 (3 + 5 equals 8, and 8 ^ 2 equals 64). However, if you perform the exponentiation first and then the addition, the result is 28 (5 ^ 2 equals 25, and 3 + 25 equals 28). Therefore, a single formula can produce multiple answers, depending on the order in which you perform the calculations.

To solve this problem, Excel evaluates a formula according to a predefined order of precedence, which is determined by the formula operators, as shown in the following table:

Operator	Operation	Precedence
( )	Parentheses	1st
−	Negation	2nd
%	Percentage	3rd
^	Exponentiation	4th
* and /	Multiplication and division	5th
+ and −	Addition and subtraction	6th
= < <= > >= <>	Comparison	7th

Build a Formula

Y ou can add a formula to a worksheet cell using a technique similar to adding data to a cell. To ensure that Excel treats the text as a formula, begin with an equal sign (=) and then type your operands and operators.

When you add a formula to a cell, Excel displays the formula result in the cell, not the actual formula. For example, if you add the formula =C3 + C4 to a cell, that cell displays the sum of the values in cells C3 and C4. To see the formula, click the cell and examine the formula bar.

Build a Formula

1 Click in the cell in which you want to build the formula.

2 Type =.

A Your typing also appears in the formula bar.

Note: You can also type the formula into the formula bar.

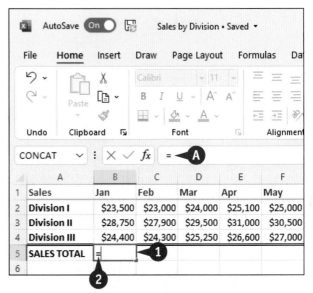

3 Type or click an operand. For example, to reference a cell in your formula, click in the cell.

B Excel inserts the address of the clicked cell into the formula.

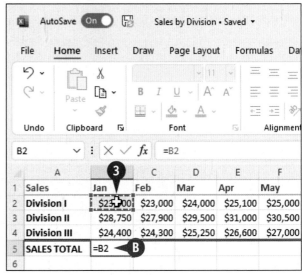

④ Type a space, type an operator, and then type another space.

Note: Typing a space before and after each operand is optional, but it's recommended because it makes your formulas easier to read.

⑤ Repeat steps **3** and **4** to add other operands and operators to your formula.

⑥ Click ✓ or press **Enter**.

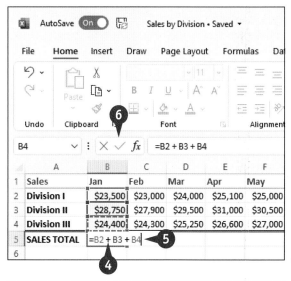

ⓒ Excel displays the formula result in the cell.

ⓓ The formula appears in the formula bar whenever you select the cell.

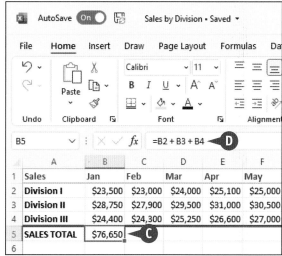

TIPS

If Excel displays only the result of the formula, how do I make changes to the formula?

Excel displays the formula result in the cell, but it still keeps track of the original formula. To display the formula again, you have two choices: Click the cell and then edit the formula using the formula bar, or double-click the cell (or press F2) to display the original formula in the cell and then edit the formula. In both cases, click ✓ or press **Enter** when you finish editing the formula.

If I have several formulas, is there an easy way to view them?

Yes. You can configure the worksheet to temporarily show the formulas instead of their results. Click the **Formulas** tab and then click **Show formulas** (🖩). To return to showing the formula results, click **Formulas** and then click 🖩 again. You can also toggle between formulas and results by pressing **Ctrl**+**`**.

To build powerful and useful formulas, you often need to include one or more Excel functions as operands. To get the most out of functions and to help you build formulas quickly and easily, you need to understand a few things about functions. For example, you need to know the advantages of using functions as well as the basic structure of every function. To help you get a sense of what is available and how you might use functions, we'll review the Excel function types.

Functions

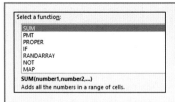

A *function* is a predefined formula that performs a specific task. For example, the SUM function calculates the total of a list of numbers, and the PMT (payment) function calculates a loan or mortgage payment. You can use functions on their own, preceded by =, or as part of a larger formula.

Function Advantages

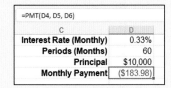

Functions are designed to take you beyond the basic arithmetic and comparison formulas by offering two main advantages. First, functions make simple but cumbersome formulas easier to use. For example, calculating a loan payment requires a complex formula, but the Excel PMT function makes this easy.

Second, functions enable you to include complex mathematical expressions in your worksheets that otherwise would be difficult or impossible to construct using simple arithmetic operators.

Function Structure

Every worksheet function has the same basic structure: NAME(Argument1, Argument2, . . .). The NAME part

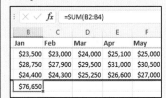

identifies the function. In worksheet formulas and custom PivotTable formulas, the function name always appears in uppercase letters: PMT, SUM, AVERAGE, and so on. The items that appear within the parentheses are the functions' *arguments*. The arguments are the inputs that functions use to perform calculations. For example, the function SUM(B2, B3, B4) adds the values in cells B2, B3, and B4.

Mathematical Functions

The following table lists some common mathematical functions:

Function	Description
MOD(number, divisor)	Returns the remainder of a number after dividing by the divisor
PI( )	Returns the value of Pi
PRODUCT(number1, number2,. . .)	Multiplies the specified numbers
RAND( )	Returns a random number between 0 and 1
RANDBETWEEN(number1, number2)	Returns a random number between the two numbers
ROUND(number, digits)	Rounds the number to a specified number of digits
SQRT(number)	Returns the positive square root of the number
SUM(number1, number2,. . .)	Adds the arguments

Statistical Functions

The following table lists some common statistical functions:

Function	Description
AVERAGE(number1, number2,. . .)	Returns the average of the arguments
COUNT(number1, number2,. . .)	Counts the numbers in the argument list
MAX(number1, number2,. . .)	Returns the maximum value of the arguments
MEDIAN(number1, number2,. . .)	Returns the median value of the arguments
MIN(number1, number2,. . .)	Returns the minimum value of the arguments
MODE.SNGL(number1, number2,. . .)	Returns the most common value of the arguments
STDEV.S(number1, number2,. . .)	Returns the standard deviation based on a sample
STDEV.P(number1, number2,. . .)	Returns the standard deviation based on an entire population

Financial Functions

Most of the Excel financial functions use the following arguments:

Argument	Description
rate	The fixed rate of interest over the term of the loan or investment
nper	The number of payments or deposit periods over the term of the loan or investment
pmt	The periodic payment or deposit
pv	The present value of the loan (the principal) or the initial deposit in an investment
fv	The future value of the loan or investment
type	The type of payment or deposit: 0 (the default) for end-of-period payments or deposits; 1 for beginning-of-period payments or deposits

The following table lists some common financial functions:

Function	Description
FV(rate, nper, pmt, pv, type)	Returns the future value of an investment or loan
IPMT(rate, per, nper, pv, fv, type)	Returns the interest payment for a specified period of a loan
NPER(rate, pmt, pv, fv, type)	Returns the number of periods for an investment or loan
PMT(rate, nper, pv, fv, type)	Returns the periodic payment for a loan or investment
PPMT(rate, per, nper, pv, fv, type)	Returns the principal payment for a specified period of a loan
PV(rate, nper, pmt, fv, type)	Returns the present value of an investment
RATE(nper, pmt, pv, fv, type, guess)	Returns the periodic interest rate for a loan or investment

To get the benefit of an Excel function, you need to use it within a formula. You can use a function as the only operand in the formula, or you can include the function as part of a larger formula. To make it easy to choose the function you need and to add the appropriate arguments, Excel offers the Insert Function feature. This is a dialog box that enables you to display functions by category and then choose the function you want from a list. You then see the Function Arguments dialog box, where you can easily see and fill in the arguments used by the function.

Add a Function to a Formula

1 Click in the cell in which you want to build the formula.

2 Type =.

3 Type any operands and operators you need before adding the function (not shown).

4 Click the **Insert Function** button (fx).

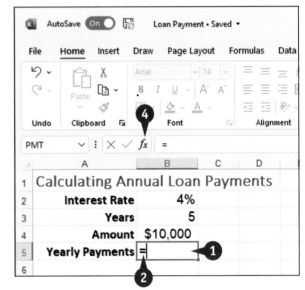

The Insert Function dialog box appears.

5 Click ⌄ and then click the category that contains the function you want to use.

6 Click the function.

7 Click **OK**.

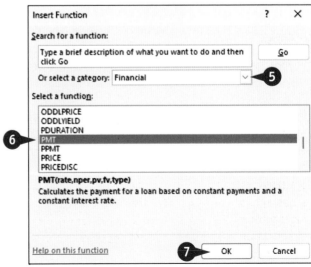

The Function Arguments dialog box appears.

⑧ Click inside an argument box.

⑨ Click the cell that contains the argument value.

You can also type the argument value.

⑩ Repeat steps **8** and **9** to fill as many arguments as you need.

Ⓐ The function result appears here.

⑪ Click **OK**.

Ⓑ Excel adds the function to the formula.

Ⓒ Excel displays the formula result.

Note: In this example, the result appears in the parentheses to indicate a negative value. In loan calculations, money that you pay out is always a negative amount.

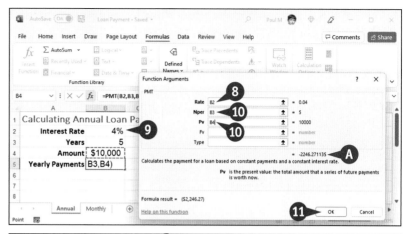

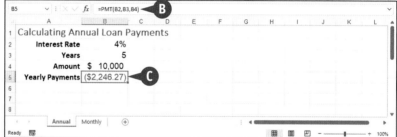

Note: If your formula requires any other operands and operators, press F2 and then type what you need to complete your formula.

TIPS

Do I have to specify a value for every function argument?

Not necessarily. Some function arguments are required to obtain a result, but others are optional. In the PMT function, for example, the rate, nper, and pv arguments are required, but the fv and type arguments are optional. When the Function Arguments dialog box displays a result for the function, you know you have entered all the required arguments.

How do I calculate a monthly financial result if I only have yearly values?

This is a common problem. For example, if your loan payment worksheet contains an annual interest rate and a loan term in years, how do you calculate the monthly payment using the PMT function? You need to convert the rate and term to monthly values. That is, you divide the annual interest rate by 12, and you multiply the term by 12. For example, if the annual rate is in cell B2, the term in years is in B3, and the loan amount is in B4, then the function PMT(B2/12, B3*12, B4) calculates the monthly payment.

Add a Range of Numbers

You can quickly add worksheet numbers by building a formula that uses the Excel SUM function. When you use the SUM function in a formula, you can specify as the function's arguments a series of individual cells. For example, SUM(A1, B2, C3) calculates the total of the values in cells A1, B2, and C3.

However, you can also use the SUM function to specify just a single argument, which is a range reference, usually to a collection of cells within a single row or column. For example, SUM(C3:C17) calculates the total of the values in all the cells in the range C3 to C17.

Add a Range of Numbers

1 Click in the cell where you want the sum to appear.

2 Type **=sum(**.

A When you begin a function, Excel displays a banner that shows you the function's arguments.

Note: In the function banner, bold arguments are required, and arguments that appear in square brackets are optional.

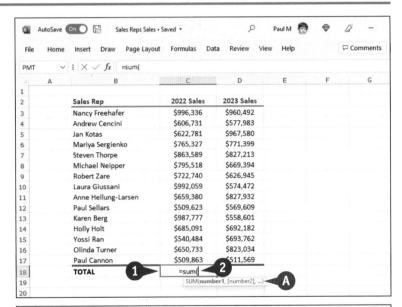

3 Use the mouse ✥ to click and drag the row or column of numbers that you want to add.

B Excel adds a reference for the range to the formula.

④ Type).

⑤ Click ✓ or press Enter.

C3	✓ : ✗ ✓ fx	=sum(C3:C17)				
	A	B	C	D	E	F	G
1							
2		Sales Rep	2022 Sales	2023 Sales			
3		Nancy Freehafer	$996,336	$960,492			
4		Andrew Cencini	$606,731	$577,983			
5		Jan Kotas	$622,781	$967,580			
6		Mariya Sergienko	$765,327	$771,399			
7		Steven Thorpe	$863,589	$827,213			
8		Michael Neipper	$795,518	$669,394			
9		Robert Zare	$722,740	$626,945			
10		Laura Giussani	$992,059	$574,472			
11		Anne Hellung-Larsen	$659,380	$827,932			
12		Paul Sellars	$509,623	$569,609			
13		Karen Berg	$987,777	$558,601			
14		Holly Holt	$685,091	$692,182			
15		Yossi Ran	$540,484	$693,762			
16		Olinda Turner	$650,733	$823,034			
17		Paul Cannon	$509,863	$511,569			
18		TOTAL	=sum(C3:C17)				
19							
20							

ⓒ Excel completes the formula.

ⓓ Excel displays the sum in the cell.

C18	✓ : ✗ ✓ fx	=SUM(C3:C17)				
	A	B	C	D	E	F	G
1							
2		Sales Rep	2022 Sales	2023 Sales			
3		Nancy Freehafer	$996,336	$960,492			
4		Andrew Cencini	$606,731	$577,983			
5		Jan Kotas	$622,781	$967,580			
6		Mariya Sergienko	$765,327	$771,399			
7		Steven Thorpe	$863,589	$827,213			
8		Michael Neipper	$795,518	$669,394			
9		Robert Zare	$722,740	$626,945			
10		Laura Giussani	$992,059	$574,472			
11		Anne Hellung-Larsen	$659,380	$827,932			
12		Paul Sellars	$509,623	$569,609			
13		Karen Berg	$987,777	$558,601			
14		Holly Holt	$685,091	$692,182			
15		Yossi Ran	$540,484	$693,762			
16		Olinda Turner	$650,733	$823,034			
17		Paul Cannon	$509,863	$511,569			
18		TOTAL	$10,908,032				
19							
20							

TIPS

Can I use the SUM function to total rows and columns at the same time?

Yes, the SUM function works not only with simple row and column ranges, but with any rectangular range. After you type **=sum(**, use the mouse ✛ to click and drag the entire range that you want to sum.

Can I use the SUM function to total only certain values in a row or column?

Yes. The SUM function can accept multiple arguments, so you can enter as many cells or ranges as you need. After you type **=sum(**, hold down Ctrl and either click each cell that you want to include in the total or use the mouse ✛ to click and drag each range that you want to sum.

You can reduce the time it takes to build a worksheet as well as reduce the possibility of errors by using the Excel AutoSum feature. This tool adds a SUM function formula to a cell and automatically adds the function arguments based on the structure of the worksheet data. For example, if there is a column of numbers above the cell where you want the SUM function to appear, AutoSum automatically includes that column of numbers as the SUM function argument.

Build an AutoSum Formula

1 Click in the cell where you want the sum to appear.

Note: For AutoSum to work, the cell you select should be below or to the right of the range you want to sum.

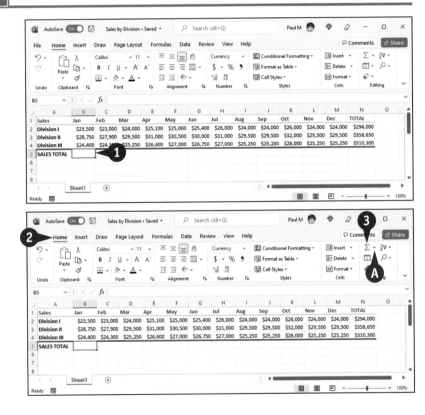

2 Click the **Home** tab.

3 Click the **Sum** button (∑).

Ⓐ If you want to use a function other than SUM, click the **Sum** ∨ and then click the operation you want to use: Average, Count Numbers, Max, or Min.

B Excel adds a SUM function formula to the cell.

Note: You can also press **Alt**+**=** instead of clicking ∑.

C Excel guesses that the range above (as shown in this example) or to the left of the cell is the one you want to add.

If Excel guessed wrong, you can select the correct range manually.

4 Click ✓ or press **Enter**.

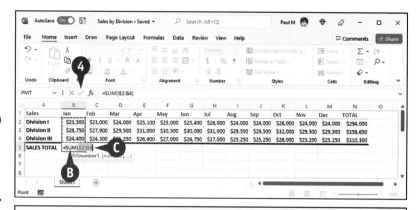

D Excel completes the formula.

E Excel displays the sum in the cell.

TIPS

Is there a way to see the sum of a range without adding an AutoSum formula?

Yes. You can use the Excel status bar to do this. When you select any range, Excel adds the range's numeric values and displays the result in the middle of the status bar — for example, Sum: 76,650. By default, Excel also displays the Average and Count. If you want to see a different calculation, right-click the result in the status bar and then click the operation you want to use: Numerical Count, Maximum, or Minimum.

Is there a faster way to add an AutoSum formula?

Yes. If you know the range you want to sum, and that range is either a vertical column with a blank cell below it or a horizontal row with a blank cell to its right, select the range (including the blank cell) and then click ∑ or press **Alt**+**=**. Excel populates the blank cell with a SUM formula that totals the selected range.

Add a Range Name to a Formula

You can make your formulas easier to build, more accurate, and easier to read by using range names as operands instead of cell and range addresses. For example, the formula =SUM(B2:B10) is difficult to decipher on its own, particularly if you cannot see the range B2:B10 to examine its values. However, if you use the formula =SUM(Expenses) instead, it becomes immediately obvious what the formula is meant to do.

See Chapter 4 to learn how to define names for ranges in Excel.

Add a Range Name to a Formula

1 Click in the cell in which you want to build the formula, type **=**, and then type any operands and operators you need before adding the range name.

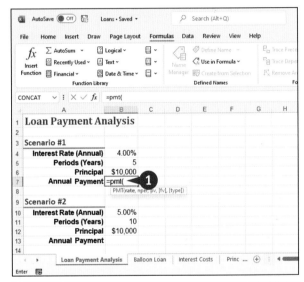

2 Click the **Formulas** tab.

3 Click **Use in Formula**.

A Excel displays a list of the range names in the current workbook.

4 Click the range name you want to use.

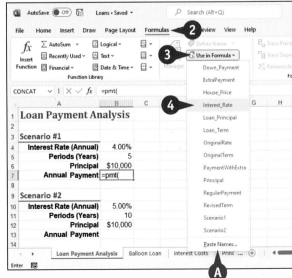

B Excel inserts the range name into the formula.

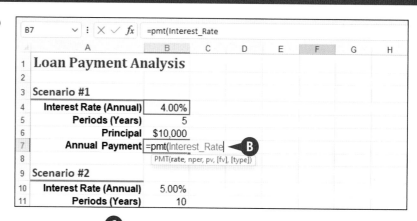

5 Type any operands and operators you need to complete your formula.

C If you need to insert other range names into your formula, repeat steps **2** to **5** for each name.

6 Click ✓ or press Enter.

Excel calculates the formula result.

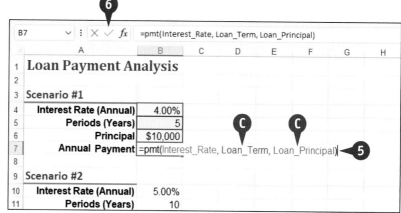

TIPS

If I create a range name after I build my formula, is there an easy way to convert the range reference to the range name?

Yes. Excel offers an Apply Names feature that replaces range references with their associated range names throughout a worksheet. Click the **Formulas** tab, click the **Define Name** ⌄, and then click **Apply Names** to open the Apply Names dialog box. In the Apply names list, click the range name you want to use, and then click **OK**. Excel replaces the associated range references with the range name in each formula in the current worksheet.

Do I have to use the list of range names to insert range names into my formula?

No. As you build your formula, you can type the range name manually, if you know it. Alternatively, as you build your formula, click the cell or select the range that has the defined name, and Excel adds the name to your formula instead of the range address. If you want to work from a list of defined range names, click an empty area of the worksheet, click **Formulas**, click **Use in Formula**, click **Paste Names**, and then click **Paste List**.

Reference Another Worksheet Range in a Formula

You can add flexibility to your formulas by adding references to ranges that reside in other worksheets. This enables you to take advantage of work you have done in other worksheets, so you do not have to waste time repeating your work in the current worksheet.

Referencing a range in another worksheet also gives you the advantage of having automatically updated information. For example, if the data in the other worksheet range changes, Excel automatically updates your formula result to include the changed data when you save your work.

Reference Another Worksheet Range in a Formula

1 Click in the cell in which you want to build the formula, type =, and then type any operands and operators you need before adding the range reference.

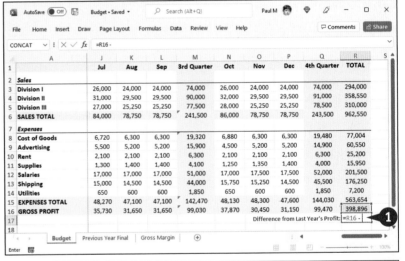

2 Press `Ctrl` + `Page down` until the worksheet you want to use appears.

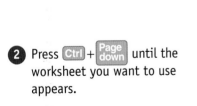

3 Select the cell or range you want to use.

4 Press `Ctrl` + `Page up` until you return to the original worksheet.

	I	J	K	L	M	N	O	P	Q	R
1	2nd Quarter	Jul	Aug	Sep	3rd Quarter	Oct	Nov	Dec	4th Quarter	TOTAL
2										
3	69,460	23,920	22,080	22,080	68,080	23,920	22,080	22,080	68,080	270,480
4	84,180	28,520	27,140	27,140	82,800	29,440	27,140	27,140	83,720	329,866
5	73,922	24,840	23,230	23,230	71,300	25,760	23,230	23,230	72,220	285,200
6	227,562	77,280	72,450	72,450	222,180	79,120	72,450	72,450	224,020	885,546
7										
8	19,115	6,492	6,086	6,086	18,663	6,646	6,086	6,086	18,818	74,386
9	16,538	5,775	5,460	5,460	16,695	4,725	5,460	5,460	15,645	63,578
10	6,615	2,205	2,205	2,205	6,615	2,205	2,205	2,205	6,615	26,460
11	4,148	1,365	1,470	1,470	4,305	1,313	1,418	1,470	4,200	16,748
12	52,500	17,850	17,850	17,850	53,550	17,850	18,375	18,375	54,600	211,575
13	46,463	15,750	15,225	15,225	46,200	16,538	16,013	15,225	47,775	185,063
14	1,890	683	630	630	1,943	683	630	630	1,943	7,560
15	147,268	50,119	48,926	48,926	147,971	49,959	50,186	49,451	149,595	585,368
16	80,294	27,161	23,524	23,524	74,209	29,161	22,264	22,999	74,425	300,178
17										
18										

Budget | Previous Year Final | Gross Margin

Point

A A reference to the range on the other worksheet appears in your formula.

5 Type any operands and operators you need to complete your formula (not shown).

6 Click ✓ or press `Enter`.

Excel calculates the formula result.

R17 f_x =R16 - 'Previous Year Final'!R16

	A	L	M	N	O	P	Q	R	S	T	U
1		Sep	3rd Quarter	Oct	Nov	Dec	4th Quarter	TOTAL			
2	Sales										
3	Division I	24,000	74,000	26,000	24,000	24,000	74,000	294,000			
4	Division II	29,500	90,000	32,000	29,500	29,500	91,000	358,550			
5	Division III	25,250	77,500	28,000	25,250	25,250	78,500	310,000			
6	SALES TOTAL	78,750	241,500	86,000	78,750	78,750	243,500	962,550			
7	Expenses										
8	Cost of Goods	6,300	19,320	6,880	6,300	6,300	19,480	77,004			
9	Advertising	5,200	15,900	4,500	5,200	5,200	14,900	60,550			
10	Rent	2,100	6,300	2,100	2,100	2,100	6,300	25,200			
11	Supplies	1,400	4,100	1,250	1,350	1,400	4,000	15,950			
12	Salaries	17,000	51,000	17,000	17,500	17,500	52,000	201,500			
13	Shipping	14,500	44,000	15,750	15,250	14,500	45,500	176,250			
14	Utilities	600	1,850	650	600	600	1,850	7,200			
15	EXPENSES TOTAL	47,100	142,470	48,130	48,300	47,600	144,030	563,654			
16	GROSS PROFIT	31,650	99,030	37,870	30,450	31,150	99,470	398,896			
17							Difference from Last Year's Profit:	=R16 - 'Previous Year Final'!R16			
18											

Budget | Previous Year Final | Gross Margin

TIPS

Can I manually reference a range in another worksheet?

Yes. Rather than selecting the other worksheet range with your mouse, you can type the range reference directly into your formula. Type the worksheet name, surrounded by single quotation marks (') if the name contains a space; type an exclamation mark (!); then type the cell or range address. Here is an example: **'Team Expenses'!B2:B10**.

Can I reference a range in another workbook in my formula?

Yes. First make sure the workbook you want to reference is open. When you reach the point in your formula where you want to add the reference, click the Excel icon (⬛) in the Windows taskbar, and then click the other workbook to switch to it. Click the worksheet that has the range you want to reference, and then select the range. Click ⬛ and then click the original workbook to switch back to it. Excel adds the other workbook range reference to your formula.

Move or Copy a Formula

You can restructure or reorganize a worksheet by moving an existing formula to a different part of the worksheet. When you move a formula, Excel preserves the formula's range references.

Excel also enables you to make a copy of a formula, which is a useful technique if you require a duplicate of the formula elsewhere or if you require a formula that is similar to an existing formula. When you copy a formula, Excel adjusts the range references to the new location.

Move or Copy a Formula

Move a Formula

1 Click the cell that contains the formula you want to move.

2 Position ⊕ over any outside border of the cell (⊕ changes to ⬚).

3 Click and drag the cell to the new location (⬚ changes to ⬚).

Ⓐ Excel displays an outline of the cell.

Ⓑ Excel displays the address of the new location.

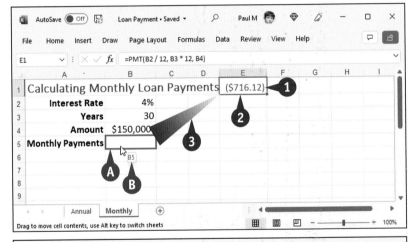

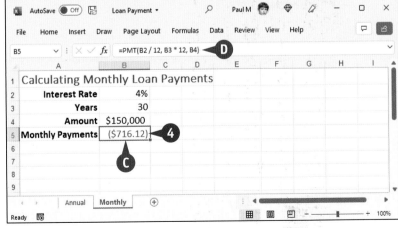

4 Release the mouse button.

Ⓒ Excel moves the formula to the new location.

Ⓓ Excel does not change the formula's range references.

Copy a Formula

1 Click the cell that contains the formula you want to copy.

2 Press and hold **Ctrl**.

3 Position ✥ over any outside border of the cell (✥ changes to ▨).

4 Click and drag the cell to the location where you want the copy to appear.

E Excel displays an outline of the cell.

F Excel displays the address of the new location.

5 Release the mouse button.

6 Release **Ctrl**.

G Excel creates a copy of the formula in the new location.

H Excel adjusts the range references.

Note: You can make multiple copies by dragging the bottom-right corner of the cell. Excel fills the adjacent cells with copies of the formula. See the following section, "Switch to Absolute Cell References," for an example.

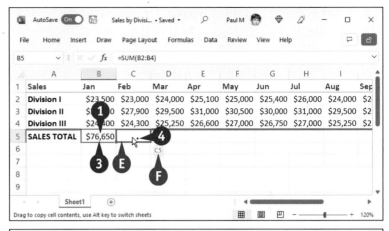

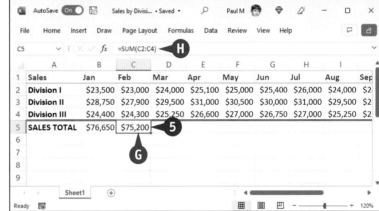

TIP

Why does Excel adjust the range references when I copy a formula?

When you make a copy of a formula, Excel assumes that you want that copy to reference different ranges than in the original formula. In particular, Excel assumes that the ranges you want to use in the new formula are positioned relative to the ranges used in the original formula, and that the relative difference is equal to the number of rows and columns you dragged the cell to create the copy.

For example, suppose your original formula references cell A1, and you make a copy of the formula in the cell one column to the right. In that case, Excel also adjusts the cell reference one column to the right, so it becomes B1 in the new formula. To learn how to control this behavior, see the following section, "Switch to Absolute Cell References."

You can make some formulas easier to copy by switching to absolute cell references. When you use a regular cell address — called a *relative cell reference* — such as A1 in a formula, Excel adjusts that reference when you copy the formula to another location. To prevent that reference from changing, you must change it to the *absolute cell reference* format: A1.

See the first tip at the end of this section to learn more about the difference between relative and absolute cell references.

Switch to Absolute Cell References

1 Double-click the cell that contains the formula you want to edit.

2 Select the cell reference you want to change.

3 Press F4.

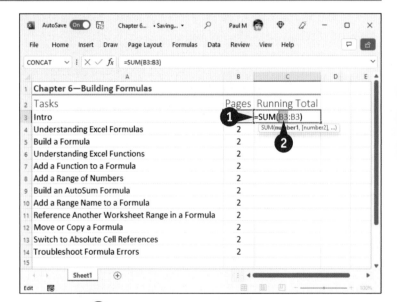

A Excel switches the address to an absolute cell reference.

4 Repeat steps **2** and **3** to switch any other cell addresses that you require in the absolute reference format.

5 Click ✓ or press Enter.

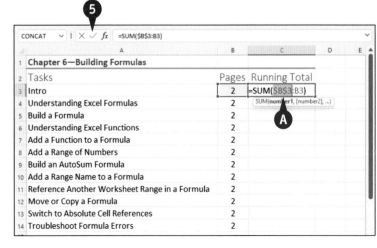

B Excel adjusts the formula.

6 Copy the formula.

Note: See the previous section, "Move or Copy a Formula," to learn how to copy a formula.

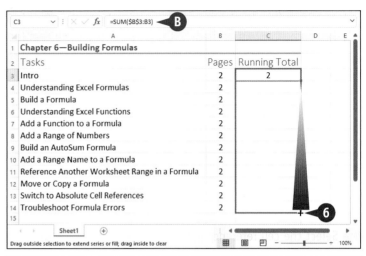

C Excel preserves the absolute cell references in the copied formulas.

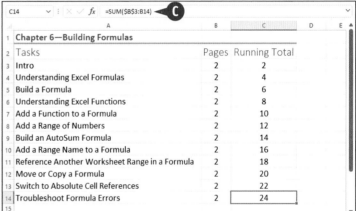

TIPS

What is the difference between absolute cell references and relative cell references?

When you use a cell reference in a formula, Excel treats that reference as being relative to the formula's cell. For example, if the formula is in cell B5 and it references cell A1, Excel effectively treats A1 as the cell four rows up and one column to the left. If you copy the formula to cell D10, then the cell four rows up and one column to the left now refers to cell C6, so in the copied formula Excel changes A1 to C6. If the original formula instead refers to A1, then the copied formula in cell D10 also refers to A1.

How do I restore a cell address back to a relative cell reference?

You can use the F4 keyboard technique, which runs the address through four different reference formats. Press F4 once to switch to the absolute cell reference format, such as A1. Press F4 again to switch to a mixed reference format that uses a relative column and absolute row (A$1). Press F4 a third time to switch to a mixed reference format that uses an absolute column and relative row ($A1). Finally, press F4 a fourth time to return to the relative cell reference (A1).

Despite your best efforts, a formula may return an inaccurate or erroneous result. To help you fix such problem formulas, there are a few troubleshooting techniques you can use, such as checking for incorrect range references or function arguments, confirming your data, and checking for punctuation errors such as missing colons or parentheses.

If Excel displays an error such as #DIV/0! instead of a result, then you also need to understand these error messages so that you can troubleshoot and correct the problem.

Confirm Range References

If your formula is returning an unexpected or inaccurate result, the first thing to check is your range and cell references. For example, if your data is in the range B9:B15, but your formula uses B9:B14, then the result will be inaccurate. The easiest way to check the range and cell references is to double-click the cell containing the formula. Excel highlights the range referenced by the formula, so you can see at a glance which range your formula is using.

	A	B	C	D
2		Jan	Feb	Mar
8	*Expenses*			
9	Cost of Goods	6,132	5,984	6,300
10	Advertising	4,600	4,200	5,200
11	Rent	2,100	2,100	2,100
12	Supplies	1,300	1,200	1,400
13	Salaries	16,000	16,000	16,500
14	Shipping	14,250	13,750	14,500
15	Utilities	500	600	600
16	**EXPENSES TOTAL**	=SUM(B9:B14)	43,834	46,600
17	**GROSS PROFIT**	32,268	30,966	32,150

Confirm Range Data

If your formula is correct but it is still producing unexpected results, the problem might lie with the data instead of the formula. Double-check your range data to make sure that it is accurate and up-to-date.

C7 fx =SUM(C4:C6)

	A	B	C	D	
2		Jan	Feb	Mar	
3	*Sales*				
4	Software	23,500	1	24,000	25
5	Books	28,750	2	29,500	31
6	Videos	24,400	3	25,250	26
7	SALES TOTAL	76,650	6	78,750	82
8	*Expenses*				

Confirm Punctuation

Many formulas produce inaccurate or erroneous results because of incorrect punctuation. Look for missing colons in range references; missing or misplaced quotation marks in string data or links to other worksheets or workbooks; and missing commas in function arguments. Also check parentheses to make sure you have one closing parenthesis for each opening parenthesis, and that your parentheses are in the correct locations within the formula.

	A	B	C	D	E
1	**Loan Payment Analysis**				
2	**Interest Rate (Annual)**	4.00%			
3	**Periods (Years)**	5			
4	**Principal**	$10,000			
5	**Balloon Payment**				
6	**Monthly Payment**	=PMT(B2 / 12 B3 * 12, B4, -B5)			
7		PMT(**rate**, nper, pv, [fv], [type])			
8					

Confirm Operator Precedence

The order in which Excel calculates numeric formulas can make a big difference to the result, particularly if you are mixing addition and subtraction with multiplication and division. Confirm the correct order of precedence that your formula requires; compare this with the natural order of operator precedence in Excel, as described in the "Understanding Excel Formulas" section earlier in this chapter; and then use parentheses to force the correct order if necessary.

	A	B	C	D	E
1					
2	Calculating the Pre-Tax Cost of an Item				
3					
4	**Variables:**		**Pre-Tax Cost Calculation:**		
5	**Total Cost**	$10.65		**Result**	**Formula in D**
6	**Tax Rate**	7%	Without controlling precedence →	$10.72	=B5 / 1 + B6
7			Controlling precedence →	$9.95	=B5 / (1 + B6)

Understand the Excel Error Values

Excel may display an error value instead of a formula result. Here are descriptions of the six main error types:

Error	Description
#DIV/0!	Your formula is dividing by zero. Check the divisor input cells for values that are either zero or blank.
#N/A	Your formula cannot return a legitimate result. Check that your function arguments are appropriate for each function.
#NAME?	Your formula uses a name that Excel does not recognize. Check your range names and function names.
#NUM!	Your formula uses a number inappropriately. Check the arguments for your mathematical functions to make sure they use the correct types of numbers.
#REF!	Your formula contains an invalid cell reference. This usually occurs when you delete a cell referenced by a formula. Adjust the formula to use a different cell.
#VALUE!	Your formula uses an inappropriate value in a function argument. Check your function arguments to make sure they use the correct data type.

CHAPTER 7

Manipulating Worksheets

An Excel worksheet is where you enter your headings and data and build your formulas. You will spend most of your time in Excel operating within a worksheet, so you need to know how to navigate and perform tasks such as renaming, moving, copying, and deleting worksheets.

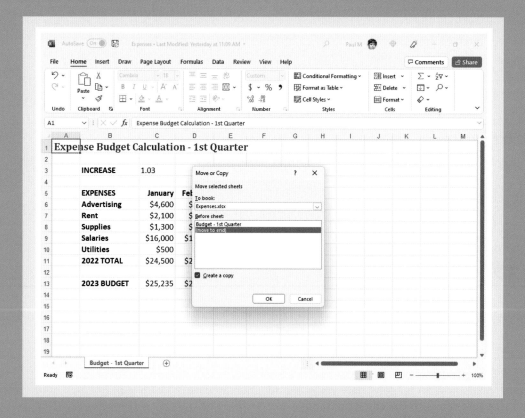

Navigate a Worksheet

You can use a few keyboard techniques that make it easier to navigate data after you have entered it in a worksheet.

It is usually easiest to use your mouse to click in the next cell you want to work with. If you are using Excel on a tablet or PC that has a touchscreen, you can tap the next cell you want to use. However, if you are entering data, using the keyboard to navigate to the next cell is often faster because your hands do not have to leave the keyboard.

Keyboard Techniques for Navigating a Worksheet	
Press	**To Move**
←	Left one cell
→	Right one cell
↑	Up one cell
↓	Down one cell
Home	To the beginning of the current row
Page down	Down one screen
Page up	Up one screen
Alt + Page down	One screen to the right
Alt + Page up	One screen to the left
Ctrl + Home	To the top-left corner of the worksheet (cell A1)
Ctrl + End	To the bottom-right corner of the used portion of the worksheet
Ctrl + arrow keys	In the direction of the arrow to the next non-blank cell if the current cell is blank, or to the last non-blank cell if the current cell is not blank

Rename a Worksheet

You can make your Excel workbooks easier to understand and navigate by providing each worksheet with a name that reflects the contents of the sheet.

Excel provides worksheets with generic names such as Sheet1 and Sheet2, but you can change these to more descriptive names such as Sales 2023, Amortization, or Budget Data. Note, however, that although worksheet names can include any combination of letters, numbers, symbols, and spaces, they cannot be longer than 31 characters.

Rename a Worksheet

1 Display the worksheet you want to rename.

2 Click the **Home** tab.

3 Click **Format**.

4 Click **Rename Sheet**.

Ⓐ You can also double-click the worksheet's tab.

Ⓑ Excel opens the worksheet name for editing and selects the text.

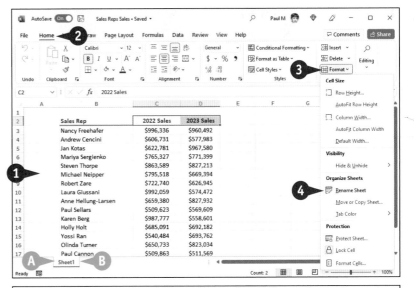

5 If you want to edit the existing name, press either ⬅ or ➡ to deselect the text.

6 Type the new worksheet name.

7 Press Enter.

Excel assigns the new name to the worksheet.

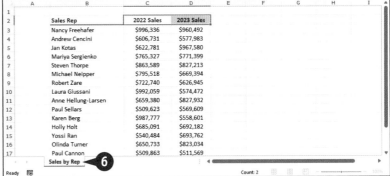

Create a New Worksheet

W hen you create a new workbook, Excel includes a single worksheet that you can use to build a spreadsheet model or to store data. If you want to build a new model or store a different set of data, and this new information is related to the existing data in the workbook, you can create a new worksheet to hold the new information. Excel supports multiple worksheets in a single workbook, so you can add as many worksheets as you need for your project or model.

In most cases, you will add a blank worksheet, but Excel also comes with several predefined worksheet templates that you can use.

Create a New Worksheet

Insert a Blank Worksheet

1 Open the workbook to which you want to add the worksheet.

2 Click the **Home** tab.

3 Click the **Insert** ⌄.

4 Click **Insert Sheet**.

A Excel inserts the worksheet.

Note: You can also insert a blank worksheet by pressing **Shift**+**F11**.

B Another way to add a blank worksheet is to click the **New sheet** button (⊕).

Insert a Worksheet from a Template

1 Open the workbook to which you want to add the worksheet.

2 Right-click a worksheet tab.

3 Click **Insert**.

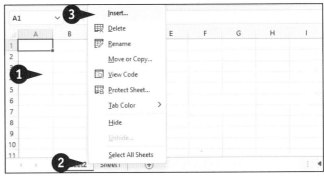

The Insert dialog box appears.

4 Click the **Spreadsheet Solutions** tab.

5 Click the type of worksheet you want to add.

C You can also click **Templates on Office.com** to download worksheet templates from the web.

6 Click **OK**.

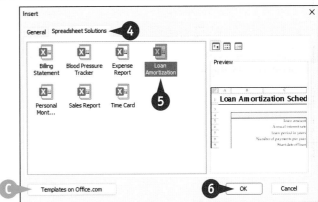

D Excel inserts the worksheet.

How do I navigate from one worksheet to another?

Click the tab of the worksheet you want to use or press Ctrl + Page down and Ctrl + Page up. You can also scroll sheets into view with the following controls:

◄	Scroll the worksheets left.
►	Scroll the worksheets right.
Ctrl + ◄	Scroll to the first worksheet.
Ctrl + ►	Scroll to the last worksheet.

Move a Worksheet

You can organize an Excel workbook and make it easier to navigate by moving your worksheets to different positions within the workbook. You can also move a worksheet to another workbook.

When you add a new worksheet to a workbook, Excel adds the sheet to the left of the existing sheets. However, it is unlikely that you will add each new worksheet in the order you want them to appear in the workbook. For example, in a budget-related workbook, you might prefer to have all the sales-related worksheets together, all the expense-related worksheets together, and so on.

Move a Worksheet

1 If you want to move the worksheet to another workbook, open that workbook and then return to the current workbook.

2 Click the tab of the worksheet you want to move.

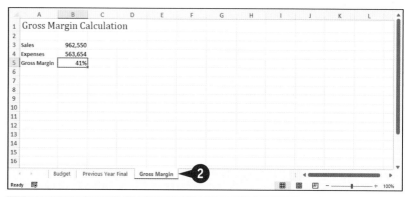

3 Click the **Home** tab.

4 Click **Format**.

5 Click **Move or Copy Sheet**.

A You can also right-click the tab and then click **Move or Copy**.

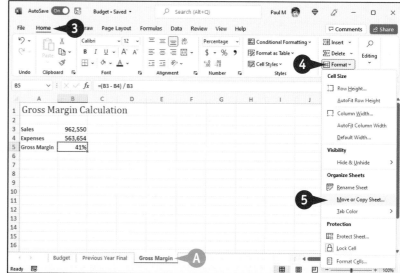

128

The Move or Copy dialog box appears.

6 If you want to move the sheet to another workbook, click the **To book** ⌄ and then click the workbook.

7 Use the **Before sheet** list to click a destination for the worksheet.

When Excel moves the worksheet, it will appear to the left of the sheet you selected in step **7**.

8 Click **OK**.

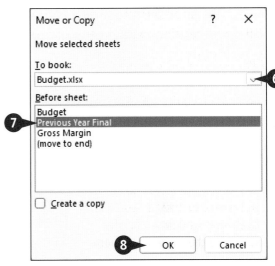

Move or Copy   ? ✕

Move selected sheets

To book:

Budget.xlsx   ⌄ —**6**

Before sheet:

Budget
Previous Year Final
Gross Margin
(move to end)

☐ Create a copy

8→ OK   Cancel

B Excel moves the worksheet.

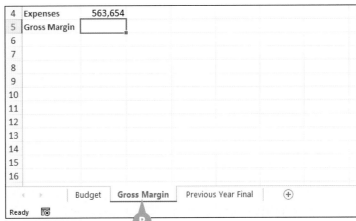

4	Expenses	563,654
5	Gross Margin	
6		
7		
8		
9		
10		
11		
12		
13		
14		
15		
16		

Budget   **Gross Margin**   Previous Year Final   ⊕

Ready

B

TIP

Is there an easier way to move a worksheet within the same workbook?

Yes. It is usually much easier to use your mouse to move a worksheet within the same workbook:

1 Move ⍗ over the tab of the workbook you want to move.

2 Click and drag the worksheet tab left or right to the new position within the workbook (⍗ changes to ⍗).

A As you drag, an arrow shows the position of the worksheet.

3 When you have the worksheet positioned where you want it, drop the worksheet tab.

Excel moves the worksheet.

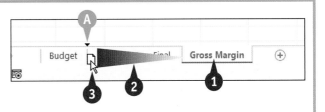

Budget   Final   **Gross Margin**   ⊕

Copy a Worksheet

Excel enables you to make a copy of a worksheet, which is a useful technique if you require a new worksheet that is similar to an existing worksheet. You can copy the sheet to the same workbook or to another workbook.

One of the secrets of productivity in Excel is to not repeat work that you have already done. For example, if you have already created a worksheet and you find that you need a second sheet that is very similar, then you should not create the new worksheet from scratch. Instead, you should copy the existing worksheet and then edit the new sheet as needed.

Copy a Worksheet

1 If you want to copy the worksheet to another workbook, open that workbook and then return to the current workbook.

2 Click the tab of the worksheet you want to copy.

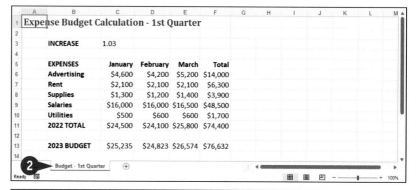

3 Click the **Home** tab.

4 Click **Format**.

5 Click **Move or Copy Sheet**.

Ⓐ You can also right-click the tab and then click **Move or Copy**.

The Move or Copy dialog box appears.

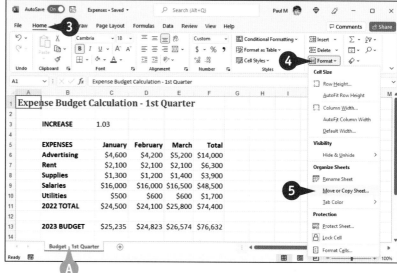

6 If you want to copy the sheet to another workbook, click the **To book** ⌄ and then click the workbook.

7 Use the **Before sheet** list to click a destination for the worksheet.

When Excel copies the worksheet, the copy will appear to the left of the sheet you selected in step **7**.

8 Click the **Create a copy** check box (☐ changes to ☑).

9 Click **OK**.

Ⓑ Excel copies the worksheet.

Ⓒ Excel gives the new worksheet the same name as the original, but with (2) appended.

Note: See the "Rename a Worksheet" section earlier in this chapter to learn how to edit the name of the copied worksheet.

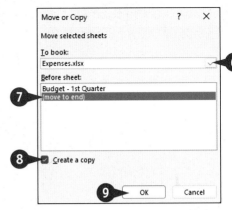

TIP

Is there an easier way to copy a worksheet within the same workbook?

Yes. It is usually much easier to use your mouse to copy a worksheet within the same workbook:

1 Move ᐅ over the tab of the workbook you want to copy.

2 Hold down **Ctrl**.

3 Click and drag the worksheet tab left or right (ᐅ changes to ᐅ).

Ⓐ As you drag, an arrow shows the position of the worksheet.

4 When you have the worksheet positioned where you want it, drop the worksheet tab.

Excel copies the worksheet.

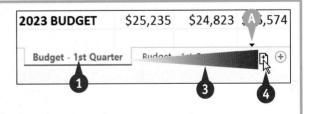

Delete a Worksheet

If you have a worksheet that you no longer need, you can delete it from the workbook. This reduces the size of the workbook and makes the workbook easier to navigate.

You cannot undo a worksheet deletion, so check the worksheet contents carefully before proceeding with the deletion. To be extra safe, save the workbook before performing the worksheet deletion. If you delete the wrong sheet accidentally, close the workbook without saving your changes.

Delete a Worksheet

1 Click the tab of the worksheet you want to delete.

2 Click the **Home** tab.

3 Click the **Delete** ∨.

4 Click **Delete Sheet**.

A You can also right-click the tab and then click **Delete**.

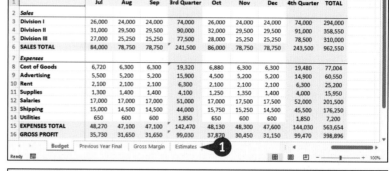

If the worksheet contains data, Excel asks you to confirm that you want to delete the worksheet.

5 Click **Delete**.

B Excel removes the worksheet.

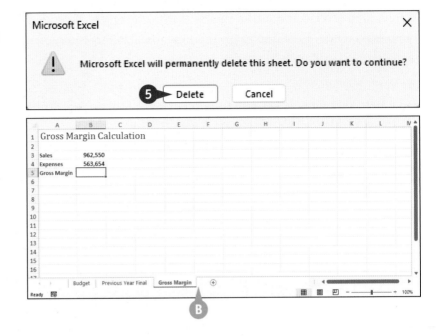

TIP

I have several worksheets that I need to delete. Do I have to delete them individually?

No. You can select all the sheets you want to remove and then run the deletion. To select multiple worksheets, click the tab of one of the worksheets, hold down <kbd>Ctrl</kbd>, and then click the tabs of the other worksheets.

If your workbook has several worksheets and you want to delete most of them, an easy way to select the sheets is to right-click any worksheet tab and then click **Select All Sheets**. Hold down <kbd>Ctrl</kbd>, and then click the tabs of the worksheets that you do not want to delete.

After you have selected your worksheets, follow steps **3** to **5** to delete all the selected worksheets at once.

Zoom In on or Out of a Worksheet

You can get a closer look at a portion of a worksheet by zooming in on that range. When you zoom in on a range, Excel increases the magnification of the range, which makes it easier to see the range data, particularly when the worksheet font is quite small.

On the other hand, if you want to get a sense of the overall structure of a worksheet, you can also zoom out. When you zoom out, Excel decreases the magnification, so you see more of the worksheet.

Zoom In on or Out of a Worksheet

1 Click the tab of the worksheet you want to zoom.

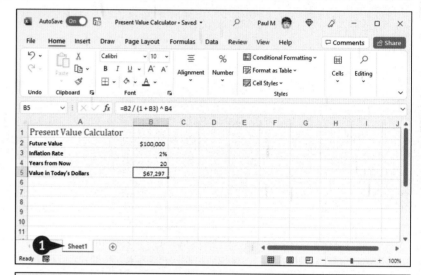

2 Click the **View** tab.

3 Click **Zoom** (🔍).

Ⓐ You can also run the Zoom command by clicking the zoom level in the status bar.

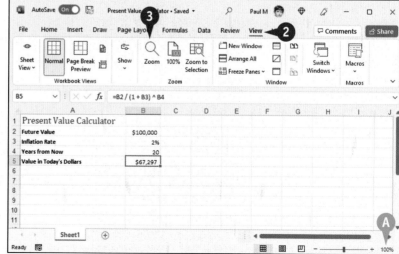

The Zoom dialog box appears.

4 Click the magnification level you want to use
(○ changes to ●).

B You can also click **Custom** (○ changes to ●) and
then type a magnification level in the text box.

Note: Select a magnification level above 100% to
zoom in on the worksheet; select a level under 100%
to zoom out of the worksheet.

5 Click **OK**.

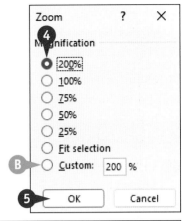

Excel changes the
magnification level and
redisplays the worksheet.

C You can click **100%** (🔲) to
return to the normal zoom
level.

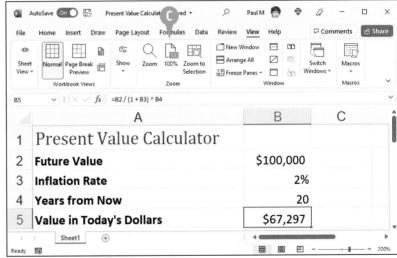

TIPS

How can I zoom in on a particular range?

Excel offers the Zoom to Selection feature that
enables you to quickly and easily zoom in on a
range. First, select the range that you want to
magnify. Click the **View** tab and then click **Zoom
to Selection** (🔍). Excel magnifies the selected
range to fill the entire Excel window.

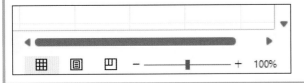

Is there an easier way to zoom in and out of a worksheet?

Yes, you can use the Zoom slider, which appears
on the far-right side of the Excel status bar. Drag
the slider ▮ to the right to zoom in on the
worksheet, or drag ▮ to the left to zoom out. You
can also click the **Zoom In** (+) or **Zoom Out** (−)
button to change the magnification.

Split a Worksheet into Two Panes

You can make it easier to examine your worksheet data by splitting the worksheet into two scrollable panes that each show different parts of the worksheet. This is useful if you have cell headings at the top of the worksheet that you want to keep in view as you scroll down the worksheet.

Splitting a worksheet into two panes is also useful if you want to keep some data or a formula result in view while you scroll to another part of the worksheet.

Split a Worksheet into Two Panes

1 Click the tab of the worksheet you want to split.

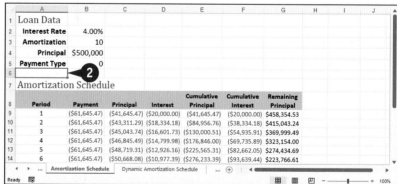

2 Select a cell in column A that is below the point where you want the split to occur.

For example, if you want to place the first five rows in the top pane, select cell A6.

3 Click the **View** tab.

4 Click **Split** (⊟).

A Excel splits the worksheet into two horizontal panes at the selected cell.

B You can adjust the size of the panes by clicking and dragging the split bar up or down.

To remove the split, either click ⊟ again or double-click the split bar.

TIPS

Can I split a worksheet into two vertical panes?

Yes. To do this, you must first select a cell in the top row of the worksheet. Specifically, select the top cell in the column to the right of where you want the split to occur. For example, if you want to show only column A in the left pane, select cell B1. When you click ⊟, Excel splits the worksheet into two vertical panes.

Can I split a worksheet into four panes?

Yes. This is useful if you have three or four worksheet areas that you want to examine separately. To perform a four-way split, first select the cell where you want the split to occur. Note that this cell must not be in either row 1 or column A. When you click ⊟, Excel splits the worksheet into four panes. The cell you selected becomes the upper-left cell in the bottom-right pane.

Hide and Unhide a Worksheet

You can hide a worksheet so that it is no longer visible in the workbook. This is useful if you need to show the workbook to other people but the workbook contains a worksheet with sensitive or private data that you do not want others to see. You might also want to hide a worksheet if it contains unfinished work that is not ready for others to view.

To learn how to protect a workbook so that other people cannot unhide a worksheet, see Chapter 16.

Hide and Unhide a Worksheet

Hide a Worksheet

1. Click the tab of the worksheet you want to hide.

2. Click the **Home** tab.

3. Click **Format**.

4. Click **Hide & Unhide**.

5. Click **Hide Sheet**.

A You can also right-click the worksheet tab and then click **Hide**.

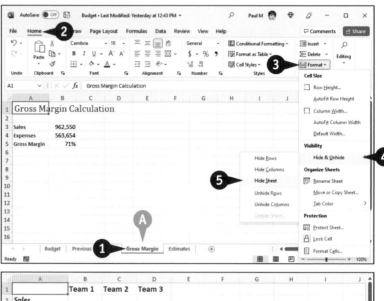

B Excel temporarily hides the worksheet in the workbook.

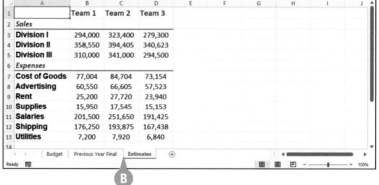

Unhide a Worksheet

1 Click the **Home** tab.

2 Click **Format**.

3 Click **Hide & Unhide**.

4 Click **Unhide Sheet**.

C You can also right-click any worksheet tab and then click **Unhide**.

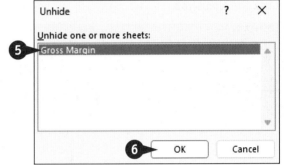

The Unhide dialog box appears.

5 Click the worksheet you want to restore.

6 Click **OK**.

D Excel returns the worksheet to the workbook.

TIP

I have several worksheets that I need to hide. Do I have to hide them individually?

No. You can select all the sheets you want to work with and then hide them. To select multiple worksheets, click the tab of one of the worksheets, hold down Ctrl, and then click the tabs of the other worksheets.

If your workbook has several worksheets and you want to hide most of them, an easy way to select the sheets is to right-click any worksheet tab and then click **Select All Sheets**. Hold down Ctrl, and then click the tabs of the worksheets that you do not want to hide.

After you have selected your worksheets, follow steps **3** to **6** to hide all the selected worksheets at once.

CHAPTER 8

Dealing with Workbooks

Everything you do in Excel takes place within a *workbook*, which is the standard Excel file. This chapter shows you how to get more out of workbooks by creating new files, saving and opening files, and finding and replacing text in a file.

Create a New Blank Workbook

To perform new work in Excel, you need to first create a new blank Excel workbook. When you launch Excel, it prompts you to create a new workbook, and you can click Blank Workbook to start with a blank file that contains a single empty worksheet. However, for subsequent files you must use the File tab to create a new blank workbook.

If you prefer to create a workbook based on one of the Excel templates, see the following section, "Create a New Workbook from a Template."

Create a New Blank Workbook

1 Click the **File** tab.

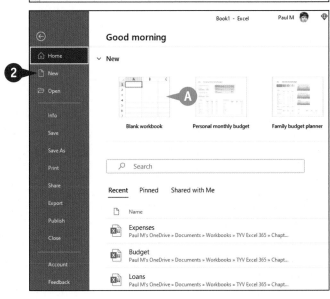

2 Click **New**.

Ⓐ You can click **Blank workbook** here and skip steps **2** and **3**.

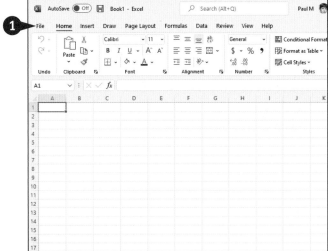

3 Click **Blank workbook**.

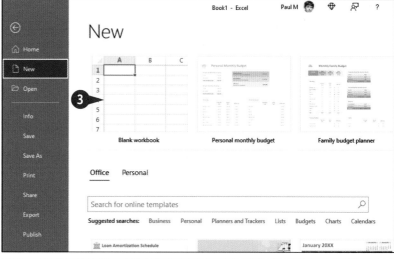

B Excel creates the blank workbook and displays it in the Excel window.

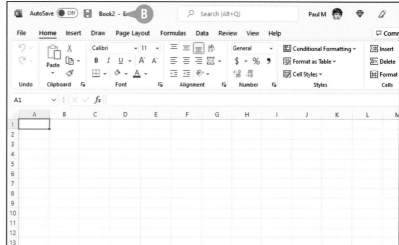

TIPS

Is there a faster method I can use to create a new workbook?
Yes. Excel offers a keyboard shortcut for faster workbook creation. Using the keyboard, press Ctrl+N.

When I start Excel and then open an existing workbook, Excel often removes the new blank workbook that it opened automatically. How can I prevent this?
Excel assumes that you want to use a fresh workbook when you start the program, so it prompts you to create a new workbook. However, if you do not make any changes to the blank workbook and then open an existing file, Excel assumes you do not want to use the new workbook, so it closes it. To prevent this from happening, make a change to the blank workbook before opening another file.

Create a New Workbook from a Template

Y ou can save time and effort by creating a new workbook based on one of the Excel template files. Each template includes a working spreadsheet model that contains predefined headings, labels, and formulas, as well as preformatted colors, fonts, styles, borders, and more. In many cases, you can use the new workbook as is and just fill in your own data.

Excel offers more than two dozen templates, and many more are available through Microsoft Office Online.

Create a New Workbook from a Template

1 Click the **File** tab.

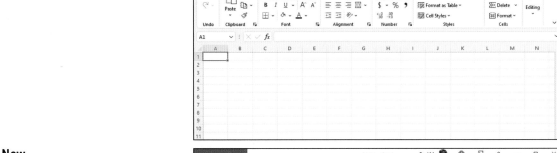

2 Click **New**.

A To use an Office Online template, use the Search for Online Templates text box to type a word or two that defines the type of template you want to use, then press Enter.

3 Click the template you want to use.

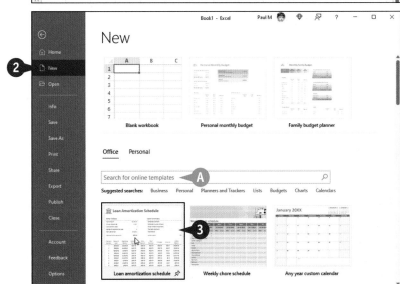

B A preview of the template appears.

4 Click **Create**.

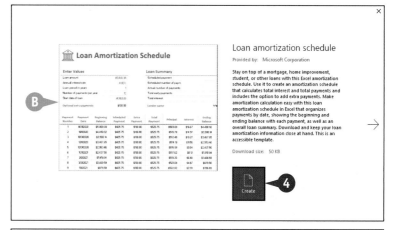

C Excel creates the new workbook and displays it in the Excel window.

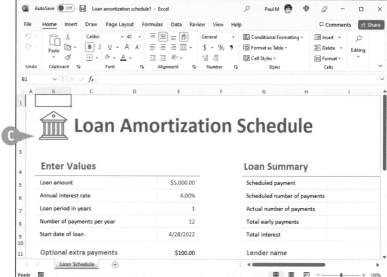

Can I create my own template?
Yes. If you have a specific workbook structure that you use frequently, you should save it as a template so that you do not have to re-create the same structure from scratch each time. Open the workbook, click **File**, click **Save As**, and then click **Browse**. In the Save As dialog box, click the **Save as type** ⌄ and then click **Excel Template**. Type a name in the **File name** text box and then click **Save**. To use the template, click **File** and click **New**; select the **Personal** tab and then click your template file.

Save a Workbook

After you create a workbook in Excel and make changes to it, you can save the document to preserve your work. When you edit a workbook, Excel stores the changes in your computer's memory, which is erased each time you shut down your computer. Saving the document preserves your changes on your computer's hard drive. To ensure that you do not lose any work if your computer crashes or Excel freezes up, you should save your work frequently, at least every few minutes.

Save a Workbook

1 Click **Save** (🖫).

You can also press **Ctrl**+**S**.

If you have saved the document previously, your changes are now preserved, and you can skip the rest of the steps in this section.

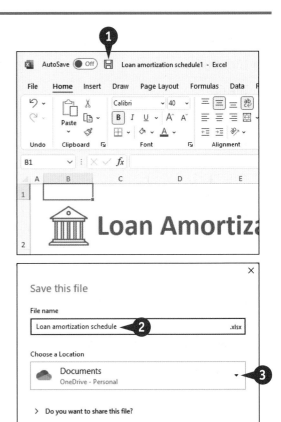

The Save This File dialog box appears.

2 Click in the **File name** text box and type the name that you want to use for the workbook.

3 If you want to use a different folder to store the file, click the **Choose a Location** ▼ and then click the folder.

4 Click **Save**.

Excel saves the file.

Note: To learn how to save a workbook in an older Excel format, see Chapter 16.

Open a Workbook

To view or make changes to an Excel workbook that you have saved in the past, you must open the workbook in Excel. To open a workbook, you must first locate it in the folder you used when you originally saved the file.

If you have used the workbook recently, you can save time by opening the workbook from the Excel Recent Workbooks menu, which displays a list of the 25 workbooks that you have used most recently.

Open a Workbook

1 Click the **File** tab (not shown).

2 Click **Open**.

The Open tab appears.

You can also press Ctrl+O.

Ⓐ You can click **Recent** to see a list of your recently used workbooks. If you see the file you want, click it and then skip the rest of these steps.

3 Click **Browse**.

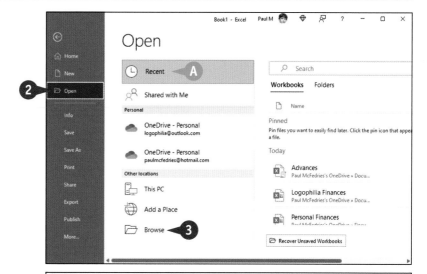

The Open dialog box appears.

4 Select the folder that contains the workbook you want to open.

5 Click the workbook.

6 Click **Open**.

The workbook appears in a window.

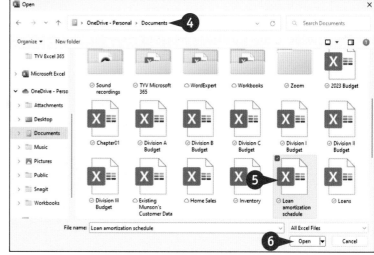

Find Text in a Workbook

Most spreadsheet models require at most a screen or two in a single worksheet, so locating the text you want is usually not difficult. However, you might be working with a large spreadsheet model that takes up either multiple screens in a single worksheet or multiple worksheets. In such large workbooks, locating specific text can be difficult and time-consuming. You can make this task easier and faster using the Excel Find feature, which searches the entire workbook in the blink of an eye.

Find Text in a Workbook

1 Click the **Home** tab.

2 Click **Find & Select**.

3 Click **Find**.

Note: You can also run the Find command by pressing Ctrl + F.

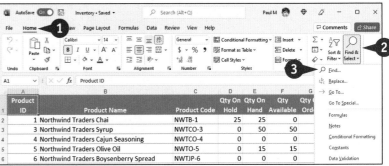

The Find and Replace dialog box appears.

4 Click in the **Find what** text box and type the text you want to find.

5 Click **Find Next**.

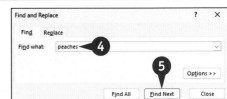

A Excel selects the next cell that contains an instance of the search text.

Note: If the search text does not exist in the document, Excel displays a dialog box to let you know.

6 If the selected instance is not the one you want, click **Find Next** until Excel finds the correct instance.

7 Click **Close** to close the Find and Replace dialog box.

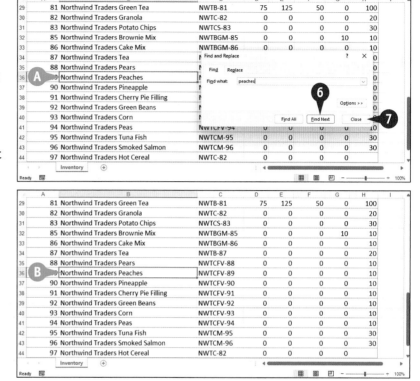

B Excel leaves the cell selected.

TIPS

When I search for a particular term, Excel only looks in the current worksheet. How can I get Excel to search the entire workbook?

In the Find and Replace dialog box, click **Options** to expand the dialog box. Click the **Within** ⌄ and then click **Workbook**. This option tells Excel to examine the entire workbook for your search text.

When I search for a name such as *Bill*, Excel also matches the non-name *bill*. Is there a way to fix this?

Yes. In the Find and Replace dialog box, click **Options** to expand the dialog box. Select the **Match case** check box (☐ changes to ☑). This option tells Excel to match the search text only if it has the same mix of uppercase and lowercase letters that you specify in the **Find what** text box. If you type **Bill**, for example, the program matches only *Bill* and not *bill*.

Replace Text in a Workbook

Do you need to replace a word or part of a word with some other text? If you only need to replace one or two instances of the text, you can usually perform the replacement quickly and easily. However, if you have many instances of the text to replace, the replacement can take a long time and the more instances there are, the more likely it is that you will make a mistake. You can save time and do a more accurate job if you let the Excel Replace feature replace the text for you.

Replace Text in a Workbook

1 Click the **Home** tab.

2 Click **Find & Select**.

3 Click **Replace**.

Note: You can also run the Replace command by pressing Ctrl + H.

The Find and Replace dialog box appears.

4 In the **Find what** text box, type the text you want to find.

5 Click in the **Replace with** text box and type the text you want to use as the replacement.

6 Click **Find Next**.

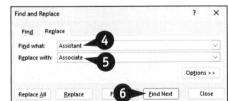

Ⓐ Excel selects the cell that contains the next instance of the search text.

Note: If the search text does not exist in the document, Excel displays a dialog box to let you know.

⑦ If the selected instance is not the one you want, click **Find Next** until Excel finds the correct instance.

⑧ Click **Replace**.

Ⓑ Excel replaces the selected text with the replacement text.

Ⓒ Excel selects the next instance of the search text.

⑨ Repeat steps **7** and **8** until you have replaced all the instances you want to replace.

⑩ Click **Close** to close the Find and Replace dialog box.

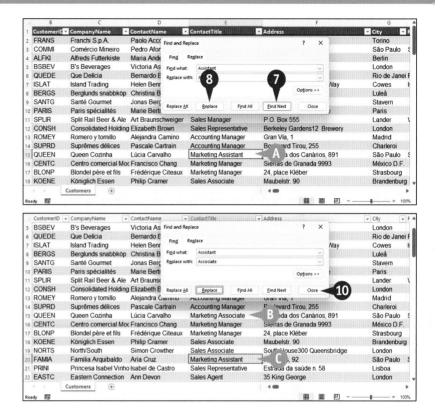

TIP

Is there a faster way to replace every instance of the search text with the replacement text?
Yes. In the Find and Replace dialog box, click **Replace All**. This tells Excel to replace every instance of the search text with the replacement text. However, you should exercise some caution with this feature because it may make some replacements that you did not intend. Click **Find Next** a few times to make sure the matches are correct. Also, consider clicking **Options** and then selecting the **Match case** check box (☐ changes to ☑), as described in the previous section, "Find Text in a Workbook."

CHAPTER 9

Formatting Workbooks

Excel offers several settings that enable you to control the look of a workbook, including the workbook colors, fonts, and special effects. You can also apply a workbook theme and add a header and footer to a workbook.

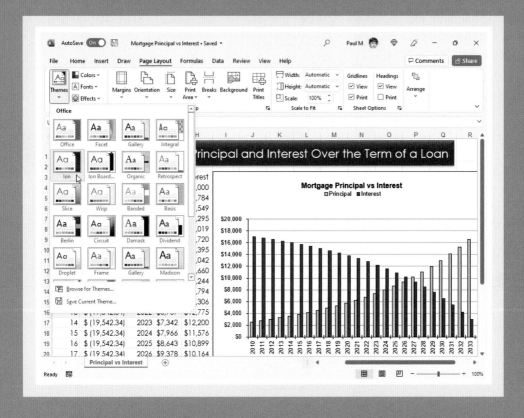

Modify the Workbook Colors

You can give your workbook a new look by selecting a different color scheme. Each color scheme affects a dozen workbook elements, including the workbook's text colors, background colors, border colors, chart colors, and more. Excel offers more than 20 color schemes. However, if none of these predefined schemes suits your needs, you can also create your own custom color scheme.

To get the most out of the Excel color schemes, you must apply styles to your ranges, as described in Chapter 5.

Modify the Workbook Colors

1 Open or switch to the workbook you want to format.

2 Click the **Page Layout** tab.

3 Click **Colors** ().

④ Click the color scheme you want to apply.

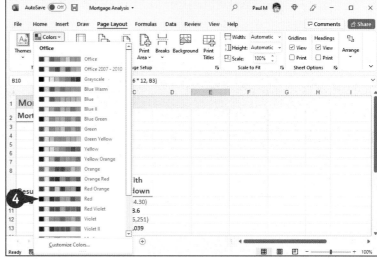

Ⓐ Excel applies the color scheme to the workbook.

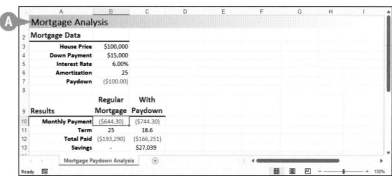

TIP

Can I create my own color scheme?
Yes, by following these steps:

① Click the **Page Layout** tab.

② Click ▦.

③ Click **Customize Colors**.

The Create New Theme Colors dialog box appears.

④ For each theme color, click ▼ and then click the color you want to use.

Ⓐ The Sample area shows what your theme colors look like.

⑤ Type a name for the custom color scheme.

⑥ Click **Save**.

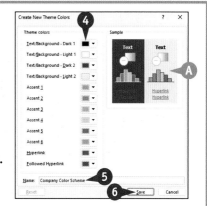

Set the Workbook Fonts

You can add visual appeal to your workbook by selecting a different font scheme. Each font scheme has two defined fonts: a *heading font* for the titles and headings, and a *body font* for the regular worksheet text. Excel offers more than 20 font schemes. However, if none of the predefined schemes is suitable, you can create a custom font scheme.

To get the most out of the Excel font schemes, particularly the heading fonts, you must apply to your ranges either styles or theme fonts, as described in Chapter 5.

Set the Workbook Fonts

1 Open or switch to the workbook you want to format.

2 Click the **Page Layout** tab.

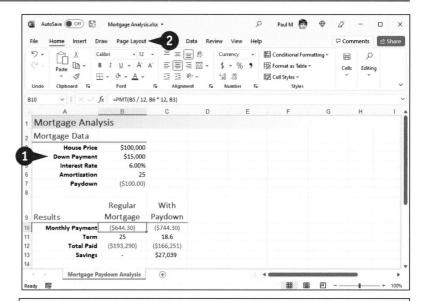

3 Click **Fonts** ().

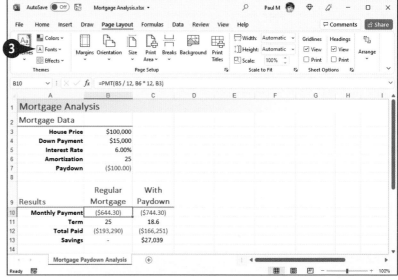

4 Click the font scheme you want to apply.

Ⓐ Excel applies the heading font to the workbook's headings.

Ⓑ Excel applies the body font to the workbook's regular text.

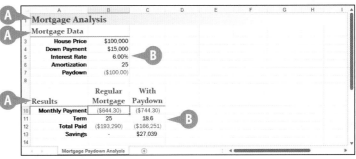

TIP

Can I create my own font scheme?

Yes, by following these steps:

1 Click the **Page Layout** tab.

2 Click A.

3 Click **Customize Fonts**.

The Create New Theme Fonts dialog box appears.

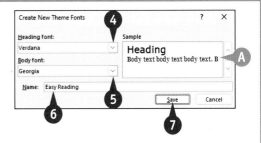

4 Click the **Heading font** ⌄ and then click the font you want to use for titles and headings.

5 Click the **Body font** ⌄ and then click the font you want to use for regular sheet text.

Ⓐ The Sample area shows what your theme fonts look like.

6 Type a name for the custom font scheme.

7 Click **Save**.

Choose Workbook Effects

Y ou can enhance the look of your workbook by selecting a different effect scheme. The effect
scheme applies to charts and graphic objects, and each scheme defines a border style, fill style,
and added effect such as a drop shadow or glow. Excel offers 15 effect schemes.

To get the most out of the Excel effect schemes, you must apply a style to your chart, as described in
Chapter 14, or to your graphic object, as described in Chapter 15.

Choose Workbook Effects

1 Open or switch to the workbook
you want to format.

2 Click the **Page Layout** tab.

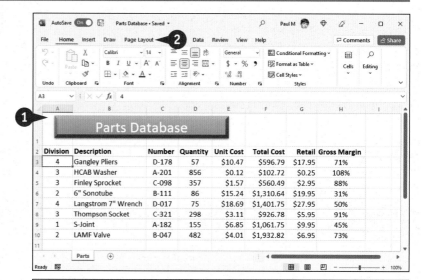

3 Click **Effects** ( ).

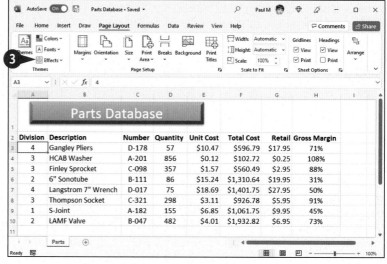

4 Click the effect scheme you want to apply.

A Excel applies the effect scheme to the workbook's charts and graphics.

	Division	Description	Number	Quantity	Unit Cost	Total Cost	Retail	Gross Margin
		Parts Database						
2	Division	Description	Number	Quantity	Unit Cost	Total Cost	Retail	Gross Margin
3	4	Gangley Pliers	D-178	57	$10.47	$596.79	$17.95	71%
4	3	HCAB Washer	A-201	856	$0.12	$102.72	$0.25	108%
5	3	Finley Sprocket	C-098	357	$1.57	$560.49	$2.95	88%
6	2	6" Sonotube	B-111	86	$15.24	$1,310.64	$19.95	31%
7	4	Langstrom 7" Wrench	D-017	75	$18.69	$1,401.75	$27.95	50%
8	3	Thompson Socket	C-321	298	$3.11	$926.78	$5.95	91%
9	1	S-Joint	A-182	155	$6.85	$1,061.75	$9.95	45%
10	2	LAMF Valve	B-047	482	$4.01	$1,932.82	$6.95	73%

TIPS

Can I create a custom effect scheme?

No. Unlike with the color schemes and font schemes described earlier in this chapter, Excel does not have a feature that enables you to create your own effect scheme.

Why are all the effect schemes the same color?

The color you see in the effect schemes depends on the color scheme you have applied to your workbook. If you apply a different color scheme, as described in the "Modify the Workbook Colors" section earlier in the chapter, you will see a different color in the effect schemes. If you want to use a custom effect color, create a custom color scheme and change the Accent 1 color to the color you want.

Apply a Workbook Theme

You can give your workbook a completely new look by selecting a different workbook theme. Each theme consists of the workbook's colors, fonts, and effects. Excel offers more than 30 predefined workbook themes.

To get the most out of the Excel workbook themes, you must apply styles to your ranges, as described in Chapter 5; to your charts, as described in Chapter 14; and to your graphic objects, as described in Chapter 15.

Apply a Workbook Theme

1 Open or switch to the workbook you want to format.

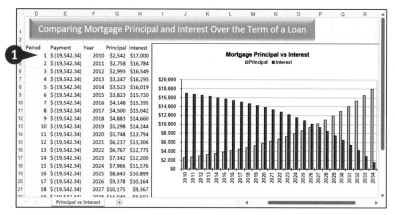

2 Click the **Page Layout** tab.

3 Click **Themes** (Aa).

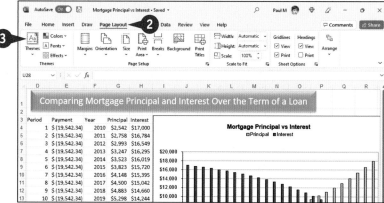

④ Click the workbook theme you want to apply.

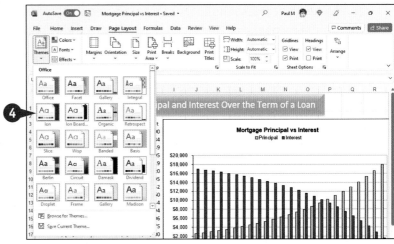

Ⓐ Excel applies the theme to the workbook.

Note: After you apply the theme, the new font size might require you to adjust the widths of columns and graphic objects to see your data properly.

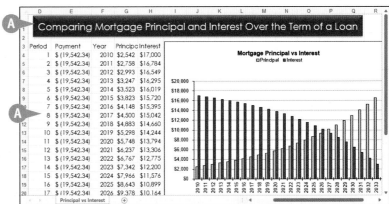

TIP

Can I create my own workbook theme?
Yes, by following these steps:

① Format the workbook with a color scheme, font scheme, and effect scheme, as described in the previous three sections.

② Click the **Page Layout** tab.

③ Click 🅰.

④ Click **Save Current Theme**.

The Save Current Theme dialog box appears.

⑤ Type a name for the custom theme.

⑥ Click **Save**.

Add a Workbook Header

If you will be printing a workbook, you can enhance the printout by building a custom header that includes information such as the page number, date, filename, or even a picture.

The *header* is an area on the printed page between the top of the page text and the top margin. Excel offers several predefined header items that enable you to quickly add data to the workbook header. If none of the predefined header items suits your needs, Excel also offers tools that enable you to build a custom header.

Add a Workbook Header

1 Click the **View** tab.

2 Click **Page Layout** (⬒).

Excel switches to Page Layout view.

Ⓐ You can also click the **Page Layout** button (▦).

3 Click the **Add header** text.

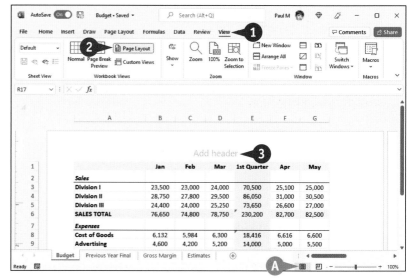

Ⓑ Excel opens the header area for editing.

Ⓒ Excel adds the Header & Footer contextual tab.

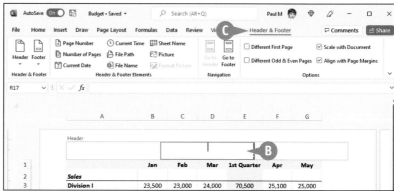

④ Type your text in the header.

Ⓓ If you want to include a predefined header item instead, click **Header** and then click the item.

Ⓔ You can also click in either of these header areas and type or insert text.

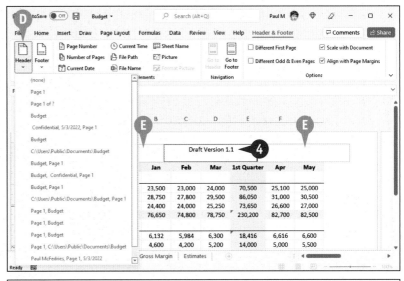

⑤ Click a button in the Header & Footer Elements group to add that element to the header.

Ⓕ Excel inserts a code into the header, such as &[Date] for the Current Date element, as shown here.

⑥ Repeat steps **4** and **5** to build the header.

⑦ Click outside the header area.

Excel applies the header. When you are in Page Layout view, you see the current values for elements such as the date.

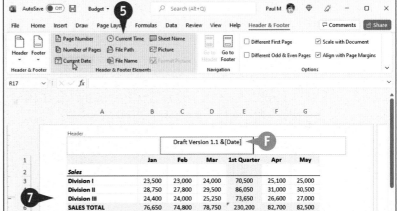

TIP

Can I have multiple headers in a workbook?

Yes. You can have a different header and footer on the first page, which is useful if you want to add a title or explanatory text to the first page. In the Header & Footer tab, click the **Different First Page** check box (☐ changes to ☑).

You can also have different headers and footers on the even and odd pages of the printout, such as showing the filename on the even pages and the page numbers on the odd pages. In the Header & Footer tab, click the **Different Odd & Even Pages** check box (☐ changes to ☑).

Add a Workbook Footer

If you will be printing a workbook, you can enhance the printout by building a custom footer that includes information such as the current page number, the total number of pages, the worksheet name, and more.

The *footer* is an area on the printed page between the bottom of the page text and the bottom margin. Excel offers several predefined footer items that enable you to quickly add data to the workbook footer. If none of the predefined footer items suits your needs, Excel also offers tools that enable you to build a custom footer.

Add a Workbook Footer

1 Click the **View** tab.

2 Click **Page Layout** (⊞).

Excel switches to Page Layout view.

Ⓐ You can also click the **Page Layout** button (▣).

3 Scroll down to the bottom of the page and click the **Add footer** text.

Note: You can also click the **Add header** text and then click the Header & Footer tab's **Go to Footer** command (▤).

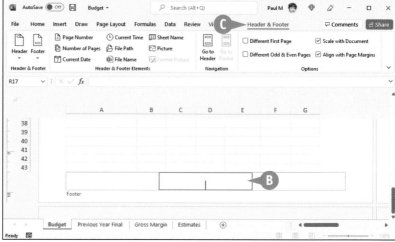

Ⓑ Excel opens the footer area for editing.

Ⓒ Excel adds the Header & Footer contextual tab.

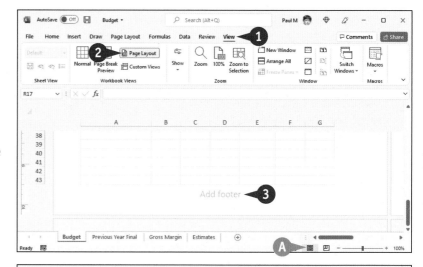

④ Type your text in the footer.

Ⓓ If you want to include a predefined footer item instead, click **Footer** and then click the item.

Ⓔ You can also click in either of these footer areas and type or insert text.

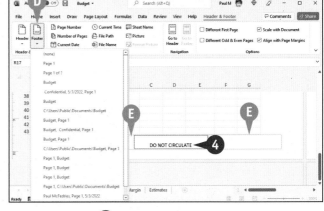

⑤ Click a button in the Header & Footer Elements group to add that element to the footer.

Ⓕ Excel inserts a code into the footer, such as &[Pages] for the Number of Pages element, as shown here.

⑥ Repeat steps **4** and **5** to build the footer.

⑦ Click outside the footer area.

Excel applies the footer. When you are in Page Layout view, you see the current values for elements such as the page number.

Can I view my headers and footers before I print the workbook?

Yes. Follow these steps:

① Click the **File** tab.

② Click **Print**.

Ⓐ The right side of the Print tab shows you a preview of the workbook printout.

Ⓑ The header appears here.

Ⓒ The footer appears here.

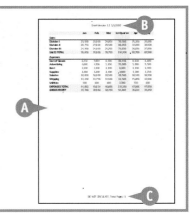

CHAPTER 10

Importing Data into Excel

Excel offers a number of tools that enable you to import external data into the program. Excel can access a wide variety of external data types. However, this chapter focuses on the six most common types: data source files, Access tables, Word tables, text files, web pages, and XML files.

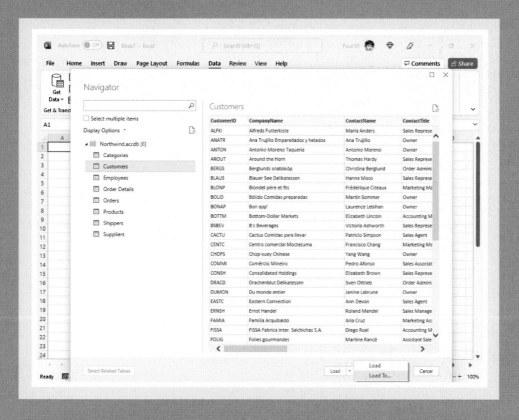

Understanding External Data

External data is data that resides outside of Excel in a file, database, server, or website. You can import external data directly into an Excel PivotTable or worksheet for additional types of data analysis.

Before you learn the specifics of importing external data into your Excel workbooks, you need to understand the various types of external data that you are likely to encounter. For the vast majority of applications, external data comes in one of the following six formats: data sources, Access tables, Word tables, text files, web pages, and XML files.

Data Source File

Open Database Connectivity (ODBC) data sources give you access to data residing in databases such as Access and dBASE, or on servers such as SQL Server and Oracle. However, there are many other data source types that connect to specific objects in a data source.

Microsoft Access Table

Microsoft Access is the Microsoft 365 suite's relational database management system, and so it is often used to store and manage the bulk of the data used by a person, team, department, or company. For more information, see the section "Import Data from an Access Table."

Microsoft Word Table

Some simple data is often stored in a table embedded in a Microsoft Word document. You can only perform so much analysis on that data within Word, and so it is often useful to import the data from the Word table into an Excel worksheet. For more information, see the section "Import Data from a Word Table."

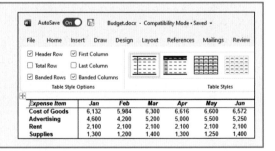

Text File

Text files often contain useful data. If that data is formatted properly — for example, each line has the same number of items, all separated by spaces, commas, or tabs — then it is possible to import that data into Excel for further analysis. For more information, see the section "Import Data from a Text File."

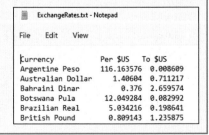

Web Page

People and companies often store useful data on web pages that reside either on the Internet or on company intranets. This data is often a combination of text and tables, but you cannot analyze web-based data in any meaningful way in your web browser. Fortunately, Excel enables you to create a web query that lets you import text and tables from a web page. For more information, see the section "Import Data from a Web Page."

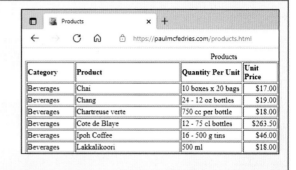

XML

XML — Extensible Markup Language — has redefined how data is stored. This is reflected in the large number of tools that Excel now has for dealing with XML data, particularly tools for importing XML data into Excel. For more information, see the section "Import Data from an XML File."

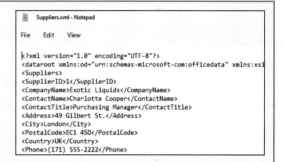

Location

To access external data, you must at least know where it is located. Here are the most common possibilities: in a file on your computer; in a file on your network; on a network server, particularly as part of a large, server-based database management system, such as SQL Server or Oracle; on a web page; or on a web server.

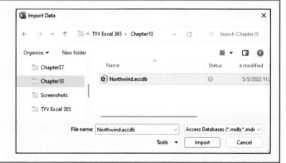

Login

Knowing where the data is located is probably all that you require if you are dealing with a local file or database or, usually, a web page. However, after you start accessing data remotely — on a network, database server, or web server — you will also require authorization to secure that access. See the administrator of the resource to obtain a username or login ID as well as a password.

Import Data from an Access Table

If you want to use Excel to analyze data from a table in an Access database, you can import the table to an Excel worksheet.

In Excel, you can use Microsoft Query to create a database query to extract records from a database, to filter and sort the records, and then to return the results to your worksheet. Excel offers tools for creating a database query for any ODBC data source, including an Access database. However, Excel also gives you an easier way to do this: You can import the table directly from the Access database.

Import Data from an Access Table

1. Click the **Data** tab.

2. Click **Get Data**.

3. Click **From Database**.

4. Click **From Microsoft Access Database**.

   The Import Data dialog box appears.

5. Open the folder that contains the database.

6. Click the file.

7. Click **Import**.

   The Navigator dialog box appears.

8. Click the table or query you want to import.

9. Click the **Load** ▼.

10. Click **Load To**.

The Import Data dialog box appears.

11 Click **Table** (○ changes to ●).

Ⓐ To import the data directly into a PivotTable, click **PivotTable Report** (○ changes to ●).

12 Select **Existing worksheet** (○ changes to ●).

13 Click the cell where you want the imported data to appear.

Ⓑ To import the data to a new sheet, click **New worksheet** (○ changes to ●).

14 Click **OK**.

Ⓒ Excel imports the data to the worksheet.

Ⓓ Excel displays the Queries & Connections task pane.

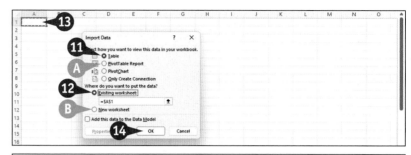

TIP

Why does Excel display the Queries & Connections task pane?
The Queries & Connections task pane enables you to quickly view your imported Access data. If you are working in another worksheet in the same Excel workbook, clicking the query in the Queries & Connections task pane takes you directly to the data. You can also right-click the query in the Queries & Connections task pane to access several commands related to the query, such as Refresh (see "Refresh Imported Data," later in this chapter) and Delete. If you find you do not use the Queries & Connections task pane, you should close it by clicking its **Close** button (✖).

Import Data from a Word Table

*W*ord tables are collections of rows, columns, and cells that look like Excel ranges but reside in a Word document. You can insert fields into Word table cells to perform calculations. In fact, Word fields support cell references, built-in functions such as SUM and AVERAGE, and operators such as addition (+) and multiplication (*), to build formulas that calculate results based on the table data.

However, even the most powerful Word formulas cannot perform the tasks available to you in Excel, which offers much more sophisticated data analysis tools. Therefore, to analyze your Word table data properly, you should import the table into an Excel worksheet.

Import Data from a Word Table

1. Launch Microsoft Word and open the document that contains the table.

2. Click a cell inside the table you want to import.

3. Click the **Layout** tab.

4. Click **Select**.

5. Click **Select Table**.

   A You can also select the table by clicking the table selection handle (⊕).

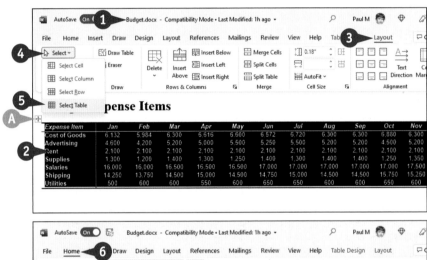

6. Click the **Home** tab.

7. Click **Copy** (📋).

   You can also press Ctrl+C.

   Word copies the table to the Clipboard.

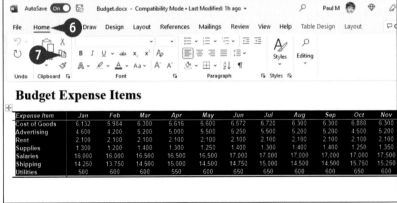

8 Switch to the Excel workbook into which you want to import the table.

9 Click the cell where you want the table to appear.

10 Click the **Home** tab.

11 Click **Paste** (📋).

You can also press `Ctrl`+`V`.

Excel pastes the Word table data.

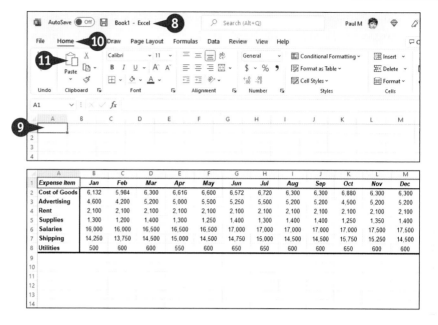

TIP

If I make changes to the Word data, are those changes automatically reflected in the Excel data?
No. If this is a concern, a better approach is to shift the data's container application from Word to Excel. That is, after you paste the table data into Excel, copy the Excel range, switch to Word, click the **Home** tab, click the **Paste** drop-down arrow (∨), and then click **Paste Special**. In the Paste Special dialog box, click **HTML Format** in the **As** list, and then click **Paste link** (○ changes to ⬤). Click **OK**, and the resulting table is linked to the Excel data. This means that any changes you make to the data in Excel automatically appear in the Word table. Note, however, that if you change the data in Word, you cannot update the original data in Excel.

Import Data from a Text File

Today, most data reside in some kind of special format, such as an Excel workbook, Access database, or web page. However, it is still relatively common to find data stored in simple text files because text is a universal format that works on any system and a wide variety of programs. You can analyze the data contained in certain text files by importing the data into an Excel worksheet.

Note, however, that although you can import any text file into Excel, you will get the best results if you only import *delimited* or *fixed-width* text files. See the tip to learn more.

Import Data from a Text File

Start the Text Import Wizard

1 Click the **Data** tab.

2 Click **From Text/CSV** (⬚).

The Import Data dialog box appears.

3 Open the folder that contains the text file.

4 Click the text file.

5 Click **Import**.

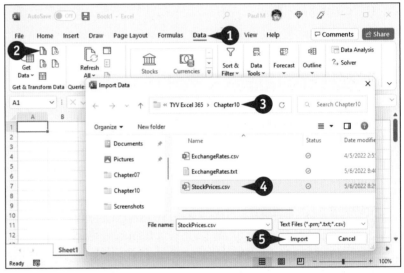

Excel displays a preview of the import.

6 Click the **Load** ▼.

7 Click **Load To**.

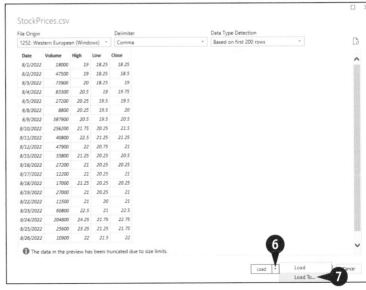

The Import Data dialog box appears.

8 Click **Table** (○ changes to ●).

Ⓐ To import the data directly into a PivotTable, click **PivotTable Report** (○ changes to ●).

9 Select **Existing worksheet** (○ changes to ●).

10 Click the cell where you want the imported data to appear.

Ⓑ To import the data to a new sheet, click **New worksheet** (○ changes to ●).

11 Click **OK**.

Ⓒ Excel imports the data to the worksheet.

Ⓓ Excel displays the Queries & Connections task pane.

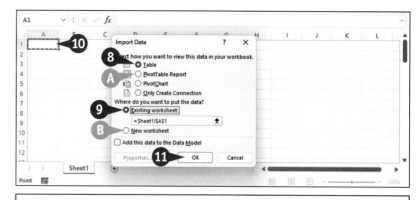

TIP

What are delimited and fixed-width text files?

A *delimited* text file uses a text structure in which each item on a line of text is separated by a character called a *delimiter*. The most common text delimiter is the comma (,). A delimited text file is imported into Excel by treating each line of text as a record and each item between the delimiter as a field.

A *fixed-width* text file uses a text structure in which all the items on a line of text use a set amount of space — say, 10 or 20 characters — and these fixed widths are the same on every line of text. A fixed-width text file is imported into Excel by treating each line of text as a record and each fixed-width item as a field.

Import Data from a Web Page

Data is often available on web pages. Although this data is usually text, some web page data comes as either a table (a rectangular array of rows and columns) or as preformatted text (text that has been structured with a predefined spacing used to organize data into columns with fixed widths).

Both types are suitable for import into Excel so that you can perform more extensive data analysis. To import web page data, you must know the web address of the page or the location of the web page file on your computer or on your network.

Import Data from a Web Page

① Click the **Data** tab.

② Click **From Web** (⬚).

The From Web dialog box appears.

③ Type the address of the web page.

④ Click **OK**.

The Access Web Content dialog box appears.

⑤ Click **Connect**.

Ⓐ If the web page requires you to log in, select the appropriate tab and then enter your credentials. See the tip for more information.

The Navigator dialog box appears.

6 Select the data you want to import.

7 Click the **Load** ▼.

8 Click **Load To**.

The Import Data dialog box appears.

9 Click **Existing worksheet** (○ changes to ●).

10 Click the cell where you want the imported data to appear.

Ⓑ If you want the data to appear in a new sheet, click **New worksheet** (○ changes to ●).

11 Click **OK**.

Ⓒ Excel imports the data to the worksheet.

Ⓓ Excel displays the Queries & Connections task pane.

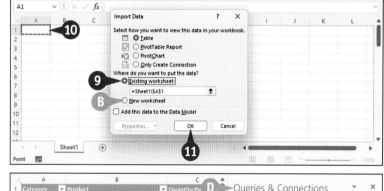

TIP

My web page requires me to log in. How do I enter my credentials?

For most web pages, you can use *anonymous access*, which means you do not have to enter any credentials to access the page. For pages that do require some kind of authentication, you need to select one of the following tabs in the Access Web Content dialog box:

• **Windows:** For a page that requires the same username and password as you use for your Windows account.

• **Basic:** For a page that requires a username and password for an account on the website.

• **Organizational account:** For a page that requires the username and password of your work account.

Import Data from an XML File

You can analyze data that currently resides in XML format by importing that data into Excel and then manipulating and analyzing the resulting table.

XML, or Extensible Markup Language, is a standard that enables the management and sharing of structured data using simple text files. These XML files organize data using *tags* that specify the equivalent of a table name and field names. Because XML is just text, if you want to perform data analysis on the XML file, you must import the XML file into an Excel table.

Import Data from an XML File

1 Click the **Data** tab.

2 Click **Get Data**.

3 Click **From File**.

4 Click **From XML**.

The Import Data dialog box appears.

5 Select the folder that contains the XML file you want to import.

6 Click the XML file.

7 Click **Import**.

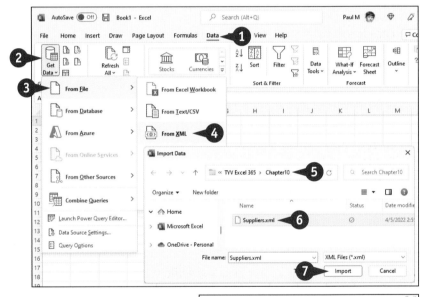

8 Click the data.

Ⓐ Excel displays a preview of the data.

9 Click the **Load** ▼.

10 Click **Load To**.

The Import Data dialog
box appears.

⑪ Click **Existing
worksheet**
(○ changes to ◉).

⑫ Click the cell where
you want the imported
data to appear.

Ⓑ If you want the data
to appear in a new sheet,
click **New worksheet**
(○ changes to ◉).

⑬ Click **OK**.

Ⓒ Excel imports the data into the
worksheet as an XML table.

Ⓓ Excel displays the Queries &
Connections task pane.

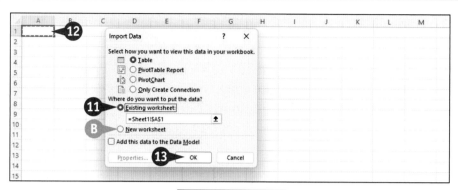

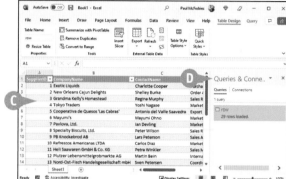

Refresh Imported Data

External data often changes; you can ensure that you are working with the most up-to-date version of the information by refreshing the imported data. Refreshing the imported data means retrieving the most current version of the source data and then updating the Excel data to reflect that version.

When you refresh imported data, you have two ways to proceed. One possibility is to refresh the data for just one import. A second possibility is to refresh the data for all the imports you've performed in the current workbook.

Refresh Imported Data

Refresh a Single Data Import

1 Click any cell inside the imported data.

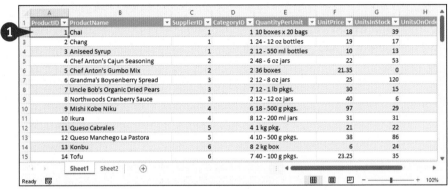

2 Click the **Data** tab.

3 Click the **Refresh All** drop-down arrow (⌄).

4 Click **Refresh** (🗐).

Note: You can also refresh the current data by pressing Alt + F5.

Excel refreshes the imported data.

Refresh All Imported Data in a Workbook

1 Click any cell inside any imported data.

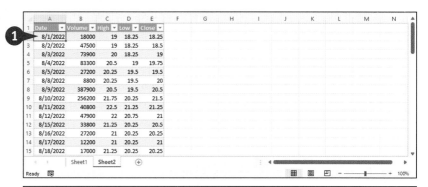

2 Click the **Data** tab.

3 Click the **Refresh All** button (🔄).

Note: You can also refresh all the imported data in the current workbook by pressing Ctrl + Alt + F5.

Excel refreshes all the imported data in the current workbook.

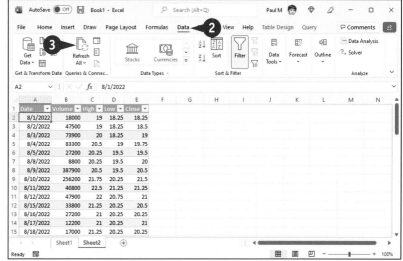

TIPS

Is there an easier way to refresh data regularly?
Yes. In most cases, you can set up a schedule that automatically refreshes the data at a specified interval. Follow steps **1** to **3** in the subsection "Refresh a Single Data Import," and then click **Connection Properties**. Click the **Refresh Every** check box (☐ changes to ☑). Use the spin box (🔼) to specify the refresh interval in minutes (not every type of imported data supports this feature).

Why does my refresh not seem to be working?
The refresh may take a long time. To check the status of the refresh, follow steps **1** to **3** in the subsection "Refresh a Single Data Import," and then click **Refresh Status** to display the External Data Refresh Status dialog box; click **Close** to continue the refresh. If the refresh is taking too long, repeat steps **1** to **3**, and then click **Cancel Refresh** to stop it.

Separate Cell Text into Columns

You can make imported data easier to analyze by separating the text in each cell into two or more columns of data.

An imported data column may contain multiple items of data. In imported contact data, for example, a column might contain each person's first and last name, separated by a space. This is problematic when sorting the contacts by last name, so you need to organize the names into separate columns. Excel makes this easy with the Text to Columns feature, which examines a column of data and then separates it into two or more columns.

Separate Cell Text into Columns

1 Insert a column to the right of the column you want to separate.

Note: If the data will separate into three or more columns, you can insert as many new columns as you need to hold the separated data.

2 Select the data you want to separate.

3 Click the **Data** tab.

4 Click **Text to Columns** (⛁).

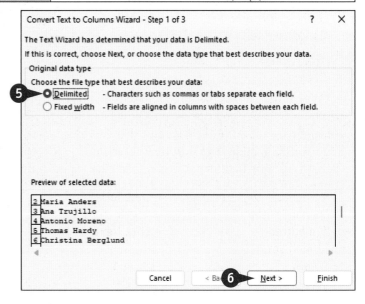

The Convert Text to Columns Wizard – Step **1** of **3** dialog box appears.

5 Click **Delimited** (○ changes to ●).

6 Click **Next**.

7 Click the check box beside the delimiter character that your text data uses (☐ changes to ☑).

A If you choose the correct delimiter, the data appears in separate columns.

8 Click **Next**.

9 Click a column.

10 Click the data format you want Excel to apply to the column (○ changes to ●).

B To prevent a column from being imported, click the **Do not import column (skip)** option (○ changes to ●).

11 Repeat steps **9** and **10** to set the data format for all the columns.

12 Specify the address of the first cell where you want the separated data to appear.

13 Click **Finish**.

Note: If Excel asks whether you want to replace the contents of the destination cells, click **Cancel** and read the second tip.

Excel separates the data.

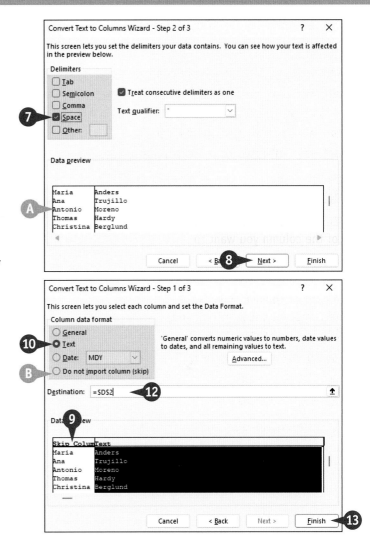

TIPS

What do I do if my column contains fixed-width text?

Follow steps **1** to **4** to start the Convert Text to Columns Wizard. Click the **Fixed width** option button (○ changes to ●). Click **Next**, and then click and drag a break line to set the width of each column. Click **Next**, and then follow steps **9** to **13** to complete the wizard.

Does Excel always create only one extra column from the data?

No, not always. For example, in a column of contact names, if any of those names use three words, Excel assumes that you want to create two extra columns for all the data. Unfortunately, this might cause Excel to overwrite some of your existing data. Therefore, before separating data into columns, check the data to see exactly how many columns Excel will create.

CHAPTER 11

Working with Tables

The forte of Excel is spreadsheet work, of course, but its row-and-column layout also makes it a natural flat-file database manager. That is, instead of entering data and then using the Excel tools to build formulas and analyze that data, you can also use Excel to store data in a special structure called a table.

Understanding Tables

I n Excel, a *table* is a rectangular range of cells used to store data. The table is a collection of related information with an organizational structure that makes it easy to find or extract data from its contents. To get the most out of Excel tables, you need to understand a few basic concepts, such as how a table is like a database, the advantages of tables, and how tables help with data analysis.

A Table Is a Database

A table is a type of database where the data is organized into rows and columns. Each column represents a database *field*, which is a single type of information, such as a name, address, or phone number; each row represents a database *record*, which is a collection of associated field values, such as the information for a specific contact.

Advantages of a Table

A table differs from a regular Excel range in that Excel offers a set of tools that makes it easier for you to work with the data within a table. As you see in this chapter, these tools make it easy to convert existing worksheet data into a table, add new records and fields to a table, delete existing records and fields, insert rows to show totals, and apply styles.

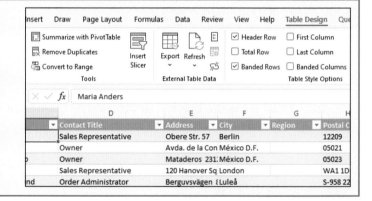

Data Analysis

Tables are also useful tools for analyzing your data. For example, as you see in Chapter 12, you can easily use a table as the basis of a PivotTable, which is a special object for summarizing and analyzing data. In Chapter 13, you also learn how to sort table records and how to filter table data to show only specific records.

Get to Know Table Features

Although a table looks much like a regular Excel range, it offers a number of features that differentiate it from a range. To understand these differences and make it as easy as possible to learn how to build and use tables, you need to know the various features in a typical table, such as the table rows and columns, the table headers, and the filter buttons.

Ⓐ Table Column

A single type of information, such as names, addresses, or phone numbers. In an Excel table, each column is the equivalent of a database field.

Ⓑ Column Headers

The unique names you assign to every table column that serve to label the type of data in each column. These names are always found in the first row of the table. If you have data above the table, it is best to include at least one blank row above the column headers.

Ⓒ Table Cell

An item in a table column that represents a single instance of that column's data, such as a name, address, or phone number. In an Excel table, each cell is equivalent to a database field value.

Ⓓ Table Row

A collection of associated table cells, such as the data for a single contact. In Excel tables, each row is the equivalent of a database record.

Ⓔ Column Filter Button

A feature that gives you access to a set of commands that perform various actions on a column, such as sorting or filtering the column data.

Convert a Range to a Table

You cannot create a table from scratch and then fill that table with data. Instead, you must first create a range that includes some or all of the data you want in your table and then convert that range to a table.

Note that you do not need to enter all your data before converting the range to a table. After you create the table, you can insert new rows and columns as needed, as described later in this chapter. Also, although it is best to include your own column headers for clarity, if you exclude headers, Excel will automatically create generic ones.

Convert a Range to a Table

1 Click a cell within the range that you want to convert to a table.

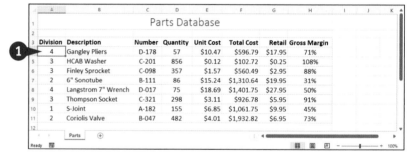

2 Click the **Insert** tab.

3 Click **Table** (▦).

Note: You can also choose the Table command by pressing Ctrl + T.

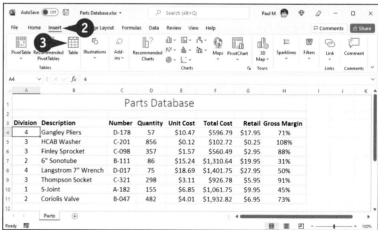

The Create Table dialog box appears.

Ⓐ Excel selects the range that it will convert to a table.

Ⓑ If you want to change the range, click ⬆, drag the mouse 🕂 over the new range, and then click ⬇ .

④ If the top row of your range has labels that you want to use as column headers, click **My table has headers** (☐ changes to ☑).

⑤ Click **OK**.

Excel converts the range to a table.

Ⓒ Excel applies a table format to the range.

Ⓓ The Table Design contextual tab appears.

Ⓔ Filter buttons appear in each column heading.

⑥ Click the **Table Design** tab to see the Excel table design tools.

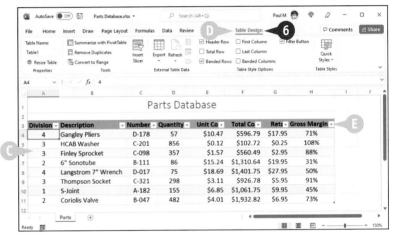

Do I need to add labels to the top of each column before converting my range to a table?

No, you do not need to add labels before performing the conversion. In this case, follow steps **1** to **3** to display the Create Table dialog box, then click **My table has headers** (☑ changes to ☐). After you click **OK**, Excel converts the range to a table and automatically adds headers to each column. These headers use the generic names Column1, Column2, and so on.

If I selected the wrong range for my table, is there a way to tell Excel the correct range?

Yes, although you cannot change the location of the headers. To redefine the range used in the table, first select any cell in the table. Click the **Table Design** tab and then click **Resize Table** (⊞) to open the Resize Table dialog box. Drag the mouse 🕂 over the new range and then click **OK**.

Select Table Data

I f you want to work with one or more table elements, you first need to select those elements. For example, if you want to apply a format to a table column or copy a couple of table rows, you first need to select that column or those rows.

The normal range-selection techniques in Excel often do not work well with a table. For example, selecting an entire worksheet column or row does not work because no table uses up an entire worksheet column or row. Instead, Excel provides several tools for selecting a table column (just the data or the data and the header), a table row, or the entire table.

Select Table Data

Select a Table Column

1 Right-click any cell in the column you want to select.

2 Click **Select**.

3 Click **Table Column Data**.

Excel selects all the column's data cells.

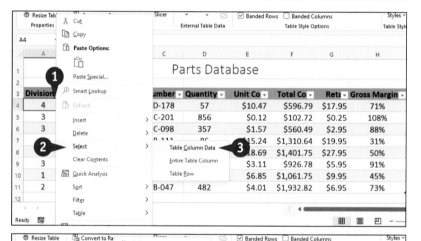

Select a Table Column and Header

1 Right-click any cell in the column you want to select.

2 Click **Select**.

3 Click **Entire Table Column**.

Excel selects the column's data and header.

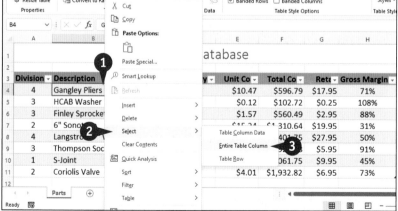

Select a Table Row

1 Right-click any cell in the row you want to select.

2 Click **Select**.

3 Click **Table Row**.

Excel selects all the data within the row.

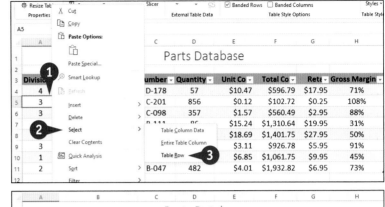

Select the Entire Table

1 Click any table header.

2 Press Ctrl + A.

Excel selects the entire table.

	Division	Description	Number	Quantity	Unit Co	Total Co	Reta	Gross Margin
				Parts Database				
4	4	Gangley Pliers	D-178	57	$10.47	$596.79	$17.95	71%
5	3	HCAB Washer	C-201	856	$0.12	$102.72	$0.25	108%
6	3	Finley Sprocket	C-098	357	$1.57	$560.49	$2.95	88%
7	2	6" Sonotube	B-111	86	$15.24	$1,310.64	$19.95	31%
8	4	Langstrom 7" Wrench	D-017	75	$18.69	$1,401.75	$27.95	50%
9	3	Thompson Socket	C-321	298	$3.11	$926.78	$5.95	91%
10	1	S-Joint	A-182	155	$6.85	$1,061.75	$9.95	45%
11	2	Coriolis Valve	B-047	482	$4.01	$1,932.82	$6.95	73%

How do I select multiple columns or rows?

To select two or more adjacent table columns, first select one cell in each of the columns that you want to include in your selection. Right-click any selected cell, click **Select**, and then click **Table Column Data** (or **Entire Table Column** to include the column headers).

To select columns that are not side by side, select the first column. Hold down Ctrl, click a cell in the next column you want to select, right-click the selected cell, click **Select**, and then click **Table Column Data** (or **Entire Table Column**). Repeat for each of the other columns you want to select.

To select two or more adjacent table rows, first select one cell in each of the rows that you want to include in your selection. Right-click any selected cell, click **Select**, and then click **Table Row**.

To select non-adjacent rows, select the first row. Hold down Ctrl, click a cell in the next row you want to select, right-click the selected cell, click **Select**, and then click **Table Row**. Repeat for each of the other rows you want to select.

Insert a Table Row

You can add a new record to your Excel table by inserting a new row. You can insert a row either within the table or at the end of the table.

Once you have entered the initial set of data into your table, you will likely add most new records within the table by inserting a new row above a current row. However, when you are in the initial data entry phase, you will most likely prefer to add new records by adding a row to the end of the table.

Insert a Table Row

1 Select a cell in the row below which you want to insert the new row.

2 Click the **Home** tab.

3 Click the **Insert** ⌄.

4 Click **Insert Table Rows Above**.

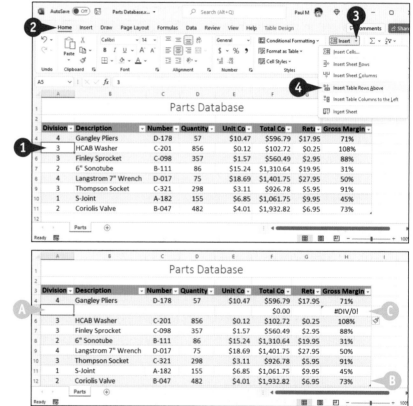

A Excel inserts the new row.

B To insert a new row at the end of the table, select the lower-right table cell and then press Tab.

C Any errors that Excel displays in the inserted row will usually be resolved after you add data to the row.

Insert a Table Column

Y ou can add a new field to your Excel table by inserting a new column. You can insert a column either within the table or at the end of the table.

To make data entry easier and more efficient, you should decide in advance all the fields you want to include in the table. However, if later you realize you forgot a particular field, you can still add it to the table. Inserting a table column is also useful if you imported or inherited the data from elsewhere and you see that the data is missing a field that you require.

Insert a Table Column

1 Select a cell in the column to the left of which you want to insert the new column.

A If you want to insert the new column at the end of the table, select a cell in the last table column.

2 Click the **Home** tab.

3 Click the **Insert** ∨.

4 Click **Insert Table Columns to the Left**.

To insert a column at the end of the table instead, click **Insert Table Columns to the Right** (not shown).

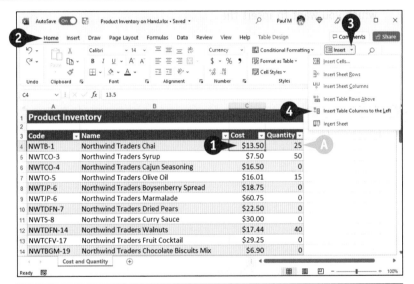

B Excel inserts the new column and gives it a generic name such as Column1.

5 Give the new field a more descriptive name by editing the column header.

Delete a Table Row

I f your table contains a record that includes inaccurate, outdated, duplicate, or unnecessary data, you should delete that row to preserve your table's data integrity.

An Excel table is a repository of data that you can use as a reference source or to analyze or summarize the data. However you use the table, it is only as beneficial as its data is accurate, so you should take extra care to ensure that the data you enter is correct. If you find that an entire record is inaccurate, duplicated, or no longer needed, Excel enables you to quickly delete that row.

Delete a Table Row

1 Select a cell in the row you want to delete.

Note: To delete multiple rows, select a cell in each row you want to delete.

2 Click the **Home** tab.

3 Click the **Delete** ∨.

4 Click **Delete Table Rows**.

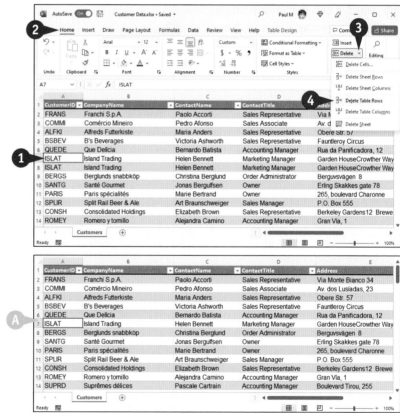

A Excel deletes the row.

Delete a Table Column

I f your table contains a field that you do not need, you should delete that column to make your table easier to work with and manage.

As you see later in this chapter and in Chapter 13, you analyze and summarize your table information based on the data in one or more fields. If your table contains a field that you never look at and that you never use for analysis or summaries, consider deleting that column to reduce table clutter and make your table easier to navigate.

Delete a Table Column

1 Select a cell in the column you want to delete.

Note: To delete multiple columns, select a cell in each column you want to delete. However, you can only delete multiple columns that are adjacent to each other.

2 Click the **Home** tab.

3 Click the **Delete ∨**.

4 Click **Delete Table Columns**.

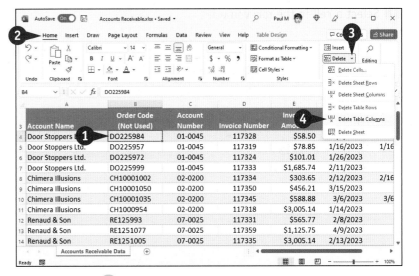

A Excel deletes the column.

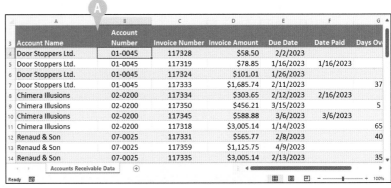

Add a Column Subtotal

Y ou can get more out of your table data by summarizing a field with a subtotal that appears at the bottom of the column.

Although the word *subtotal* implies that you are summing the numeric values in a column, Excel uses the term more broadly. That is, a subtotal can be not only a numeric sum, but also an average, a maximum or minimum, or a count of the values in the field. You can also choose more advanced subtotals such as a standard deviation or a variance.

Add a Column Subtotal

1 Select all the data in the column you want to total.

Note: See the "Select Table Data" section earlier in the chapter to learn how to select column data.

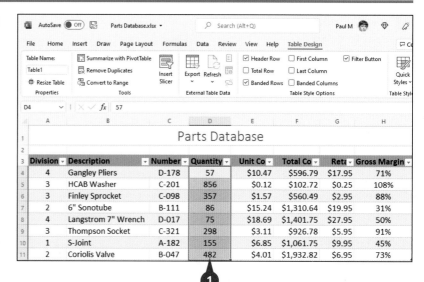

2 Click the **Quick Analysis** button (📈).

Note: If you do not see 📈, move the mouse ✛ over the selected column data.

The Quick Analysis options appear.

3 Click **Totals**.

4 Click the type of calculation you want to use.

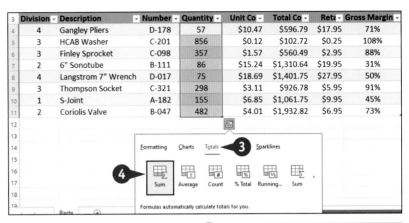

Ⓐ Excel adds a Total row to the bottom of the table.

Ⓑ Excel inserts a SUBTOTAL function to perform the calculation you chose in step **4**.

Ⓒ Click the cell's ▼ to choose a different type of subtotal.

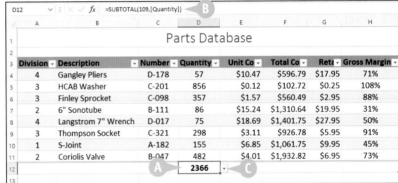

TIP

Is there a quick way to insert a total row in my table?
Yes. You can add the total row and include a subtotal function for any column in that row with just a few mouse clicks:

1 Click any cell within the table.

2 Click the **Table Design** tab.

3 Click the **Total Row** check box (☐ changes to ☑).

Ⓐ Excel automatically inserts a row named Total at the bottom of the table.

Ⓑ Excel adds a SUBTOTAL function below the last column.

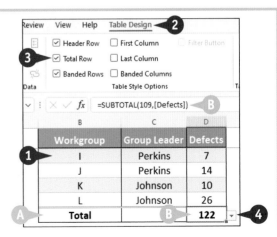

4 In the Total row, click any cell's ▼ and then click the type of subtotal you want to use.

Convert a Table to a Range

If you no longer require the Excel table tools, you can convert a table to a normal range. After the conversion, the Table Design contextual tab no longer appears when you click inside the range.

Tables are extremely useful Excel features, but they can occasionally be bothersome. For example, if you click a table cell, click the Table Design tab, and then click a cell outside the table, Excel automatically switches to the Home tab. If you then click a table cell again, Excel automatically switches back to the Table Design tab. If you are not using the table features in the Table Design tab, this behavior can be annoying, but you can prevent it from happening by converting the table to a normal range.

Convert a Table to a Range

1 Click a cell inside the table.

2 Click the **Table Design** tab.

3 Click **Convert to Range** (🔁).

Excel asks you to confirm.

4 Click **Yes**.

Excel converts the table to a normal range.

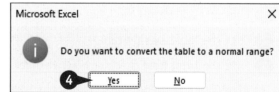

Apply a Table Style

You can give an Excel table more visual appeal and make it easier to read by applying one of Excel's predefined table styles.

A table style is a combination of formatting options that Excel applies to 13 different table elements, including the first and last columns, the header row, the total row, and the entire table. For each element, Excel applies one or more of the following formatting options: the font, including the typeface, style, size, color, and text effects; the border; and the background color and fill effects.

Apply a Table Style

1 Click a cell inside the table.

2 Click the **Table Design** tab.

3 Click the **Table Styles** ⇩.

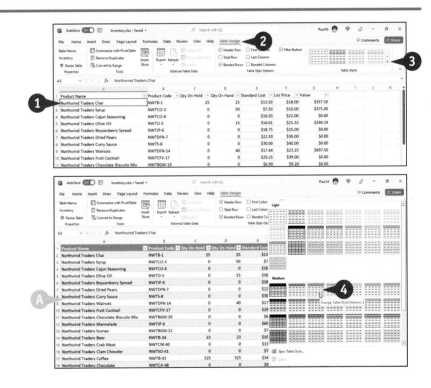

The Table Styles gallery appears.

4 Click the table style you want to use.

Ⓐ Excel applies the style to the table.

CHAPTER 12

Analyzing with PivotTables

A PivotTable is a powerful data analysis tool that automatically groups large amounts of data into smaller, more manageable categories. In this chapter, you learn how to create PivotTables, edit them, pivot them, format them, calculate with them, and much more.

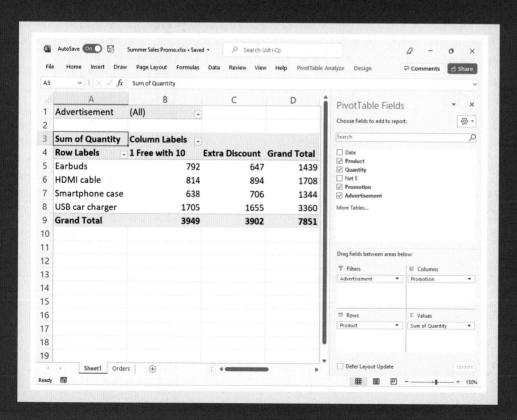

Understanding PivotTables

Tables and external databases can contain thousands of records. Analyzing that much data can be a nightmare without the right tools. Excel offers a powerful data analysis tool called a *PivotTable*, which enables you to summarize hundreds of records in a concise tabular format. You can then manipulate the layout of — or *pivot* — the table to see different views of your data.

PivotTables help you analyze large amounts of data by performing three operations: grouping the data into categories, summarizing the data using calculations, and filtering the data to show just the records with which you want to work.

Grouping

A PivotTable is a powerful data analysis tool in part because it automatically groups large amounts of data into smaller, more manageable categories. Suppose you have a data source with a Region field in which each cell contains one of four values: East, Midwest, South, or West. The original data may contain thousands of records, but if you build your PivotTable using the Region field, the resulting table has only four rows — one for each of the four Region values in your data.

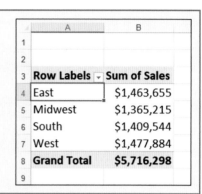

	A	B
1		
2		
3	Row Labels ▾	Sum of Sales
4	East	$1,463,655
5	Midwest	$1,365,215
6	South	$1,409,544
7	West	$1,477,884
8	**Grand Total**	**$5,716,298**
9		

Summarizing

Excel also displays summary calculations for each group. The default calculation is Sum, which means for each group Excel totals all the values in some specified field. For example, if your data has a Region field and a Sales field, a PivotTable can group the unique Region values and display the total of the Sales values for each one. Other summary calculations include Count, Average, Maximum, Minimum, and Standard Deviation.

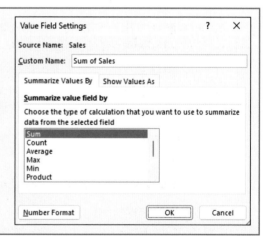

Filtering

A PivotTable also enables you to view just a subset of the data. For example, if your data contains a Sales Rep field, a PivotTable can filter the data to show the results for just a single sales rep. Each PivotTable comes with a filter area that enables you to apply a filter to the entire PivotTable.

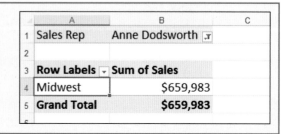

	A	B	C
1	Sales Rep	Anne Dodsworth ▾	
2			
3	Row Labels ▾	Sum of Sales	
4	Midwest	$659,983	
5	**Grand Total**	**$659,983**	

You can get up to speed with PivotTables very quickly after you learn a few key concepts. You need to understand the features that make up a typical PivotTable, particularly the four areas — row, column, data, and filter — to which you add fields from your data.

You also need to understand some important PivotTable terminology that you will encounter throughout this book, including terms such as *source data*, *pivot cache*, and *summary calculation*.

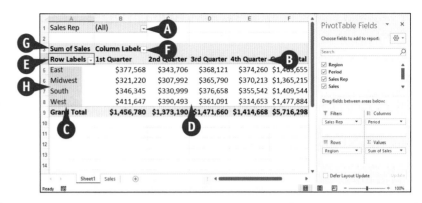

Build a PivotTable from an Excel Range or Table

If the data you want to analyze exists as an Excel range or table, you can use the PivotTable command to quickly build a PivotTable report based on your data. You need only specify the location of your source data and then choose the location of the resulting PivotTable.

Excel creates an empty PivotTable in a new worksheet or in the location you specify. Excel also displays the PivotTable Fields task pane, which contains four areas: Filters, Columns, Rows, and Values. To complete the PivotTable, you must populate some or all of these areas with one or more fields from your data.

Build a PivotTable from an Excel Range or Table

1 Click a cell within the range or table that you want to use as the source data.

2 Click the **Insert** tab.

3 Click **PivotTable** (⊞).

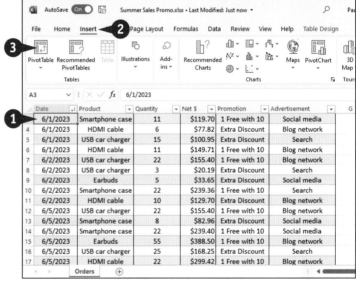

The PivotTable from Table or Range dialog box appears.

4 Click **New Worksheet** (○ changes to ◉).

A If you want to place the PivotTable in an existing location, click **Existing Worksheet** (○ changes to ◉). Then, use the **Location** range box to select the worksheet and cell where you want the PivotTable to appear.

5 Click **OK**.

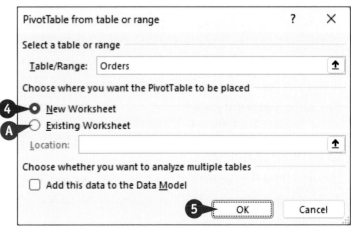

Ⓑ Excel creates a blank PivotTable.

Ⓒ Excel displays the PivotTable Fields task pane.

⑥ Click and drag a field and drop it inside the Rows area.

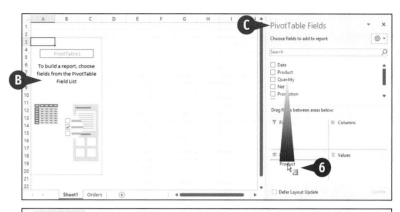

Ⓓ Excel adds the field's unique values to the PivotTable's row area.

⑦ Click and drag a numeric field and drop it inside the Values area.

Ⓔ In the PivotTable's data area, Excel sums the numeric values based on the row values.

⑧ If desired, click and drag fields and drop them in the Columns area and the Filters area.

Each time you drop a field in an area, Excel updates the PivotTable to include the new data.

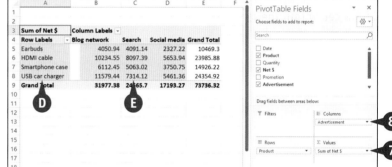

TIPS

Are there faster ways to build a PivotTable?

Yes. In the PivotTable Fields task pane, click a check box for a text or date field (☐ changes to ☑) and Excel adds the field to the Rows area. Click a check box for a numeric field (☐ changes to ☑) and Excel adds the field to the Values area. You can also right-click a field, and then click the area that you want to use.

What is the purpose of the Filters box?

To add a filter field to the PivotTable, which enables you to display a subset of the data that consists of one or more unique values from the filter field. For more details, see the section "Apply a PivotTable Filter" later in this chapter.

You can ensure that the data analysis represented by the PivotTable remains up-to-date by refreshing the PivotTable.

Whether your PivotTable is based on financial results, survey responses, or a database of collectibles such as books or CDs, the underlying data is probably not static. That is, the data changes over time as new results come in, new surveys are undertaken, and new items are added to the collection. You will need to refresh the PivotTable to ensure that it is current. Excel offers two methods for refreshing a PivotTable: manual and automatic.

Refresh PivotTable Data

Refresh Data Manually

1 Click any cell inside the PivotTable.

2 Click the **PivotTable Analyze** contextual tab.

3 Click **Refresh** (🔄).

You can also press **Alt**+**F5**.

Ⓐ To update every PivotTable in the workbook, click the **Refresh** ∨ and then click **Refresh All**.

You can also update all PivotTables by pressing **Ctrl**+**Alt**+**F5**.

Excel updates the PivotTable data.

Refresh Data Automatically

1 Click any cell inside the PivotTable.

2 Click the **PivotTable Analyze** contextual tab.

3 Click **PivotTable** (🗔).

4 Click **Options**.

Note: You can also right-click any cell in the PivotTable and then click **PivotTable Options**.

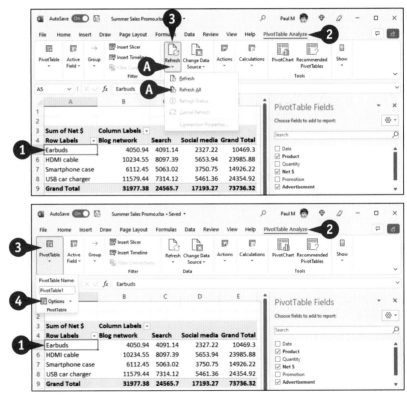

The PivotTable Options dialog box appears.

5 Click the **Data** tab.

6 Click **Refresh data when opening the file**
(☐ changes to ☑).

7 Click **OK**.

Excel applies the new setting and will now refresh
the PivotTable automatically each time you open
the workbook.

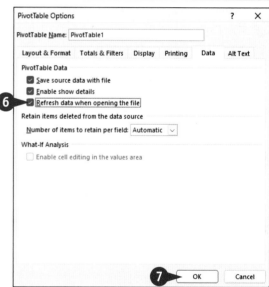

TIPS

Is there a drawback to using an automatic refresh?

Yes, you might find that your workbook takes too long to open because the PivotTable source data is very large. In that case, you might prefer to turn off the automatic refresh and, instead, run a manual refresh when you will not be working with the file for a while.

My PivotTable refresh is taking a very long time. Can I cancel it?

Yes. A very long refresh can occur if the PivotTable source data is very large or is in a different workbook. If you find the refresh is taking too long, you can cancel it by clicking the **PivotTable Analyze** contextual tab, clicking the **Refresh ∨**, and then clicking **Cancel Refresh**.

You can add multiple fields to any of the PivotTable areas. This is a powerful technique that enables you to perform further analysis of your data by viewing the data differently.

For example, suppose that you are analyzing the results of a sales campaign that ran several types of advertisements. A basic PivotTable might show you the sales for each Product (the row field) according to the Advertisement used (the column field). You might also be interested in seeing the breakdown in sales for each promotion. You can do that by adding the Promotion field to the row area.

Add Multiple Fields to the Row or Column Area

Add a Field to the Rows Area

1 Click a cell within the PivotTable.

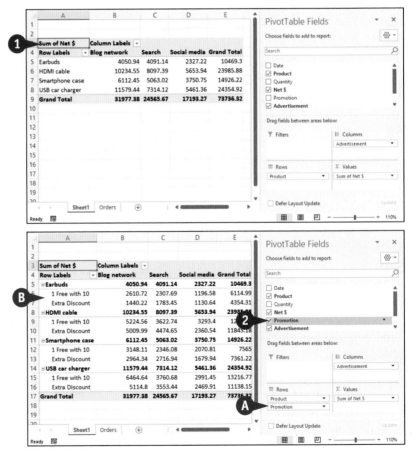

2 Select the check box of the text or date field that you want to add (☐ changes to ☑).

A Excel adds the field to the Rows box.

B Excel adds the field's unique values to the PivotTable's row area.

Add a Field to the Rows or Columns Area

1. Click a cell within the PivotTable.

2. In the PivotTable Fields task pane, drag the field that you want to add and drop the field in either the Rows box or the Columns box.

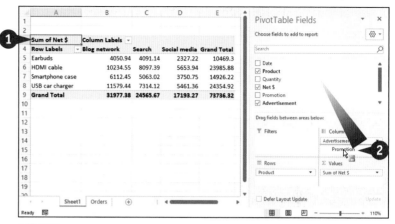

C. Excel adds the field to the Rows or Columns box.

D. Excel adds the field's unique values to the PivotTable's row or column area.

TIPS

Can I change the field positions within the row or column area?
Yes. After you add a second field to the row or column area, you can change the field positions to change the PivotTable view. In the PivotTable Fields task pane, use the Rows or Columns box to click and drag the button of the field you want to move, and then drop the field above or below an existing field button.

Can I only add two fields to the row or column area?
No, Excel does not restrict you to just two fields in the row or column area. Depending on your data analysis requirements, you are free to add three, four, or more fields to the row area or to the column area.

Excel enables you to add multiple fields to the PivotTable's data area, which enhances your analysis by enabling you to see multiple summaries at one time.

Suppose you are analyzing the results of a sales campaign. A basic PivotTable might show you the sum of the Quantity sold. You might also be interested in seeing the net dollar amount sold. You can do that by adding the Net $ field to the data area, as shown in the example in this section. You can use either of the techniques in this section to add multiple fields to the data area.

Add Multiple Fields to the Data Area

Add a Field to the Data Area with a Check Box

1 Click a cell within the PivotTable.

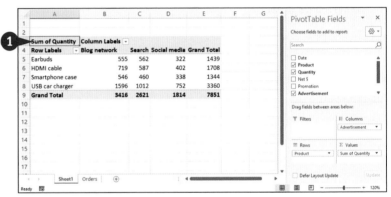

2 Select the check box of the field you want to add to the data area (☐ changes to ☑).

Ⓐ Excel adds the field to the Values box.

Ⓑ Excel adds the field's data to the PivotTable's data area.

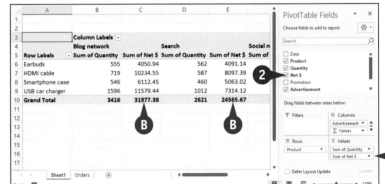

Add a Field to the Data Area by Dragging

1. Click a cell within the PivotTable.

2. In the PivotTable Fields task pane, drag the field you want to add and drop the field in the Values box.

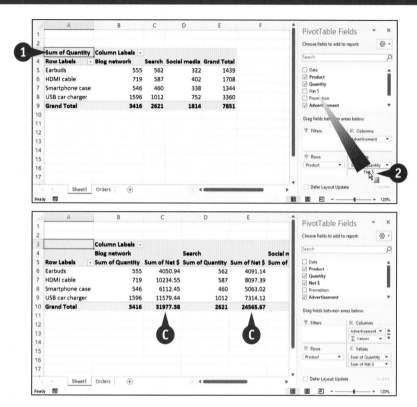

C Excel adds the field to the PivotTable's data area.

Why does Excel add a Values button to the Columns box?

When you add a second field to the data area, Excel moves the labels (for example, Sum of Quantity and Sum of Net $) into the column area for easier reference. Excel also adds a Values button in the Columns box of the PivotTable Fields task pane to enable you to pivot the values within the report. For more information, see the following section, "Move a Field to a Different Area."

Can I add only two fields to the data area?

No, Excel does not restrict you to just two fields in the data area. You are free to add three, four, or more data fields to enhance your analysis of the data.

Move a Field to a Different Area

A PivotTable is not a static collection of worksheet cells. You can move a PivotTable's fields from one area of the PivotTable to another. This enables you to view your data from different perspectives, which can help you analyze the data. Moving a field within a PivotTable is called *pivoting* the data.

The most common way to pivot the data is to use the PivotTable Fields task pane to move fields between the row and column areas. However, you can also pivot data by moving a row or column field to the filter area.

Move a Field to a Different Area

Move a Field Between the Row and Column Areas

1 Click a cell within the PivotTable.

2 Click and drag a Columns field button and drop it within the Rows box.

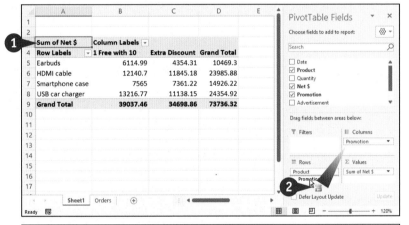

A Excel displays the field's values within the row area.

You can also drag a field button from the Rows box area and drop it within the Columns box.

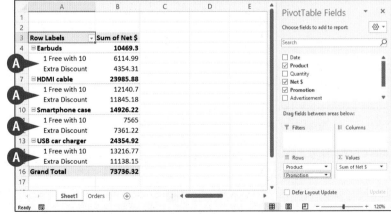

Move a Row or Column Field to the Filters Area

① Click a cell within the PivotTable.

② Click and drag a field from the Rows box and drop it within the Filters box.

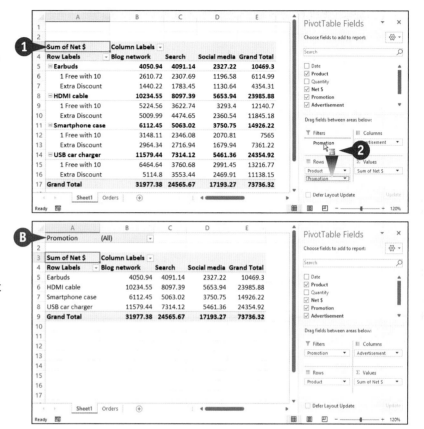

Ⓑ Excel moves the field button to the report filter.

You can also drag a field button from the Columns box and drop it within the Filters box.

To make a PivotTable with a large number of row or column items easier to work with, you can group the items together. For example, you can group months into quarters, thus reducing the number of items from twelve to four. A report that lists dozens of countries can group them by continent, thus reducing the number of items to four or five, depending on where the countries are located. If you use a numeric field in the row or column area, you may have hundreds of items, one for each numeric value. You can improve the report by creating just a few numeric ranges.

Group PivotTable Values

1 Click any item in the numeric field that you want to group.

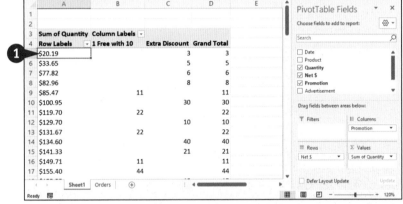

2 Click the **PivotTable Analyze** tab.

3 Click **Group Field** (⬚).

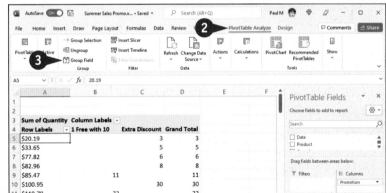

The Grouping dialog box appears.

4 Type the starting numeric value.

A Alternatively, click **Starting at** (☐ changes to ☑) to have Excel use the minimum value of the numeric items as the starting value.

5 Type the ending numeric value.

B Alternatively, click **Ending at** (☐ changes to ☑) to have Excel use the maximum value of the numeric items as the ending value.

6 Type the size that you want to use for each grouping.

7 Click **OK**.

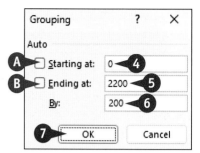

C Excel groups the numeric values.

3	Sum of Quantity	Column Labels		
4	Row Labels	1 Free with 10	Extra Discount	Grand Total
5	0-200	187	203	390
6	200-400	429	430	859
7	400-600	638	619	1257
8	600-800	363	286	649
9	800-1000	440	791	1231
10	1000-1200	473	632	1105
11	1200-1400	429	293	722
12	1400-1600	473	120	593
13	1600-1800	110	254	364
14	1800-2000	132	274	406
15	2000-2200	275		275
16	Grand Total	3949	3902	7851

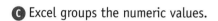

TIPS

How do I group date and time values?
Click any item in the date field that you want to group. Click the **PivotTable Analyze** tab and then click **Group Field**. In the Grouping dialog box, type the start date or time and the end date or time. In the **By** list, click the type of grouping that you want, such as **Months** or **Quarters**. Click **OK**.

How do I group text values?
You must create custom groups. Begin by selecting the items that you want to include in a group. Click the **PivotTable Analyze** tab and then click **Group Selection**. Click the group label, type a new name for the group, and then press [Enter]. Repeat for each custom group that you want to create.

By default, each PivotTable displays a summary for all the records in your source data. However, there may be situations in which you need to focus more closely on some aspect of the data. You can focus on a specific item from one of the source data fields by taking advantage of the PivotTable's filter field.

For example, suppose you are dealing with a PivotTable that summarizes data from a sales promotion by showing the net amount sold by product and promotion. To break down this summary by advertisement, you could add that field to the filter area.

Apply a PivotTable Filter

Apply a Report Filter

1 Add a field to the Filters box.

2 Click the drop-down arrow (▼) in the filter field.

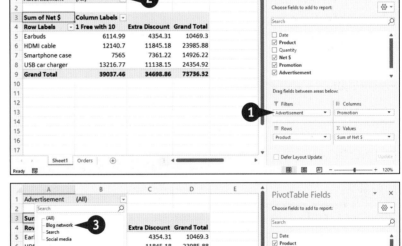

Excel displays a list of the report filter field values.

3 Click the item that you want to use as a filter.

Ⓐ If you want to display data for two or more report filters, click **Select Multiple Items** (☐ change to ☑). Repeat step **3** to select the other filters.

4 Click **OK**.

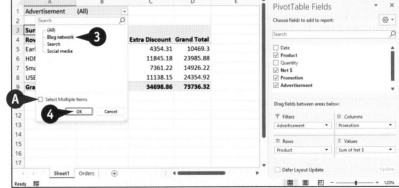

216

B Excel filters the PivotTable to show only the data for the item that you selected.

C The filter field drop-down arrow (▼) changes to the Filter button (🔽).

Remove the Filter

1 Click the **Filter** button (🔽) in the report filter field.

Excel displays a list of the report filter field values.

2 Click **All**.

3 Click **OK**.

Excel removes the filter from the PivotTable.

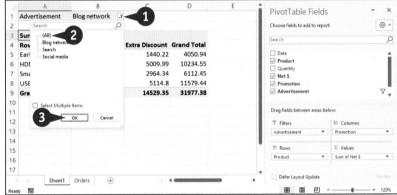

TIP

Can I add multiple fields to the filter area?

Yes. This enables you to apply multiple filters to the data. For example, suppose you have a PivotTable that summarizes sales promotion data by showing the total amount sold for each product, and that you have a filter field with Advertisement data that enables you to isolate the sales by product for a specific type of advertising used in the promotion. You could extend your analysis to look at the advertisement-specific sales by product for individual promotions.

To do this, add the Promotion field as a second field in the Filters box and then follow the steps in this section to choose a specific advertisement and a specific promotion. It does not matter which order the fields appear in the filter because the filtering comes out the same in the end.

CHAPTER 13

Analyzing Data

You can get more out of Excel by performing *data analysis*, which is the application of tools and techniques to organize, study, and reach conclusions about a specific collection of information. In this chapter, you learn data analysis techniques such as sorting and filtering a range, setting validation rules, and using subtotals and conditional formatting.

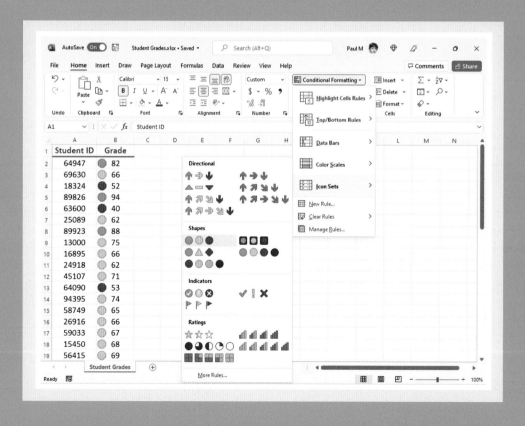

Sort a Range or Table

You can make a range or table easier to read and analyze by sorting the data based on the values in one or more columns.

You can sort the data in either ascending or descending order. An ascending sort arranges the values alphabetically from A to Z, or numerically from 0 to 9; a descending sort arranges the values alphabetically from Z to A, or numerically from 9 to 0.

Sort a Range or Table

1 Click any cell in the range you want to sort.

2 Click the **Data** tab.

3 Click **Sort** (⬛).

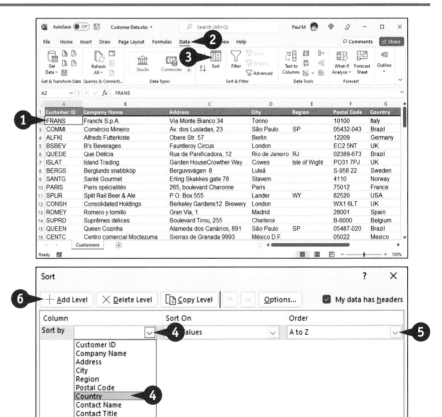

The Sort dialog box appears.

4 Click the **Sort by** ⌄ and then click the field you want to use for the main sort level.

5 Click the **Order** ⌄ and then click a sort order for the field.

6 To sort on another field, click **Add Level**.

Ⓐ Excel adds another sort level.

⑦ Click the **Then by** ▾ and then click the field you want to use for the sort level.

⑧ Click the **Order** ▾ and then click a sort order for the field.

⑨ Repeat steps **6** to **8** to add more sort levels as needed.

⑩ Click **OK**.

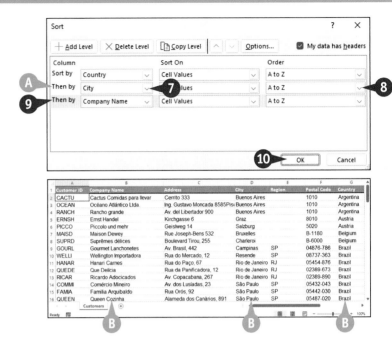

Ⓑ Excel sorts the range.

Is there a faster way to sort a range?

Yes, as long as you only need to sort your range on a single column. First, click in any cell inside the column you want to use for the sort. Click the **Data** tab and then click one of the following buttons in the Sort & Filter group:

A↓Z	Click for an ascending sort.
Z↓A	Click for a descending sort.

How do I sort a range using the values in a row instead of a column?

Excel normally sorts a range from top to bottom based on the values in one or more columns. However, you can tell Excel to sort the range from left to right based on the values in one or more rows. Follow steps **1** to **3** to display the Sort dialog box. Click **Options** to display the Sort Options dialog box, select the **Sort left to right** option (○ changes to ◉), and then click **OK**.

Filter a Range or Table

You can analyze table data much faster by only viewing those table records that you want to work with. In Excel, this is called *filtering* a range.

The easiest way to filter a range is to use the Filter buttons, each of which presents you with a list of check boxes for each unique value in a column. You filter the data by activating the check boxes for the rows you want to see. If you have converted the range to a table, as described in Chapter 11, the Filter buttons for each column are displayed automatically.

Filter a Range or Table

Display the Filter Buttons

Note: If you are filtering a table, you can skip directly to the "Filter the Data" subsection.

1 Click inside the range.

2 Click the **Data** tab.

3 Click **Filter** (⧩).

Ⓐ Excel adds a Filter button (▼) to each field.

Filter the Data

1 Click ▼ for the field you want to use as the filter.

B Excel displays a list of the unique values in the field.

2 Click the check box for each value you want to see (☐ changes to ☑).

C You can toggle all the check boxes on and off by clicking **Select All**.

3 Click **OK**.

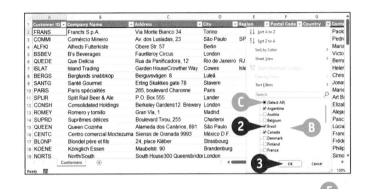

D Excel filters the table to show only those records that have the field values you selected.

E Excel displays the number of records found.

F The field's drop-down list displays a filter icon (🔽).

To remove the filter, click the **Data** tab and then click **Clear** (🔽; not shown).

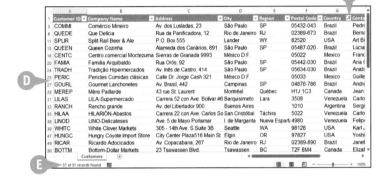

TIP

Can I create more sophisticated filters?
Yes, by using a second technique called *quick filters*, which enables you to specify criteria for a field:

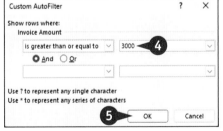

1 Click 🔽 for the field you want to use as the filter.

2 Click **Number Filters**.

Note: If the field is a date field, click **Date Filters**; if the field is a text field, click **Text Filters**.

3 Click the filter you want to use.

4 Enter the value you want to use.

5 Click **OK**.

Set Data Validation Rules

You can make Excel data entry more efficient by setting up data entry cells to accept only certain values. To do this, you can set up a cell with data validation criteria that specify the allowed value or values. This is called a *data validation rule*.

Excel also lets you tell the user what to enter by defining an input message that appears when the user selects the cell. You can also configure the data validation rule to display a message when the user tries to enter an invalid value.

Set Data Validation Rules

1 Click the cell you want to restrict.

2 Click the **Data** tab.

3 Click **Data Validation** (⊞).

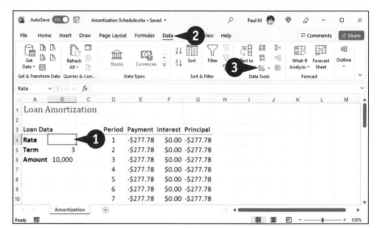

The Data Validation dialog box appears.

4 Click the **Settings** tab.

5 Click the **Allow** ☑ and then select the type of data you want to allow in the cell.

6 Click the **Data** ☑ and then select the operator you want to use to define the allowable data.

7 Specify the validation criteria, such as the **Minimum** and **Maximum** allowable values shown here.

Note: The criteria boxes you see depend on the operator you chose in step **6**.

8 Click the **Input Message** tab.

9 Make sure the **Show input message when cell is selected** check box is selected (☑).

10 Type a message title in the **Title** text box.

11 Type the message you want to display in the **Input message** text box.

12 Click **OK**.

Excel configures the cell to accept only values that meet your criteria.

Ⓐ When the user selects the cell, the input message appears.

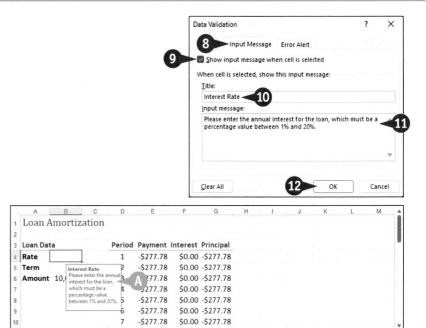

TIPS

Can I configure the cell to display a message if the user tries to enter an invalid value?
Yes. Follow steps **1** to **3** to open the Data Validation dialog box, and then click the **Error Alert** tab. Make sure the **Show error alert after invalid data is entered** check box is selected (☑), and then specify the **Style**, **Title**, and **Error message**. Click **OK**.

How do I remove data validation from a cell?
If you no longer need to use data validation on a cell, you should clear the settings. Follow steps **1** to **3** to display the Data Validation dialog box and then click **Clear All**. Excel removes all the validation criteria, as well as the input message and the error alert. Click **OK**.

Create a Data Table

If you are interested in studying the effect a range of values has on the formula, you can set up a *data table*. This is a table that consists of the formula you are using and multiple input values for that formula. Excel automatically creates a solution to the formula for each different input value.

Do not confuse data tables with the Excel tables that you learned about in Chapter 11. A data table is a special range that Excel uses to calculate multiple solutions to a formula.

Create a Data Table

1 Type the input values:

To enter the values in a column, start the column one cell down and one cell to the left of the cell containing the formula, as shown here.

To enter the values in a row, start the row one cell up and one cell to the right of the cell containing the formula.

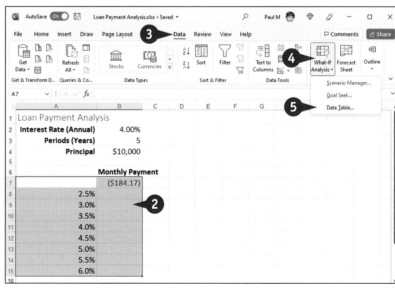

2 Select the range that includes the input values and the formula.

3 Click the **Data** tab.

4 Click **What-If Analysis** (⊞).

5 Click **Data Table**.

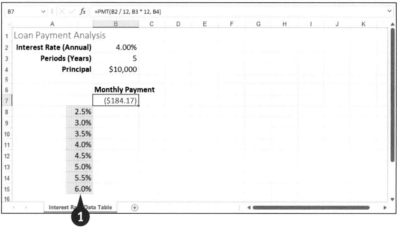

The Data Table dialog box appears.

6 Specify the formula cell you want to use as the data table's input cell:

If the input values are in a column, enter the input cell's address in the **Column input cell** text box.

If you entered the input values in a row, enter the input cell's address in the **Row input cell** text box.

7 Click **OK**.

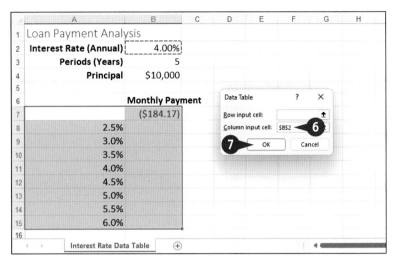

A Excel displays the results.

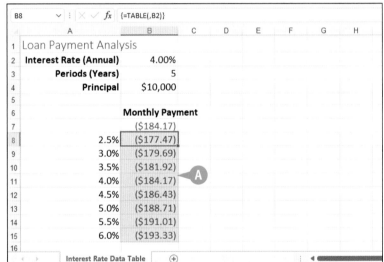

What is what-if analysis?

The technique called *what-if analysis* is perhaps the most basic method for analyzing worksheet data. With what-if analysis, you first calculate a formula D, based on the input from variables A, B, and C. You then say, "What happens to the result if I change the value of variable A?", "What happens if I change B or C?", and so on.

When I try to delete part of the data table, I get an error. Why?

The data table results are created as an *array formula*, which is a special formula that Excel treats as a unit. This means that you cannot move or delete part of the results. If you need to work with the data table results, you must first select the entire results range (B8:B15 in this section's example).

Summarize Data with Subtotals

Although you can use formulas and worksheet functions to summarize your data in various ways, including sums, averages, counts, maximums, and minimums, if you are in a hurry, or if you just need a quick summary of your data, you can get Excel to do most of the work for you. The secret here is a feature called *automatic subtotals*, which are formulas that Excel adds to a worksheet automatically.

Excel cannot apply subtotals to tables, so if your data is in table format, you need to convert it to a range, as described in Chapter 11.

Summarize Data with Subtotals

1 Click a cell within the range you want to subtotal.

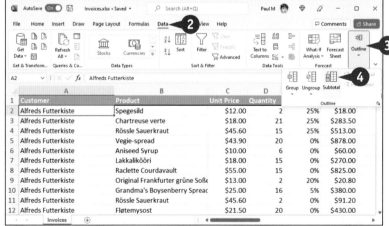

2 Click the **Data** tab.

3 Click **Outline**.

4 Click **Subtotal** (⊞).

The Subtotal dialog box appears.

5 Click the **At each change in**
☑ and then click the column
you want to use to group the
subtotals.

6 In the **Add subtotal to** list, click
the check box for the column you
want to summarize (☐ changes
to ☑).

Note: Be sure to also deselect the
check box for any column you do
not want to summarize (☑ changes
to ☐).

7 Click **OK**.

Ⓐ Excel calculates the subtotals and
adds them into the range.

Ⓑ Excel adds outline symbols to the
range.

Note: See the next section, "Group
Related Data," to learn more about
outlining in Excel.

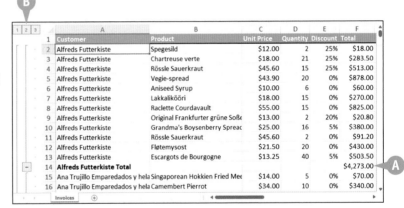

Do I need to prepare my worksheet to use subtotals?

Yes. Excel sets up automatic subtotals based on data groupings in a selected field. For example, if you ask for subtotals based on the Customer field, Excel runs down the Customer column and creates a new subtotal each time the name changes. To get useful summaries, you need to sort the range on the field containing the data groupings you are interested in.

Can I only calculate totals?

No. The word *subtotal* here is a bit misleading because you can summarize more than just totals. You can also count values, calculate the average of the values, determine the maximum or minimum value, and more. To change the summary calculation, follow steps **1** to **5**, click the **Use function** ☑, and then click the function you want to use for the summary.

Group Related Data

You can control a worksheet range display by grouping the data based on the worksheet formulas and data.

Grouping the data creates a worksheet outline, which you can use to "collapse" sections of the sheet to display only summary cells, or "expand" hidden sections to show the underlying detail. Note that when you add subtotals to a range as described in the previous section, "Summarize Data with Subtotals," Excel automatically groups the data and displays the outline tools.

Group Related Data

Create the Outline

1. Display the worksheet you want to outline.

2. Click the **Data** tab.

3. Click **Outline**.

4. Click the **Group** ∨.

5. Click **Auto Outline**.

Note: The Auto Outline command will be disabled if your data is in a table format. To use Auto Outline, you must first convert your table to a range, as described in Chapter 11.

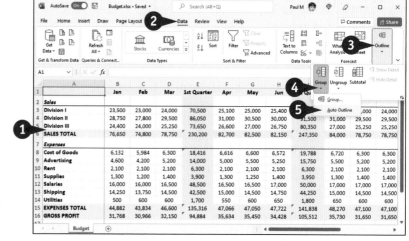

A. Excel outlines the worksheet data.

B. Excel uses level bars to indicate the grouped ranges.

C. Excel displays level symbols to indicate the various levels of detail that are available in the outline.

Using the Outline to Control the Range Display

1 Click a **Collapse** symbol (⊟) to hide the range indicated by the level bar.

D You can also collapse multiple ranges that are on the same outline level by clicking the appropriate level symbol.

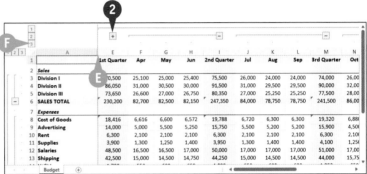

E Excel collapses the range.

2 Click the **Expand** symbol (⊞) to view the range again.

F You can also show multiple ranges that are on the same outline level by clicking the appropriate level symbol.

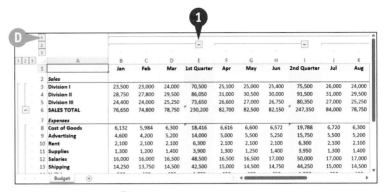

Do I have to prepare my worksheet before I can group the data?

Yes. Not all worksheets can be grouped, so you need to make sure your worksheet is a candidate for outlining. First, the worksheet must contain formulas that reference cells or ranges directly adjacent to the formula cell. Worksheets with SUM functions that subtotal cells above or to the left are particularly good candidates for outlining.

Second, there must be a consistent pattern to the direction of the formula references. For example, a worksheet with formulas that always reference cells above or to the left can be outlined. Excel will not outline a worksheet with, say, SUM functions that reference ranges above and below a formula cell.

Analyze Data with Goal Seek

$\mathbf{I}$f you already know the formula result you want but you must find an input value that produces that result, you can use the Excel Goal Seek tool to solve the problem. You tell Goal Seek the final value you need and which variable to change, and it finds a solution for you.

For example, you might know that, 18 years from now, you want to have $50,000 saved for a child's college, so you need to calculate how much to invest each year.

Analyze Data with Goal Seek

1 Set up your worksheet model.

Note: See the first tip to learn more about setting up a worksheet for Goal Seek.

Ⓐ This model uses Excel's FV function, which calculates the future value of an investment given an interest rate (cell C4), investment period (C5), and the amount deposited regularly (C6).

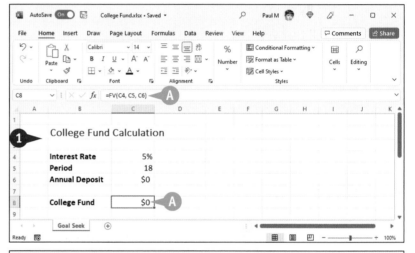

2 Click the **Data** tab.

3 Click **What-If Analysis** (▦).

4 Click **Goal Seek**.

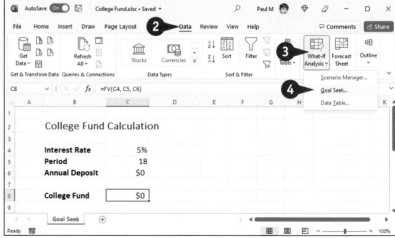

The Goal Seek dialog box appears.

5 Click inside the **Set cell** box.

6 Click the cell that contains the formula you want Goal Seek to work with.

7 Use the **To value** text box to type the value that you want Goal Seek to find.

8 Click in the **By changing cell** box.

9 Click the cell that you want Goal Seek to modify.

10 Click **OK**.

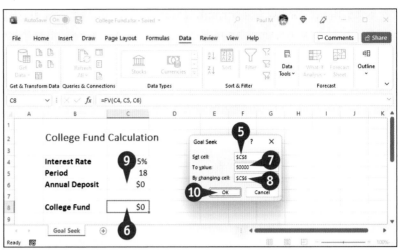

B Goal Seek adjusts the changing cell value until it reaches a solution.

C The formula now shows the value you entered in step **7**.

11 Click **OK**.

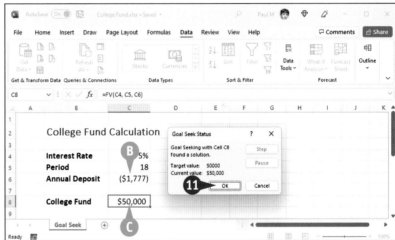

TIPS

How do I set up my worksheet to use Goal Seek?
Setting up your worksheet model for Goal Seek means doing three things. First, set up one cell as the *changing cell*, which is the value that Goal Seek will manipulate to reach the goal. Enter an initial value (such as 0) in the cell. Second, set up the other input values for the formula and give them proper initial values. Third, create a formula for Goal Seek to use to reach the goal.

What other types of problems can Goal Seek solve?
One common problem is called a *break-even analysis*, where you determine the number of units you must sell of a product so that your total profits are 0. In this case, the changing cell is the number of units sold and the formula is the profit calculation. You can also use Goal Seek to determine which price (the changing cell) is required to return a particular profit margin (the formula).

Highlight Cells That Meet Some Criteria

A *conditional format* is formatting that Excel applies only to cells that meet the criteria you specify. For example, you can tell Excel to apply the formatting only if a cell's value is greater or less than some specified amount, between two specified values, or equal to some value. You can also look for cells that contain specified text, dates that occur during a specified timeframe, and more.

You can specify the font, border, and background pattern, which helps to ensure that the cells that meet your criteria stand out from the other cells in the range.

Highlight Cells That Meet Some Criteria

1 Select the range with which you want to work.

2 Click the **Home** tab.

3 Click **Conditional Formatting** (▦).

4 Click **Highlight Cells Rules**.

5 Click the operator you want to use for the condition.

A dialog box appears, the name of which depends on the operator you clicked in step **5**.

6 Type the value you want to use for the condition.

Ⓐ You can also click **Collapse Dialog** (↥), click a worksheet cell, and then click **Restore Dialog** (▥).

Depending on the operator, you may need to specify two values.

7 Click this drop-down arrow (⌄), and then click the formatting you want to use.

Ⓑ To create your own format, click **Custom Format**.

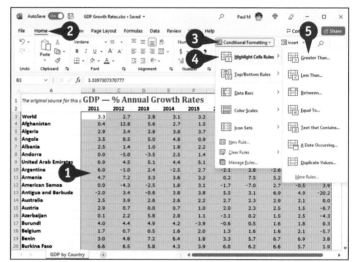

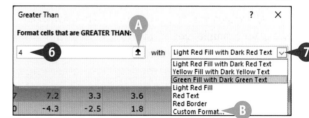

8 Click **OK**.

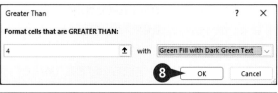

C Excel applies the formatting to cells that meet the condition you specified.

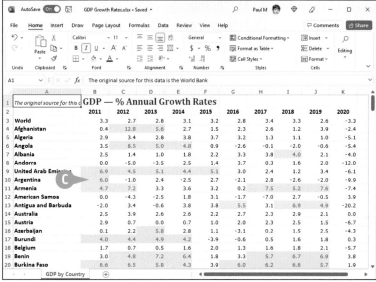

TIPS

Can I set up more than one conditional format on a range?

Yes, Excel enables you to specify multiple conditional formats. For example, you could set up one condition for cells that are greater than some value, and a separate condition for cells that are less than some other value. You can apply unique formats to each condition. Follow steps **1** to **8** to configure the new condition.

How do I remove a conditional format?

If you no longer require a conditional format, you can delete it. Follow steps **1** to **3** to select the range and display the Conditional Formatting drop-down menu, and then click **Manage Rules**. Excel displays the Conditional Formatting Rules Manager dialog box. Click the conditional format you want to remove and then click **Delete Rule**.

Highlight the Top or Bottom Values in a Range

When analyzing worksheet data, it is often useful to look for items that stand out from the norm. For example, you might want to know which sales reps sold the most last year, or which departments had the lowest gross margins.

You can do this by setting up *top/bottom rules*, where Excel applies a conditional format to those items that are at the top or bottom of a range of values. For the top or bottom values, you can specify a number, such as the top 5 or 10, or a percentage, such as the bottom 20 percent.

Highlight the Top or Bottom Values in a Range

1 Select the range with which you want to work.

2 Click the **Home** tab.

3 Click **Conditional Formatting** (▦).

4 Click **Top/Bottom Rules**.

5 Click the type of rule you want to create.

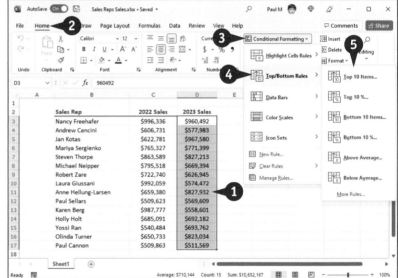

A dialog box appears, the name of which depends on the type of rule you clicked in step **5**.

6 Type the value you want to use for the condition.

7 Click this drop-down arrow (⌄), and then click the formatting you want to use.

A To create your own format, click **Custom Format**.

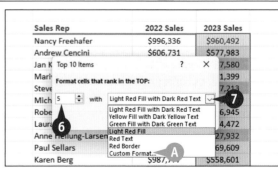

236

8 Click **OK**.

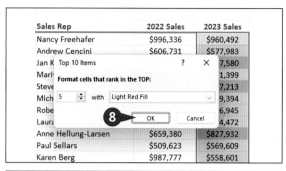

B Excel applies the formatting to cells that meet the condition you specified.

Can I highlight cells that are above or below the average?
Yes, Excel also enables you to create top/bottom rules based on the average value in the range. First, follow steps **1** to **4** to select the range and display the Top/Bottom Rules menu. Then click either **Above Average** to format those values that exceed the range average, or **Below Average** to format those values that are less than the range average.

How do I remove a top/bottom rule?
If you no longer require a top/bottom rule, you can delete it. Follow steps **1** to **3** to select the range and display the Conditional Formatting drop-down menu. Click **Clear Rules**, and then click **Clear Rules from Selected Cells**. Excel removes the rule from the range.

Analyze Cell Values with Data Bars

In some data analysis scenarios, you might be interested more in the relative values within a range than the absolute values. For example, if you have a table of products that includes a column showing unit sales, how do you compare the relative sales of all the products?

This sort of analysis is often easiest if you visualize the relative values. You can do that by using *data bars*. Data bars are a data visualization feature that applies colored, horizontal bars to each cell in a range of values, and these bars appear "behind" the values in the range.

Analyze Cell Values with Data Bars

1 Select the range with which you want to work.

2 Click the **Home** tab.

3 Click **Conditional Formatting** (▦).

4 Click **Data Bars**.

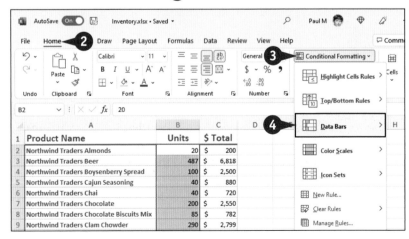

⑤ Click the fill type of data bars you want to create:

Ⓐ Gradient Fill data bars begin with a solid color, and then gradually fade to a lighter color.

Ⓑ Solid Fill data bars are a solid color.

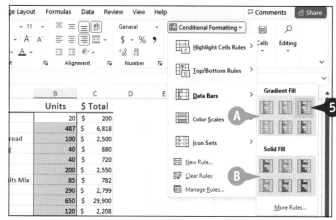

Ⓒ Excel applies the data bars to each cell in the range.

How do data bars work?

The length of the data bar that appears in each cell depends on the value in that cell; the larger the value, the longer the data bar. The cell with the highest value has the longest data bar, the cell with the lowest value has the shortest data bar, and the other cells have data bars with lengths that reflect each cell's value.

How do I delete data bars from a range?

If you no longer require the data bars, you can remove them. Follow steps **1** to **3** to select the range and display the Conditional Formatting drop-down menu, and then click **Manage Rules**. Excel displays the Conditional Formatting Rules Manager dialog box. Click the data bar rule you want to remove, click **Delete Rule**, and then click **OK**.

Analyze Cell Values with Color Scales

When analyzing worksheet data, it is often useful to get some idea about the overall distribution of the values. For example, it might be useful to know whether a range has a lot of low values and just a few high values.

You can analyze your worksheet data by using a conditional format called *color scales*. A color scale compares the relative values of cells in a range by applying shading to each cell, where the shading color reflects the cell's value.

Analyze Cell Values with Color Scales

1 Select the range with which you want to work.

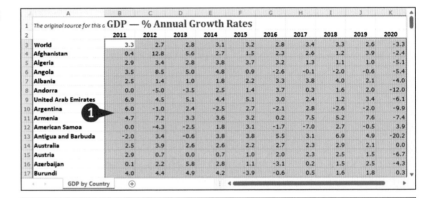

2 Click the **Home** tab.

3 Click **Conditional Formatting** (⊞).

4 Click **Color Scales**.

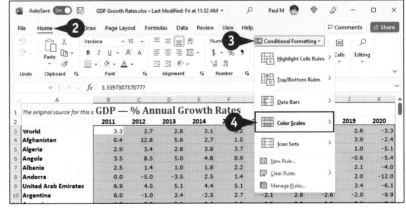

5 Click the color scale that has the color scheme you want to apply.

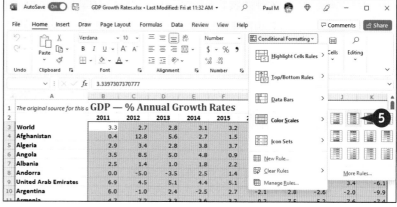

A Excel applies the color scales to each cell in the range.

In what other situations are color scales useful?

Besides showing patterns, color scales can also tell you whether your data includes any *outliers*, values that are much higher or lower than all or most of the others. Similarly, you can also use color scales to make value judgments about your data. For example, high sales and low numbers of product defects are good, whereas low margins and high employee turnover rates are bad.

When should I use a three-color scale versus a two-color scale?

If your goal is to look for outliers or to make value judgments about your data, go with a three-color scale because outliers stand out more, and you can assign your own values to the colors (such as positive, neutral, and negative). Use a two-color scale when you want to look for patterns in the data, as a two-color scale offers less contrast.

Analyze Cell Values with Icon Sets

When you are trying to make sense of a large data set, symbols that have common or well-known associations are often useful for clarifying the data. For example, for most people a check mark means something is good or finished or acceptable, whereas an X means something is bad or unfinished or unacceptable; a green circle is positive, whereas a red circle is negative (think traffic lights).

Excel puts these and many other symbolic associations to good use with the *icon sets* feature. You use icon sets to visualize the relative values of cells in a range.

Analyze Cell Values with Icon Sets

1 Select the range with which you want to work.

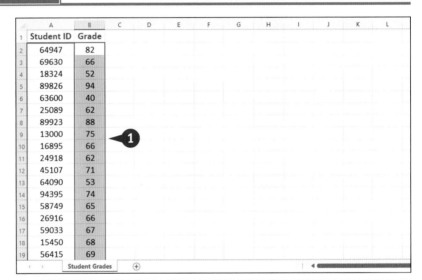

2 Click the **Home** tab.

3 Click **Conditional Formatting** (▦).

4 Click **Icon Sets**.

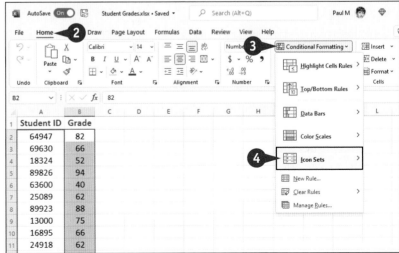

242

5 Click the type of icon set you want to apply.

The categories include Directional, Shapes, Indicators, and Ratings.

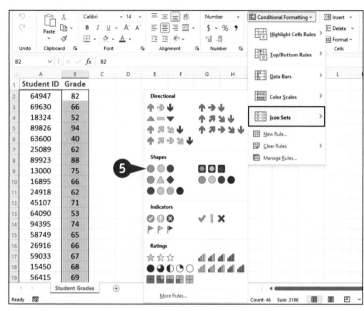

A Excel applies the icons to each cell in the range.

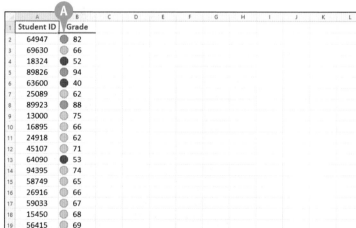

TIPS

How do icon sets work?

With icon sets, Excel adds a particular icon to each cell in the range, and that icon tells you something about the cell's value relative to the rest of the range. For example, the highest values might be assigned an upward-pointing arrow, the lowest values a downward-pointing arrow, and the values in between a horizontal arrow.

How do I use the different icon set categories?

The Excel icon sets come in four categories: Directional, Shapes, Indicators, and Ratings. Use Directional icon sets for indicating trends and data movement; use Shapes for pointing out the high (green) and low (red) values; use Indicators to add value judgments; and use Ratings to show where each cell resides in the overall range of data values.

CHAPTER 14

Visualizing Data with Charts

You can take a worksheet full of numbers and display them as a chart. Visualizing your data in this way makes the data easy to understand and analyze. To help you see your data exactly the way you want, Excel offers a wide variety of chart types, and a large number of chart options.

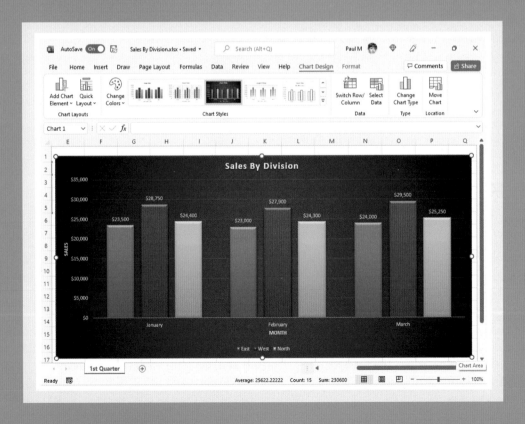

Examine Chart Elements

One of the best ways to analyze your worksheet data — or get your point across to other people — is to display your data visually in a *chart*, which is a graphic representation of spreadsheet data. As the data in the spreadsheet changes, the chart also changes to reflect the new numbers.

You have dozens of different chart formats to choose from, and if none of the built-in Excel formats is just right, you can further customize these charts to suit your needs. To get the most out of charts, you should familiarize yourself with the basic chart elements.

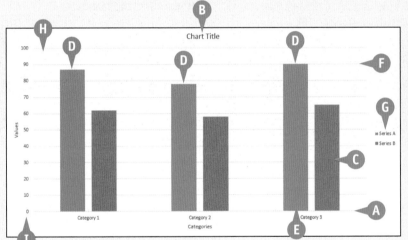

A Category Axis

The axis (usually the X-axis) that contains the category groupings.

B Chart Title

The title of the chart.

C Data Marker

A symbol, such as a column, that represents a specific data value. The symbol used depends on the chart type.

D Data Series

A collection of related data values. Normally, the marker for each value in a series has the same pattern.

E Data Value

A single piece of data, also called a *data point*.

F Gridlines

Optional horizontal and vertical extensions of the axis tick marks. These lines make data values easy to read.

G Legend

A guide that shows the colors, patterns, and symbols used by the markers for each data series.

H Plot Area

The area bounded by the category and value axes. It contains the data points and gridlines.

I Value Axis

The axis (usually the Y-axis) that contains the data values.

Understanding Chart Types

Excel offers 16 different types of charts, including column charts, bar charts, and line charts. The chart type you use depends on the type of data and how you want to present that data visually.

Chart Types

Chart Type	Description
Area chart	Shows the relative contributions over time that each data series makes to the whole picture.
Bar chart	Compares distinct items or shows single items at distinct intervals. A bar chart is laid out with categories along the vertical axis and values along the horizontal axis.
Box & Whisker chart	Visualizes several statistical values for the data in each category, including the average, the range, the minimum, and the maximum.
Column chart	Compares distinct items or shows single items at distinct intervals. A column chart is laid out with categories along the horizontal axis and values along the vertical axis.
Funnel	Shows how values change across multiple stages of a process.
Histogram	Groups the category values into ranges — called *bins* — and shows the frequency with which the data values fall within each bin.
Line chart	Shows how a data series changes over time. The category (X) axis usually represents a progression of even increments (such as days or months), and the series points are plotted on the value (Y) axis.
Map chart	Compares values and categories across geographical regions, such as countries, states, provinces, counties, or postal codes.
Pie chart	Shows the proportion of the whole that is contributed by each value in a single data series. The whole is represented as a circle (the "pie"), and each value is displayed as a proportional "slice" of the circle.
Radar chart	Makes comparisons within a data series and between data series relative to a center point. Each category is shown with a value axis extending from the center point.
Stock chart	Designed to plot stock-market prices, such as a stock's daily high, low, and closing values.
Sunburst chart	Displays hierarchical data as a series of concentric circles. The top level is the innermost circle; each circle is divided proportionally according to the values in that level.
Surface chart	Analyzes two sets of data and determines the optimum combination of the two.
Treemap chart	For hierarchical data, shows a large rectangle for each item in the top level, then divides each rectangle proportionally based on the value of each item in the next level.
Waterfall chart	Shows a running total as category values are added (positive values) or subtracted (negative values).
XY chart (or scatter chart)	Shows the relationship between numeric values in two different data series. It can also plot a series of data pairs in XY coordinates.

Create a Chart

You can create a chart from your Excel worksheet data with just a few mouse clicks. Excel offers nearly 100 default chart configurations, so there should always be a type that best visualizes your data. If you would prefer to let Excel suggest a chart type based on your data, see the following section, "Create a Recommended Chart."

Regardless of the chart type you choose originally, you can change to a different chart type at any time. See the "Select a Different Chart Type" section later in this chapter.

Create a Chart

1 Select the data that you want to visualize in a chart.

A If your data includes headings, be sure to include those headings in the selection.

Note: If your data includes totals, you must exclude those totals from the selection.

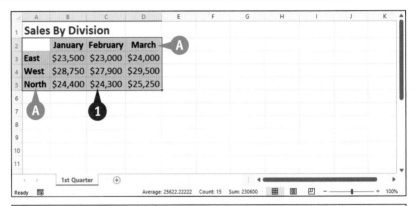

2 Click the **Insert** tab.

3 Click a chart type.

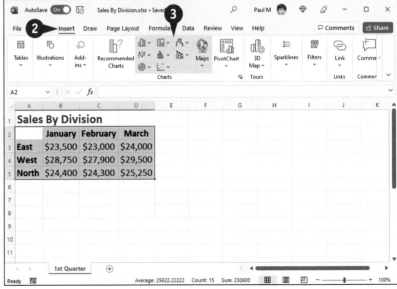

B Excel displays a gallery of configurations for the chart type.

4 Click the chart configuration you want to use.

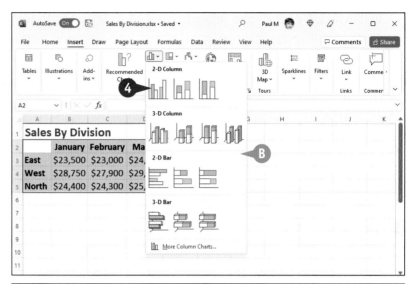

C Excel inserts the chart.

The sections in the rest of this chapter show you how to configure, format, and move the chart.

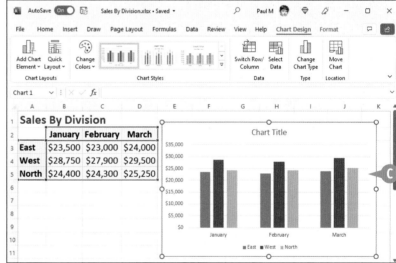

TIP

Is there a way to create a chart on a separate sheet?

Yes. You can use a special workbook sheet called a *chart sheet*. If you have not yet created your chart, select the worksheet data, right-click any worksheet tab, and then click **Insert** to display the Insert dialog box. Click the **General** tab, click **Chart**, and then click **OK**. Excel creates a new chart sheet and inserts the chart.

If you have already created your chart, you can move it to a separate chart sheet. See the first tip in the "Move or Resize a Chart" section later in this chapter.

Create a Recommended Chart

You can make it easier and faster to create a chart by choosing from one of the chart configurations recommended by Excel.

With close to 100 possible chart configurations, the Excel chart tools are certainly comprehensive. However, that can be an overwhelming number of choices if you're not sure which type would best visualize your data. Rather than wasting a great deal of time looking at dozens of different chart configurations, the Recommended Charts command examines your data and then narrows down the possible choices to about ten configurations that would work with your data.

Create a Recommended Chart

1 Select the data that you want to visualize in a chart.

A If your data includes headings, be sure to include those headings in the selection.

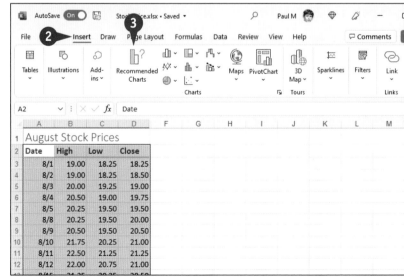

2 Click the **Insert** tab.

3 Click **Recommended Charts** (📊).

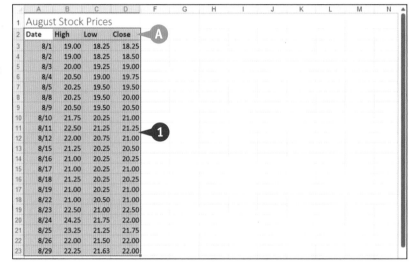

The Insert Chart dialog box appears with the Recommended Charts tab displayed.

④ Click the chart type you want to use.

Ⓑ A preview of the chart appears here.

⑤ Click **OK**.

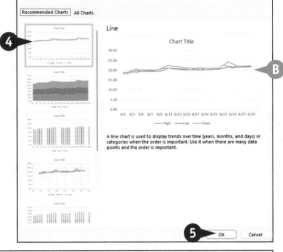

Ⓒ Excel inserts the chart.

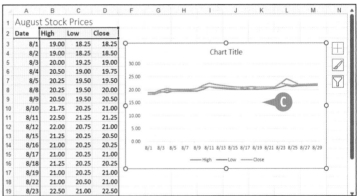

TIP

Is there a faster way to insert a recommended chart?

Yes, you can use the Quick Analysis feature in Excel:

① Select the data that you want to visualize in a chart, including the headings, if any.

② Click the **Quick Analysis** button (▣).

③ Click **Charts**.

Excel displays the chart types recommended for your data.

④ Click the chart type you want to use.

Excel inserts the chart.

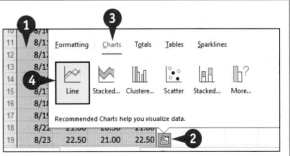

Add Chart Titles

You can make your chart easier to understand by adding chart titles, which are labels that appear in specific sections of the chart. When you include descriptive titles, people can see at a glance what your chart is visualizing.

There are three types of chart titles that you can add. The first type is the overall chart title, which usually appears at the top of the chart. You can also add a title for the horizontal axis to describe the chart categories, as well as a title for the vertical axis, which describes the chart values.

Add Chart Titles

1. Click the chart.
2. Click the **Chart Design** tab.
3. Click **Add Chart Element** (▯).
4. Click **Chart Title**.
5. Click **Above Chart**.

Ⓐ Excel adds the title box.

6. Type the title.

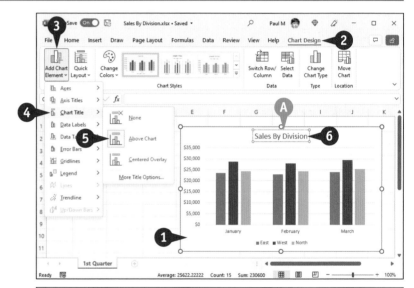

7. Click **Add Chart Element** (▯).
8. Click **Axis Titles**.
9. Click **Primary Horizontal**.

Ⓑ Excel adds the title box.

10. Type the title.
11. Click **Add Chart Element** (▯).
12. Click **Axis Titles**.
13. Click **Primary Vertical**.

Ⓒ Excel adds the title box.

14. Type the title.

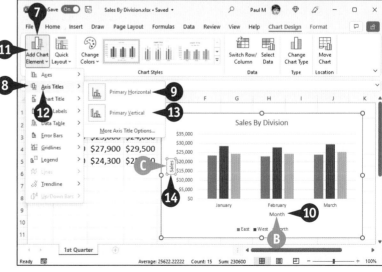

Add Data Labels

You can make your chart easier to read by adding data labels. A *data label* is a small text box that appears in or near a data marker and displays the value of that data point.

Excel offers several position options for the data labels, and these options depend on the chart type. For example, with a column chart you can place the data labels within or above each column, and for a line chart you can place the labels to the left or right, or above or below, the data marker.

Add Data Labels

1 Click the chart.

2 Click the **Chart Design** tab.

3 Click **Add Chart Element** (◫).

4 Click **Data Labels**.

5 Click the position you want to use for the data labels.

Note: Remember that the position options you see depend on the chart type.

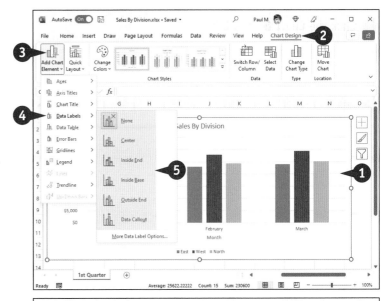

A Excel adds the labels to the chart.

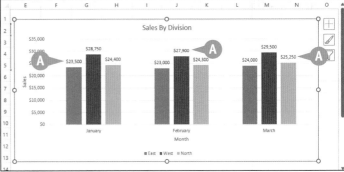

Position the Chart Legend

You can change the position of the chart *legend*, which identifies the colors associated with each data series in the chart. The legend is a crucial chart element for interpreting and understanding your chart, so it is important that you place it in the best position. For example, you might find the legend easier to read if it appears to the right of the chart. Alternatively, if you want more horizontal space to display your chart, you can move the legend above or below the chart.

Position the Chart Legend

1 Click the chart.

2 Click the **Chart Design** tab.

3 Click **Add Chart Element** (graphic).

4 Click **Legend**.

5 Click the position you want to use for the legend.

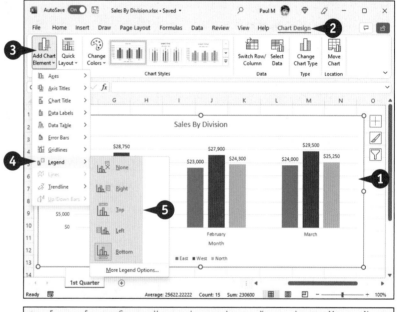

A Excel moves the legend.

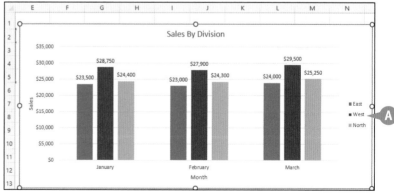

Display Chart Gridlines

You can make your chart easy to read and analyze by adding gridlines. Horizontal gridlines extend from the vertical (value) axis and are useful with area, bubble, and column charts. Vertical gridlines extend from the horizontal (category) axis and are useful with bar and line charts.

Major gridlines are gridlines associated with the *major units* (the values you see displayed on the vertical and horizontal axes), whereas *minor gridlines* are gridlines associated with the *minor units* (values between each major unit).

Display Chart Gridlines

1 Click the chart.

2 Click the **Chart Design** tab.

3 Click **Add Chart Element** (⬚).

4 Click **Gridlines**.

5 Click the horizontal gridline option you prefer.

Ⓐ Excel displays the horizontal gridlines.

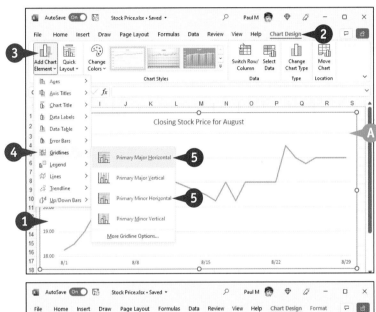

6 Click **Add Chart Element** (⬚).

7 Click **Gridlines**.

8 Click the vertical gridline option you prefer.

Ⓑ Excel displays the vertical gridlines.

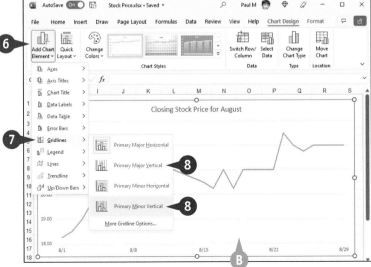

Display a Data Table

You can make it easy for yourself and others to interpret your chart by adding a data table. A *data table* is a tabular grid where each row is a data series from the chart, each column is a chart category, and each cell is a chart data point.

Excel gives you the option of displaying the data table with or without *legend keys*, which are markers that identify each series.

Display a Data Table

1 Click the chart.

2 Click the **Chart Design** tab.

3 Click **Add Chart Element** (⌷).

4 Click **Data Table**.

5 Click **With Legend Keys**.

Ⓐ If you prefer not to display the legend keys, click **No Legend Keys**.

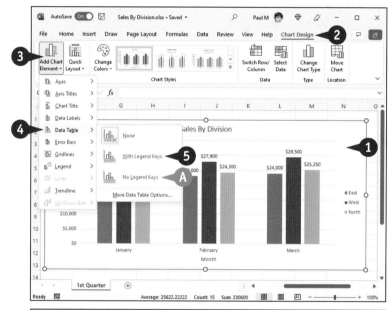

Ⓑ Excel adds the data table below the chart.

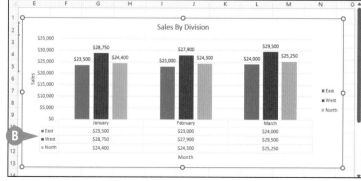

Change the Chart Layout and Style

You can quickly format your chart by applying a different chart layout and chart style. The chart layout includes elements such as the titles, data labels, legend, gridlines, and data table. The Quick Layouts feature in Excel enables you to apply these elements in different combinations with just a few mouse clicks. The chart style represents the colors used by the chart data markers and background.

Change the Chart Layout and Style

1 Click the chart.

2 Click the **Chart Design** tab.

3 Click **Quick Layout** (▦).

4 Click the layout you want to use.

A Excel applies the layout.

5 Click the **Chart Styles** (▾).

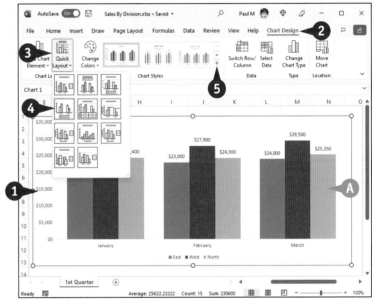

6 Click the chart style you want to use.

B Excel applies the style to the chart.

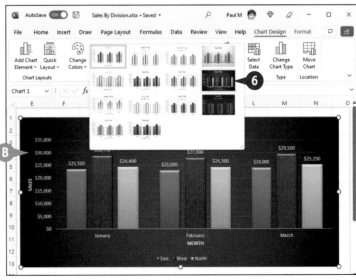

Select a Different Chart Type

If you feel that the current chart type is not showing your data in the best way, you can change the chart type. This enables you to experiment not only with the 16 different chart types offered by Excel, but also with its nearly 100 chart type configurations.

For example, if you are graphing a stock's high, low, and closing prices, a line chart shows you each value, but a stock chart gives you a better sense of the daily price movements. Similarly, if you are using a bar chart to show percentages of some whole, you would more readily visualize the data by switching to a pie chart.

Select a Different Chart Type

1 Click the chart.

2 Click the **Chart Design** tab.

3 Click **Change Chart Type** (⬛).

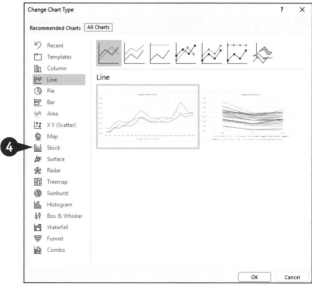

The Change Chart Type dialog box appears.

4 Click the chart type you want to use.

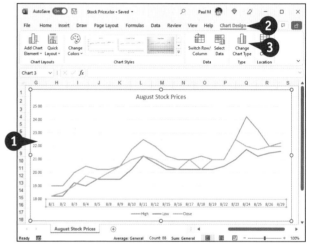

Excel displays the subtypes of the chart type you selected.

⑤ Click the subtype you want to use.

Excel displays the subtype configurations.

⑥ Click the configuration you want to use.

⑦ Click **OK**.

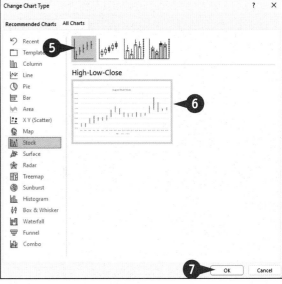

Ⓐ Excel applies the new chart type.

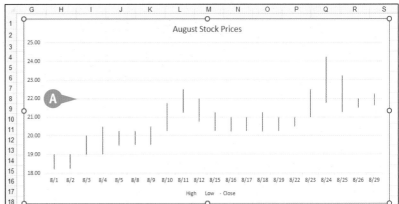

Change the Chart Source Data

In Excel, a chart's *source data* is the original range used to create the chart. You can keep your chart up-to-date and accurate by adjusting the chart when its source data changes.

You normally do this when the structure of the source data changes. For example, if the source range adds a row or column, you can adjust the chart to include the new data. However, you do not need to make any adjustments if just the data within the original range changes. In such cases, Excel automatically adjusts the chart to display the new data.

Change the Chart Source Data

1 Click the chart to select it.

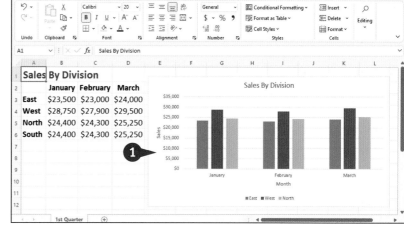

Ⓐ Excel selects the chart's source data.

2 Move the mouse ✥ over the lower-right corner of the range.

✥ changes to ↖.

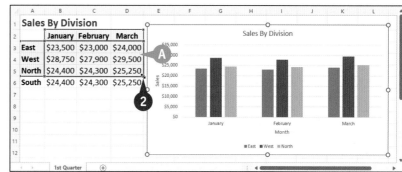

3 Click and drag ⬉ until the selection encompasses all the data you want to include in the chart.

B Excel extends the blue outline to show you the new selection.

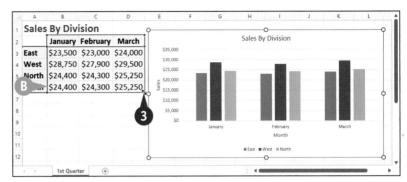

4 Release the mouse button.

C Excel redraws the chart to include the new data.

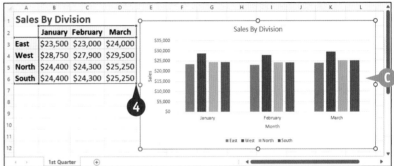

| TIPS |

Is there a way to swap the chart series with the chart categories without modifying the source data?

Yes. Excel has a feature that enables you to switch the row and column data, which swaps the series and categories without affecting the source data. First click the chart to select it, and then click the **Chart Design** tab. Click **Switch Row/Column** (⬛). Excel swaps the series and categories. Click ⬛ again to return to the original layout.

Is there a way to remove a series from a chart without deleting the data from the source range?

Yes. You can use the Select Data Source dialog box to remove individual series. Click the chart to select it, and then click the **Chart Design** tab. Click **Select Data** (⬛) to open the Select Data Source dialog box. In the **Legend Entries (Series)** list, click the series you want to get rid of, and then click **Remove**. Click **OK**.

Move or Resize a Chart

Y ou can move a chart to another part of the worksheet. This is useful if the chart is blocking the worksheet data or if you want the chart to appear in a particular part of the worksheet.

You can also resize a chart. For example, if you find that the chart is difficult to read, making the chart bigger often solves the problem. Similarly, if the chart takes up too much space on the worksheet, you can make it smaller.

Move or Resize a Chart

Move a Chart

1 Click the chart.

A Excel displays a border around the chart.

2 Move ⌖ over an empty area of the chart that is outside of the plot area.

⌖ changes to ✛.

Note: Do not position the mouse pointer over a corner or over the middle of any side of the border.

3 Click and drag the chart to the location you want.

4 Release the mouse button.

B Excel moves the chart.

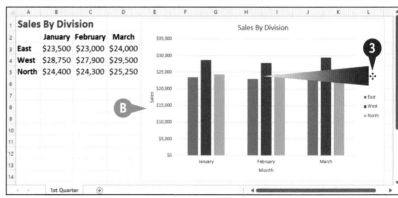

Resize a Chart

1 Click the chart.

C Excel displays a border around the chart.

D The border includes sizing handles on the corners and sides.

2 Move ⌖ over a sizing handle.

⌖ changes to ↔ (left or right), ↕ (top or bottom), or ⤢ (corner).

3 Click and drag the handle (the mouse pointer changes to + as you drag).

E Excel displays a gray outline of the new chart size.

4 Release the mouse button.

F Excel resizes the chart.

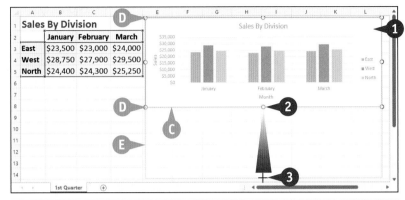

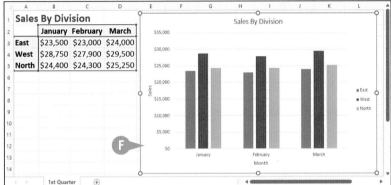

TIPS

Can I move a chart to a separate sheet?
Yes. In the "Create a Chart" section earlier in this chapter, you learned how to create a new chart in a separate sheet. If your chart already exists on a worksheet, you can move it to a new sheet. Click the chart, click the **Chart Design** tab, and then click **Move Chart** (⊞) to open the Move Chart dialog box. Select the **New sheet** option (○ changes to ◉). In the **New sheet** text box, type a name for the new sheet, and then click **OK.**

How do I delete a chart?
How you delete a chart depends on whether your chart exists as an object on a worksheet or in its own sheet. If the chart is on a worksheet, click the chart and then press `Delete`. If the chart exists on a separate sheet, right-click the sheet tab, click **Delete**, and then click **Delete.**

CHAPTER 15

Adding Worksheet Graphics

You can enhance the visual appeal and effectiveness of your Excel worksheets by incorporating graphic objects such as shapes, online images, pictures, or SmartArt graphics. This chapter shows you not only how to insert graphics on your worksheets, but also how to edit and format those graphics.

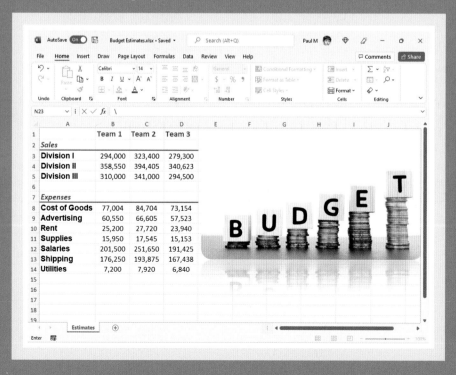

Draw a Shape

You can add visual appeal or enhance the readability of your worksheets by adding one or more shapes. The Excel Shapes gallery comes with more than 150 predefined objects called *shapes* (or sometimes *AutoShapes*) that enable you to quickly draw anything from simple geometric figures such as lines, rectangles, and ovals to more elaborate items such as starbursts, flowchart symbols, and callout boxes. You can add these shapes to a worksheet either to enhance the aesthetics of your data or to help other people read and understand your work.

Draw a Shape

1 Display the worksheet on which you want to draw the shape.

2 Click the **Insert** tab.

3 Click **Illustrations**.

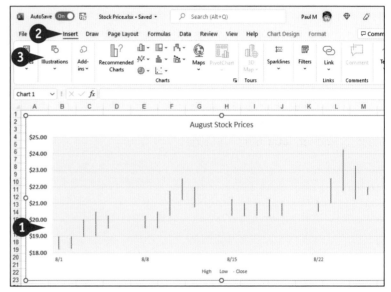

4 Click **Shapes** (⬭).

5 Click the shape you want to draw.

⬩ changes to ╋.

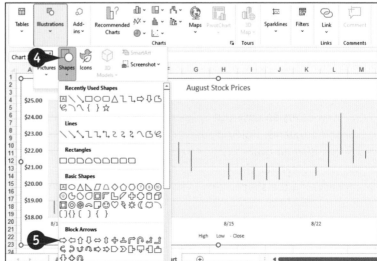

6 Click and drag the mouse **+** to draw the shape.

7 When the shape is the size you want, release the mouse button.

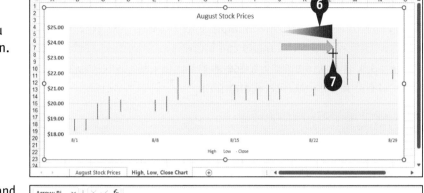

A The program draws the shape and adds sizing handles around the shape's edges.

Note: If you need to move or size the shape, see the "Move or Resize a Graphic" section later in this chapter.

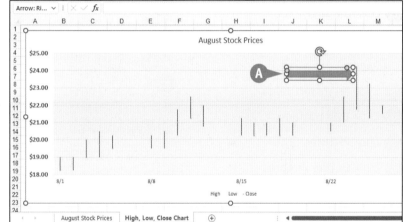

TIPS

Is there an easy way to draw a perfect circle or square?

Yes, Excel offers an easy technique for drawing circles and squares. Hold down the Shift key as you click and drag an oval or rectangle to constrain the shape into a perfect circle or square. When you finish drawing the shape, release the Shift key.

Can I add text to a shape?

Yes. You can add text to the interior of any 2-D shape (that is, any shape that is not a line). After you draw the shape, right-click the shape, click **Edit Text**, and then type your text inside the shape. You can use the Home tab's Font controls to format the text. When you finish, click outside of the shape.

Insert an Online Image

You can improve the look of an Excel worksheet by adding an online image to the sheet. Online images are photos, illustrations, or other artwork that you can insert into your documents. Excel does not come with its own images, but it does give you access to online image collections that contain thousands of images from various categories, such as animals, money, flowers, and people. By default, these images are licensed under Creative Commons (see the first tip), so you can use them without charge.

Insert an Online Image

1 Display the worksheet on which you want to insert the clip art image.

2 Click the cell where you want the upper-left corner of the image to appear.

3 Click the **Insert** tab.

4 Click **Illustrations**.

5 Click **Pictures** (⊡).

6 Click **Online Pictures**.

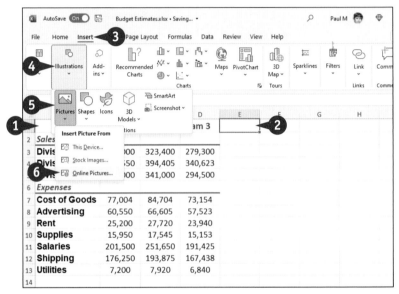

The Online Pictures window appears.

7 Use the text box to type a word that describes the kind of clip art image you want to insert.

A Alternatively, click one of the displayed categories.

8 Press Enter.

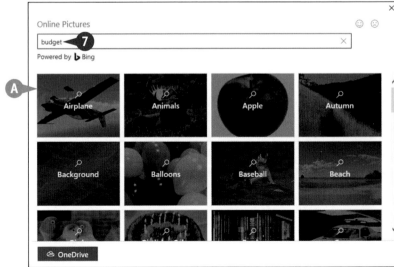

Ⓑ Excel displays a list of online images that match your search term.

❾ Click the online image you want to use.

Note: To insert multiple images, click each image you want to use.

❿ Click **Insert**.

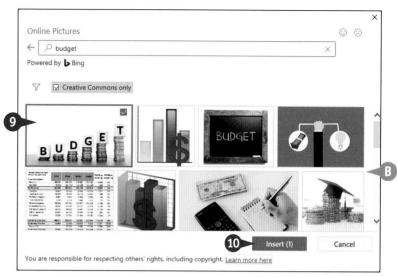

Ⓒ Excel inserts the clip art.

Ⓓ This link takes you to the website that is the source of the image.

Note: If you need to move or size the clip art, see the "Move or Resize a Graphic" section later in this chapter.

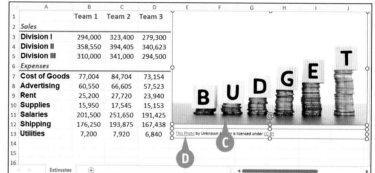

What is a Creative Commons license?
Creative Commons (see http://creativecommons. org) is a nonprofit organization that enables artists to license their works for other people to use free of charge. There are several different Creative Commons licenses, so you should visit the website that offers the image you select to check the specifics of the license.

Is there a way to narrow my search for online images?
Yes. Above the search results, click **Filter** (▽) and use the menu that appears to narrow your search. For example, in the Size section, you can click Small to see only small images; in the Type section, click the type of image you want, such as Photograph or Line drawing; in the Layout section, select your preferred image layout, such as Square.

Insert a Photo from Your PC

You can enhance the visual appeal and strengthen the message of an Excel worksheet by adding a photo to the file.

Excel can work with the most popular picture formats, including BMP, JPEG, TIFF, PNG, and GIF. This means that you can insert almost any photo that you have stored on your computer. If you would like to insert a photo that is located online instead, see the tips in the previous section, "Insert an Online Image."

Insert a Photo from Your PC

1 Open the worksheet where you want to insert the photo.

2 Click the cell where you want the upper-left corner of the photo to appear.

3 Click the **Insert** tab.

4 Click **Illustrations**.

5 Click **Pictures**.

6 Click **This Device**.

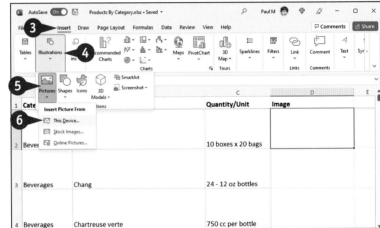

The Insert Picture dialog box appears.

7 Open the folder that contains the photo you want to insert.

8 Click the photo.

9 Click **Insert**.

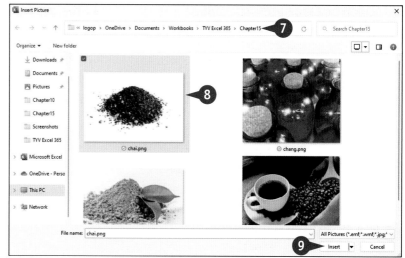

Ⓐ Excel inserts the photo into the worksheet.

Note: If you need to move or size the photo, see the "Move or Resize a Graphic" section later in this chapter.

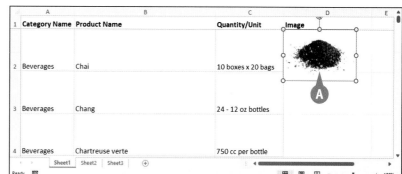

TIPS

My photo has a distracting background. Can I remove it?

Yes. Excel comes with a Background Removal feature that can eliminate the background in most photos. Click the photo, click the **Picture Format** tab, and then click **Remove Background** (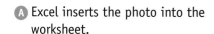). If part of the foreground is in the removal color, click **Mark Areas to Keep** and then click and drag a line through the part you want to retain. When you are finished, click **Keep Changes**.

Is there a way to reduce the size of a workbook that has a lot of photos?

Yes, you can use the Compress Pictures feature to convert the photos to a lower resolution and so reduce the size of the workbook. Click any image in the workbook, click the **Picture Format** tab, and then click **Compress Pictures** (🖾). Click **Apply only to this picture** (☑ changes to ☐), click a **Resolution** (◯ changes to ◉), and then click **OK**.

Insert a SmartArt Graphic

You can add a SmartArt graphic to a workbook to help present information in a compact, visual format. A SmartArt graphic is a collection of *nodes* — shapes with some text inside — that enables you to convey information visually.

For example, you can use a SmartArt graphic to present a company organization chart, the progression of steps in a workflow, the parts that make up a whole, and much more.

Insert a SmartArt Graphic

1 Open the worksheet in which you want to insert the SmartArt graphic.

2 Click the **Insert** tab.

3 Click **Illustrations**.

4 Click **SmartArt** (🖼️).

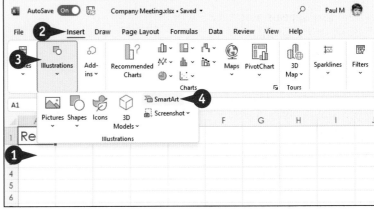

The Choose a SmartArt Graphic dialog box appears.

5 Click a SmartArt category.

6 Click the SmartArt style you want to use.

7 Click **OK**.

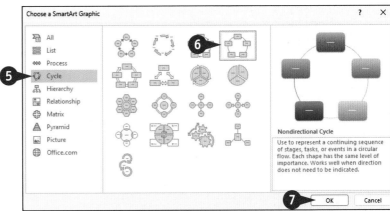

Ⓐ The SmartArt graphic appears in the document.

Ⓑ You use the Text pane to type the text for each node and to add and delete nodes.

8 Click a node in the Text pane.

9 Type the text that you want to appear in the node.

Ⓒ The text appears automatically in the associated shape.

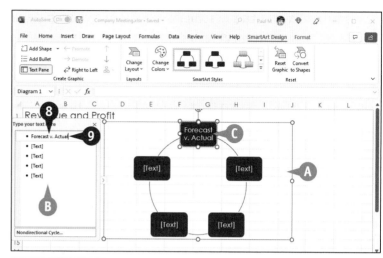

10 Repeat steps **8** and **9** to fill in the other nodes in the SmartArt graphic.

Ⓓ In the SmartArt Design tab, you can click **Text Pane** (⊞) to hide the Text pane.

Note: You will likely have to move the SmartArt graphic into position; see the following section, "Move or Resize a Graphic."

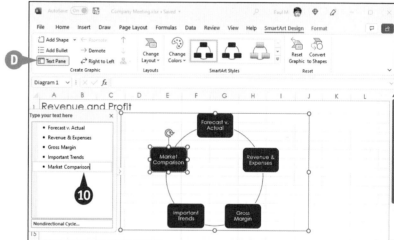

TIPS

How do I add a node to my SmartArt graphic?
To add a node to the SmartArt graphic, first decide where you want that node to appear in the current image. That is, decide which existing node you want the new node to come before or after. Click the existing node, click the **SmartArt Design** tab, click the ⌄ beside **Add Shape** (⊡), and then click **Add Shape After**. (If you want the new node to appear before the existing node, click **Add Shape Before**.)

Can I use shapes other than the ones supplied in the default SmartArt graphics?
Yes. Begin by clicking the node you want to change. Click the **Format** tab, and then click **Change Shape** (⬡) to display the Shapes gallery. Click the shape you want to use. Excel updates the SmartArt graphic node with the new shape.

Move or Resize a Graphic

To ensure that a graphic is ideally placed within an Excel worksheet, you can move the graphic to a new location or you can resize the graphic in its current location. For example, you might want to move or resize a graphic so that it does not cover existing worksheet data. Similarly, you might want to move or resize a graphic so that it is positioned near a particular worksheet element or fits within an open worksheet area. You can move or resize any graphic, including shapes, illustrations, photos, and SmartArt graphics.

Move or Resize a Graphic

Move a Graphic

1 Move the mouse pointer over an edge of the graphic you want to move.

The mouse ⊕ changes to ⊹.

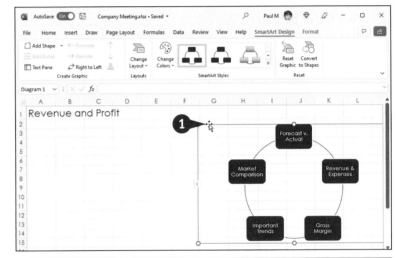

2 Drag the graphic to the location you prefer.

A Excel moves the graphic to the new location.

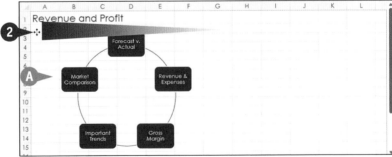

Resize a Graphic

1 Click the graphic.

B Sizing handles appear around the edges.

2 Move the mouse ✛ over a sizing handle.

C Use a left or right handle (✛ changes to ↔) to adjust the width.

D Use a top or bottom handle (✛ changes to ↕) to adjust the height.

E Use a corner handle (✛ changes to ⤢) to adjust the two sides adjacent to the corner.

3 Drag the sizing handle (the mouse pointer changes to ✚).

4 Release the mouse button when the handle is in the position you want.

F Excel resizes the graphic.

5 Repeat steps 2 to 4 to resize other sides of the graphic, as necessary.

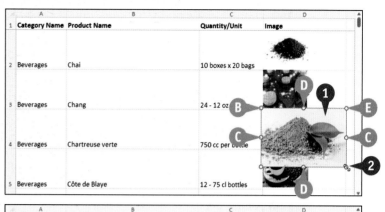

TIPS

Can I rotate a graphic?

Yes. Most graphic objects come with a rotate handle. Follow these steps:

1 Move the mouse ✛ over the rotate handle (↻).

2 Click and drag the rotate handle clockwise or counterclockwise to rotate the graphic.

3 Release the mouse button when the graphic is in the position you want.

Is it possible to resize a graphic in all directions at once to keep the proportions the same?

Yes. You normally resize one side at a time by dragging a side handle, or two sides at a time by dragging a corner handle. To resize all four sides at once, hold down the Ctrl key and then click and drag any corner handle.

Format a Picture

You can enhance your shapes, online images, photos, and SmartArt graphics by formatting the images. For example, Excel offers more than two dozen picture styles, which are predefined formats that apply various combinations of shadows, reflections, borders, and layouts.

Excel also offers a dozen picture effects, which are preset combinations of special effects such as glows, soft edges, bevels, and 3-D rotations.

Format a Picture

Apply a Picture Style

1 Click the picture you want to format.

2 Click the **Picture Format** tab.

3 Click the **Picture Styles** ⮟.

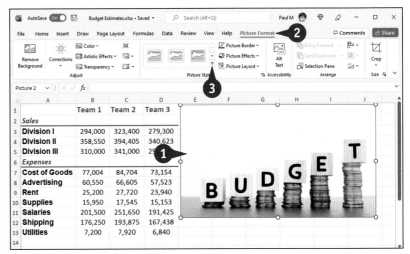

Ⓐ Excel displays the Picture Styles gallery.

4 Click the picture style you want to use.

Ⓑ Excel applies the style to the picture.

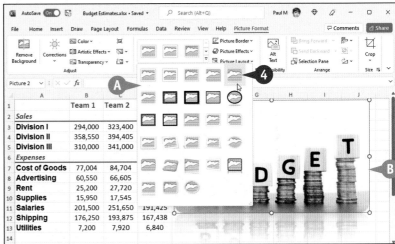

Apply a Picture Effect

1 Click the picture you want to format.

2 Click the **Picture Format** tab.

3 Click the **Picture Effects** button (⌀).

Note: If the image is a shape, the ⌀ button is named **Shape Effects** in the **Shape Format** tab.

4 Click **Preset**.

5 Click the effect you want to apply.

C Excel applies the effect to the picture.

Note: To change an image but preserve any formatting you've applied, click the existing picture, click the **Picture Format** tab, click **Change Picture** (⌧), then click the method you want to use.

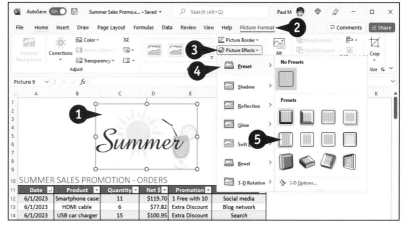

TIPS

Can I crop an image?
Yes. To crop out unwanted elements of an image, click the image, click the **Picture Format** tab, then click the **Crop** button (⌐). Excel adds crop handles around the image. Click and drag one or more crop handles to define the part of the image you want to keep, then click ⌐.

If I do not like the formatting that I have applied to a picture, can I return the picture to its original look?
Yes. If you have not performed any other tasks since applying the formatting, click **Undo** (↺) until Excel has removed the formatting. Alternatively, click the **Picture Format** tab, click **Picture Effects** (⌀), click **Preset**, and then click the icon in the **No Presets** section. To reverse all the changes you have made to a picture since you inserted the image, click the picture, click **Picture Format**, and then click **Reset Picture** (⌧).

CHAPTER 16

Collaborating with Others

If you want to collaborate with other people on a workbook, Excel gives you several ways to do this, including adding comments, marking up a workbook with a digital pen, and even working on a spreadsheet online. You can also control your collaborations by protecting worksheet data and a workbook's structure.

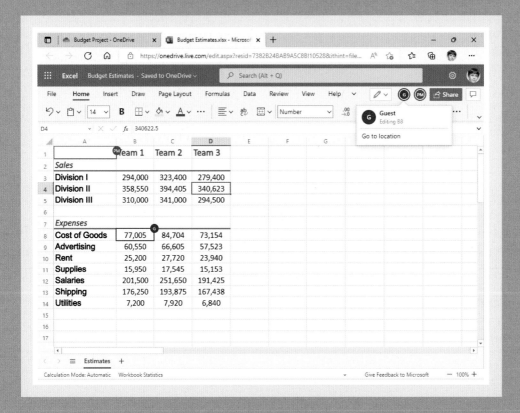

Add a Comment to a Cell

If you have received a workbook from another person, you can provide feedback to that person by adding a comment to a cell in the workbook. A comment is often the best way to provide corrections, questions, critiques, and other feedback because it does not change anything on the actual worksheet.

Each comment is attached to a particular cell, and Excel uses a comment indicator to mark which cells have comments. When you view a comment, Excel displays the comment in a pop-up window. You can also use the Comments pane to view all the comments in a worksheet.

Add a Comment to a Cell

Add a Comment

1 Click the cell you want to comment on.

2 Click the **Review** tab.

3 Click **New Comment** (🗨).

Note: You can also right-click the cell and then click **New Comment**.

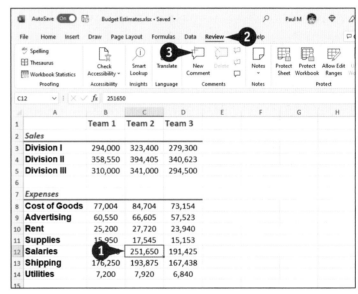

Excel displays a comment window.

Ⓐ Excel labels the comment with your Excel username.

Note: See the second tip to learn how to change your Excel username.

4 Type your comment.

5 Click **Post** (➤).

6 Click outside the comment window.

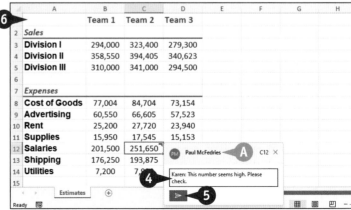

Ⓑ Excel adds a comment indicator (🚩) to the top-right corner of the cell.

View Comments

① Move the mouse ⬥ over the cell.

Ⓒ Excel displays the comment in a window.

Ⓓ In the Review tab, you can also click **Next** (🗨) and **Previous** (🗨) to run through the comments.

Ⓔ In the Review tab, you can also click **Show Comments** (🗨) or click **Comments** to display the Comments task pane, which includes every comment in the current worksheet.

TIPS

Can I edit or remove a comment?
Yes. To edit an existing comment, move the mouse ⬥ over the cell, click **Edit** in the comment window, edit the comment text, and then click **Save**. To remove a comment, click the cell that contains the comment, click the **Review** tab, and then click **Delete** (🗨) in the Comments group.

How do I change my Excel username?
When collaborating, your username is important because it tells other people who added the comments. To change it, click **File** and then click **Options** to open the Excel Options dialog box. Click the **General** tab and then use the **User name** text box to edit the name. Click **OK**, then save, close, and reopen your workbook to put the change into effect. Note, however, that this does not change your username in any existing comments.

Protect a Worksheet's Data

If you will be distributing a workbook to other people, you can enable the options in Excel for safeguarding worksheet data by activating the sheet's protection feature. You can also configure the worksheet to require a password to unprotect it.

There are two main methods you can use to safeguard worksheet data: You can unlock only those cells that users are allowed to edit, and you can configure a range to require a password before it can be edited.

Protect a Worksheet's Data

1 Display the worksheet you want to protect.

2 Click the **Review** tab.

3 Click **Protect Sheet** (⊞).

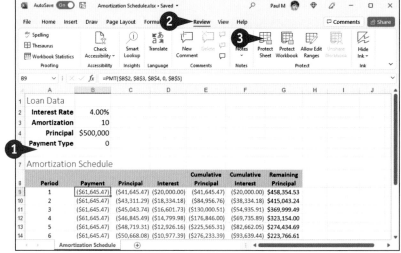

Excel displays the Protect Sheet dialog box.

4 Use the **Password to unprotect sheet** text box to type a password.

5 Make sure the **Protect worksheet and contents of locked cells** check box is selected (☑).

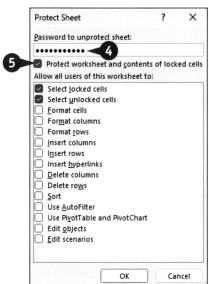

6 Click the check box beside each action that you want to allow unauthorized users to perform (☐ changes to ✅).

7 Click **OK**.

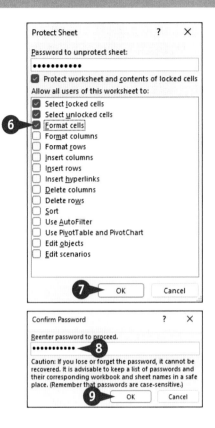

Excel asks you to confirm the password.

8 Type the password.

9 Click **OK**.

If you want to make changes to a worksheet, click the **Review** tab, click **Unprotect Sheet** (▦), type the unprotect password, and then click **OK**.

TIPS

When I protect a worksheet, no one can edit any of the cells. Is there a way to allow users to edit some of the cells?

Yes. This is useful if you have a data entry area or other range that you want other people to be able to edit but you do not want them to alter any other part of the worksheet. First, unprotect the sheet if it is currently protected. Select the range you want to unlock, click **Home**, click **Format**, and then click **Lock Cell** to turn off that option for the selected range.

When I protect a worksheet, can I configure a range to require a password before a user can edit the range?

Yes. First, unprotect the sheet if it is currently protected. Select the range you want to protect, click the **Review** tab, and then click **Allow Edit Ranges** (▦). In the Allow Users to Edit Ranges dialog box, click **New** to open the New Range dialog box. Type a title for the range, use the **Range password** text box to type a password, and then click **OK**. When Excel prompts you to reenter the password, type the password, click **OK**, and then click **OK** again.

Protect a Workbook's Structure

Y ou can prevent unwanted changes to a workbook by activating protection for the workbook's structure. You can also configure the workbook to require a password to unprotect it.

Protecting a workbook's structure means preventing users from inserting new worksheets, renaming or deleting existing worksheets, moving or copying worksheets, hiding or unhiding worksheets, and more. See the tips to learn which commands Excel disables when you protect a workbook's structure.

Protect a Workbook's Structure

1 Display the workbook you want to protect.

2 Click the **Review** tab.

3 Click **Protect Workbook** (⊞).

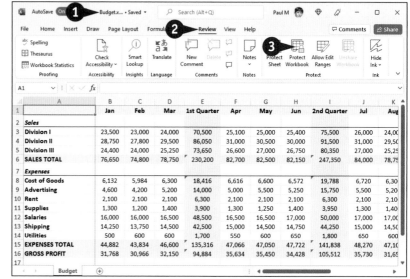

Excel displays the Protect Structure and Windows dialog box.

4 Type a password in the **Password** text box, if required.

5 Click the **Structure** check box (☐ changes to ☑).

6 Click **OK**.

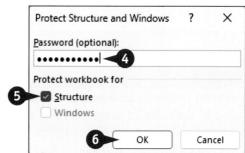

If you specified a password,
Excel asks you to confirm it.

7 Type the password.

8 Click **OK**.

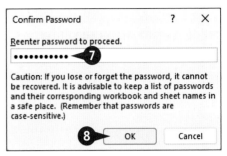

A Excel disables most worksheet-related commands on the Ribbon.

B Excel disables most worksheet-related commands on the worksheet shortcut menu.

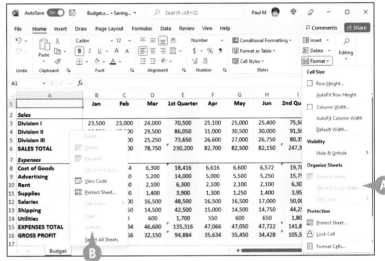

What happens when I protect a workbook's structure?

Excel disables most worksheet-related commands, including Insert Sheet, Delete Sheet, Rename Sheet, Move or Copy Sheet, Tab Color, Hide Sheet, and Unhide Sheet. Excel also prevents the Scenario Manager from creating a summary report.

How do I remove workbook structure protection?

If you no longer require your workbook structure to be protected, you can remove the protection by following steps **1** to **3**. If you protected your workbook with a password, type the password and then click **OK**. Excel removes the workbook's structure protection.

Save a Workbook to Your OneDrive

If you are using Windows under a Microsoft account, then as part of that account you get a free online storage area called *OneDrive*. You can use Excel to add any of your workbooks to your OneDrive. This is useful if you are going to be away from your computer but still require access to a workbook. Because OneDrive is accessible anywhere you have web access, you can view and work with your spreadsheet without using your computer.

Save a Workbook to Your OneDrive

1 Open the workbook you want to save to your OneDrive.

2 Click the **File** tab.

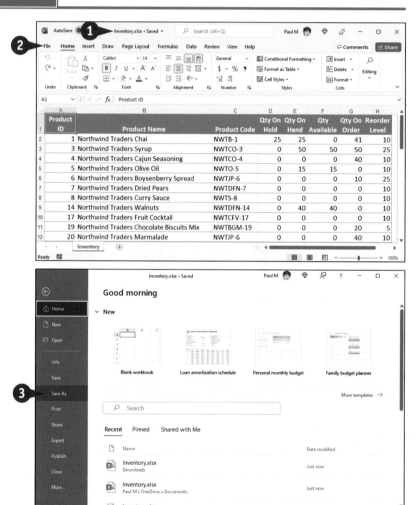

3 Click **Save As**.

The Save As tab appears.

4 Click **OneDrive**.

5 Click the OneDrive folder you want to use to store the workbook.

A If you want to use a subfolder to store the workbook, click the subfolder.

6 Click **Save**.

Excel saves the workbook to your OneDrive.

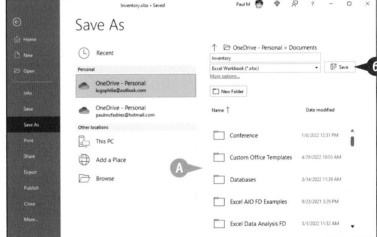

TIP

How do I open a workbook that has been saved to my OneDrive?

Follow these steps:

1 Click the **File** tab.

2 Click **Open**.

3 Click **OneDrive**.

4 Click the OneDrive folder that contains the workbook.

5 Click the workbook.

Excel opens the OneDrive workbook.

Send a Workbook as an Email Attachment

I f you want to send an Excel workbook to another person, you can attach the workbook to an email message and send it to that person's email address.

A typical email message is fine for short notes, but you may have something more complex to communicate, such as budget numbers or a loan amortization. Instead of trying to copy that information to an email message, you can send the recipient a workbook that contains the data. That way, the other person can then open the workbook in Excel after receiving your message.

Send a Workbook as an Email Attachment

1 Open the workbook you want to send.

2 Click the **File** tab.

Ⓐ Alternatively, click **Share** (🖻) and skip to step **4**.

3 Click **Share**.

Excel displays the Share dialog box.

④ Click **Excel Workbook**.

Share

×

Please upload your workbook to share it.

OneDrive - Personal
logophilia@outlook.com

Attach a copy instead

④

Excel
Workbook

PDF

A new Outlook email message appears.

Ⓑ Outlook attaches the workbook to the message.

⑤ In the To field, start typing the name of the recipient.

⑥ Click the recipient when they appear in the search results.

Note: Alternatively, you can type the email address of the recipient in the To field.

⑦ Type your message text.

⑧ Click **Send**.

Outlook sends the message.

TIPS

Are there any restrictions related to sending file attachments?

There is no practical limit to the number of workbooks you can attach to a message. However, you should be careful with the total size of the files you send. If you or the recipient has a slow Internet connection, sending or receiving the message can take an extremely long time. Also, many Internet service providers (ISPs) place a limit on the size of a message's attachments, which is usually between 2 and 20MB.

What can I do if the recipient does not have Excel?

If the other person does not use Excel, you can send the workbook in a different format. One possibility would be to save the workbook as a web page (see the following section, "Save Excel Data as a Web Page"). Alternatively, if your recipient can view PDF (Portable Document Format) files, follow steps **1** to **3** to display the Share dialog box, and then click **PDF**.

Save Excel Data as a Web Page

I f you have an Excel range, worksheet, or workbook that you want to share on the web, you can save that data as a web page that you can then upload to your website.

When you save a document as a web page, you can also specify the title text that appears in the browser's title bar and the keywords that search engines use to index the page. You can also choose whether you want to publish the entire workbook to the web, just a single worksheet, or just a range of cells.

Save Excel Data as a Web Page

1 Open the workbook that contains the data you want to save as a web page.

A If you want to save a worksheet as a web page, click the worksheet tab.

B If you want to save a range as a web page, select the range.

2 Click the **File** tab.

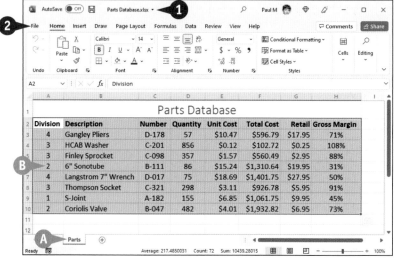

3 Click **Save As**.

Note: If your workbook is stored on your OneDrive, click **Save a Copy** instead.

4 Click **This PC**.

5 Click **More options**.

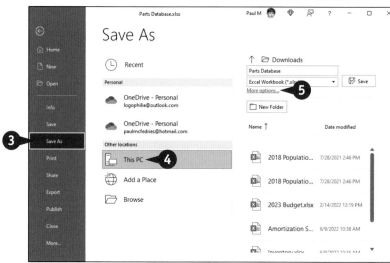

The Save As dialog box appears.

6 Click the **Save as type** ⌄ and then click **Web Page**.

7 Select the folder where you want to store the web page file.

8 Click **Change Title**.

The Enter Text dialog box appears.

9 Type the page title in the **Page title** text box.

10 Click **OK**.

11 Click **Tags** and then type one or more keywords, separated by semicolons.

12 Choose which part of the file you want to save as a web page (◯ changes to ◉):

C Click **Entire Workbook** to save the whole workbook.

D Click **Selection** to save either the current worksheet or the selected cells.

13 Click **Save**.

14 If you see a dialog box warning you that some workbook features might be lost, click **Yes** (not shown).

Excel saves the data as a web page.

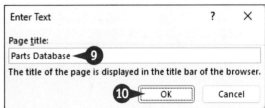

TIP

If I make frequent changes to the workbook, do I have to go through this procedure after every change?

No, you can configure the workbook to automatically save your changes to the web page file. This is called AutoRepublish. To set it up, follow steps **1** to **11** to get the workbook ready for the web and then click **Publish**. In the Publish as Web Page dialog box, click **AutoRepublish every time this workbook is saved** (☐ changes to ☑). Click **Publish**. Excel saves the workbook as a web page and will now update the web page file each time you save the workbook.

Make a Workbook Compatible with Earlier Versions of Excel

You can save an Excel workbook in a special format that makes it compatible with earlier versions of Excel. This enables you to share your workbook with other Excel users.

If you have another computer that uses a version of Excel prior to Excel 2007, or if the people you work with use earlier Excel versions, those programs cannot read documents in the standard format used by Excel 2007 and later versions of the program. By saving a workbook using the Excel 97-2003 Workbook file format, you make that file compatible with earlier Excel versions.

Make a Workbook Compatible with Earlier Versions of Excel

1 Open the workbook you want to make compatible.

2 Click **File**.

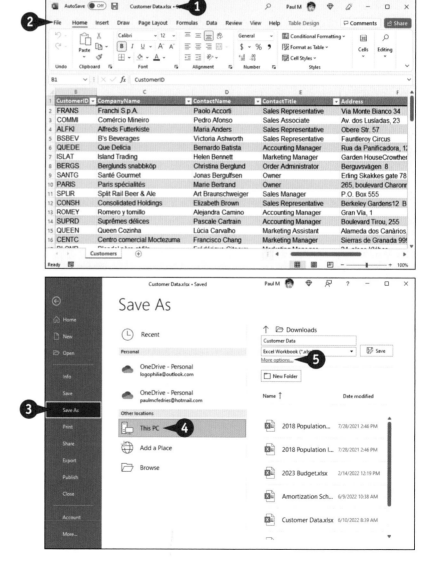

3 Click **Save As**.

Note: If your workbook is stored on your OneDrive, click **Save a Copy** instead.

4 Click **This PC**.

5 Click **More options**.

The Save As dialog box appears.

6 Select the folder in which you want to store the new workbook.

7 Click in the **File name** text box and type the name that you want to use for the new workbook.

8 Click the **Save as type** ⌄.

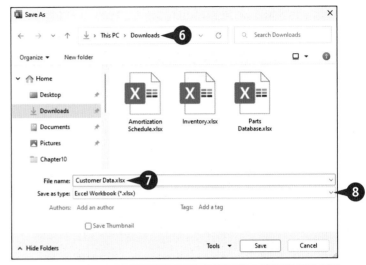

9 Click the **Excel 97-2003 Workbook** file format.

10 Click **Save**.

11 If you see the Compatibility Checker dialog box, click **Continue** (not shown).

Excel saves the file using the Excel 97-2003 Workbook format.

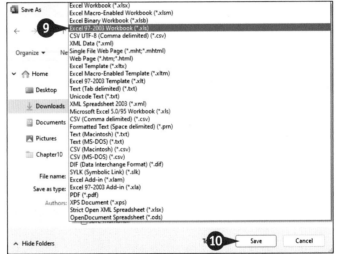

TIPS

Can people using Excel 2019, Excel 2016, Excel 2013, Excel 2010, or Excel 2007 open my Excel 365 workbooks?

Yes. The default file format used by all versions of the program since Excel 2007 is the same as the one used by Excel 365. If you only work with people who use these Excel versions, then you should stick with the default file format — which is called Excel Workbook — because it offers many benefits in terms of Excel features.

Which versions of Excel are compatible with the Excel 97-2003 Workbook file format?

For Windows, the Excel 97-2003 Workbook file format is compatible with Excel 97, Excel 2000, Excel XP, and Excel 2003. For the Mac, the Excel 97-2003 Workbook file format is compatible with Excel 98, Excel 2001, and Office 2004. In the unlikely event that you need to share a document with someone using either Excel 5.0 or Excel 95, use the Microsoft Excel 5.0/95 Workbook file format instead.

Mark Up a Worksheet with Digital Ink

Excel comes with a digital ink feature that enables you to give feedback by marking up a worksheet with pen marks and highlights. This is often easier than adding comments or cell text.

To use digital ink on a worksheet, it is easiest if you have either a tablet PC or an external graphics tablet connected to your PC, each of which comes with a pressure-sensitive screen. You can then use a digital pen — or sometimes your finger — to draw directly on the screen, a technique known as *digital inking*. However, you can also use a mouse to mark up a worksheet with digital ink.

Mark Up a Worksheet with Digital Ink

Change Input Mode to Draw

1 Tap the **Draw** tab.

Note: If you do not see the Draw tab, right-click the Ribbon, click **Customize the Ribbon**, click the **Draw** check box (☐ changes to ☑), and then click **OK**.

2 Tap **Draw** (✐).

Note: You only see the Draw button if you have a touch screen or tablet. If you do not see this button, you can still go ahead with the rest of the steps in this section.

Excel changes to draw input mode and enables the drawing tools.

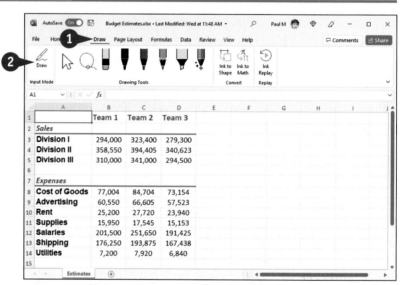

Mark Up with a Pen

1 Tap the **Draw** tab.

2 Tap the drawing tool you want to use.

3 Tap the selected drawing tool's ∨.

4 Tap a dot to set the drawing thickness.

5 Tap a swatch to set the drawing color.

6 Use your digital pen (or your finger or mouse) to write your marks or text on the worksheet.

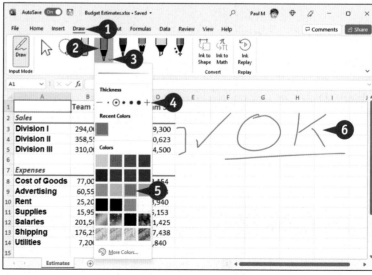

Mark Up with a Highlighter

1 Tap the **Draw** tab.

2 Tap **Highlighter** (🖊).

3 Click the **Highlighter** ⌄ to select a highlighter color and thickness.

4 Use your digital pen (or your finger or mouse) to highlight the worksheet text.

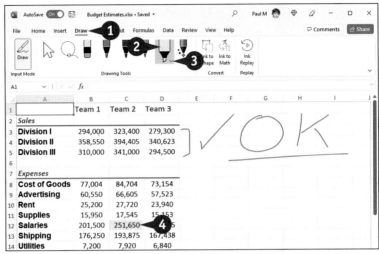

Erase Digital Ink

1 Tap the **Draw** tab.

2 Tap **Eraser** (🖊).

3 Use your digital pen (or your finger or mouse) to tap the ink you want to remove.

Excel erases the ink.

Note: You can also click the **Review** tab, click the **Hide Ink** ⌄, and then click either **Delete All Ink on Sheet** (🗒) or **Delete All Ink in Workbook** (📄).

Ⓐ When you no longer need to mark up the worksheet with digital ink, tap **Draw** (✏).

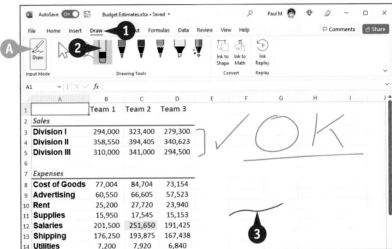

TIP

Is there a way to hide a worksheet's digital ink without deleting that ink?
Yes. This is a good idea if you want to show the worksheet to other people but you do not want them to see the digital ink, either because it contains sensitive information or because it makes the worksheet harder to read. To toggle your digital ink off and on, click the **Review** tab and then click **Hide Ink** (📝).

Collaborate on a Workbook Online

If you have a Microsoft account, you can use the OneDrive feature to store an Excel workbook in an online folder (see the "Save a Workbook to Your OneDrive" section earlier in this chapter) and then allow other users to collaborate on that workbook using the Excel for the Web app.

Collaboration here means that you and the other users can edit the workbook online at the same time. To allow another person to collaborate with you on your online workbook, it is not necessary that the person have a Microsoft account. However, you can make your online workbooks more secure by requiring collaborators to have a Microsoft account.

Collaborate on a Workbook Online

1 Use a web browser to navigate to https://onedrive.live.com.

Note: If you are not already logged in, you are prompted to log on to your Microsoft account.

Your OneDrive appears.

2 Click the folder that contains the workbooks you want to share.

3 Click **Share**.

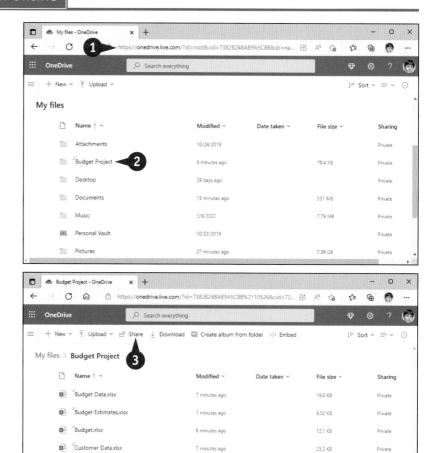

The Send Link dialog box appears.

4 In the To field, start typing the name of the recipient.

5 Click the recipient when they appear in the search results.

Note: Alternatively, you can type the email address of the recipient in the To field.

6 Repeat steps **4** and **5** as needed to share the folder with multiple people.

7 Type a message to the user.

8 Click **Send**.

OneDrive sends an email message to the user. The user clicks the link in that message, optionally logs on with a Microsoft account, and can then edit a workbook in the shared folder.

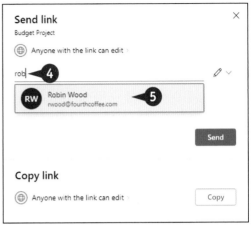

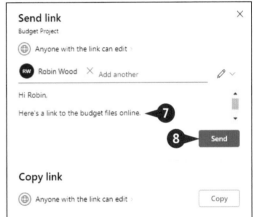

TIP

How do I know when other people are also using a workbook online?

When you open a workbook using the Excel for the Web app, examine the upper-right corner of the Excel screen. If to the left of the Share button (⬛) you see one or more icons with initials, each of those icons represents another person who is collaborating on the workbook with you. To see who they are, click an icon (Ⓐ). Excel displays the person's name (or Guest if the person does not have a Microsoft account, as shown here) and which cell the person is currently editing.

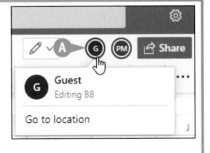

Index

Symbols

+ (addition) operator, 100, 101

, (comma), 175

=<<=>>=<> (comparison), 101

/ (division) operator, 101

! (exclamation mark), 115

= (equal to), 101

^ (exponentiation) operator, 101

> (greater than), 101

>= (greater than or equal to), 101

< (less than), 101

<= (less than or equal to), 101

* (multiplication) operator, 100, 101

<> (not equal to), 101

() (parentheses), 101

% (percentage) operator, 101

' (single quotation marks), 115

- (subtraction/negation) operator, 101

A

absolute cell references, 118–119

access, to external data, 169

Access tables, 168

accuracy, of range names, 52

adding

    background color to ranges, 78–79

    borders to ranges, 94–95

    chart titles, 246, 252

    charts, 5

    column subtotals, 196–197

    columns of numbers, 109

    comments to cells, 280–281

    data, 4

    data labels, 253

    fields

        to columns area in PivotTables, 209

        to data area in PivotTables, 210–211

        to row area in PivotTables, 208–209

    formulas, 4

    functions

        about, 4

        to formulas, 106–107

    nodes to SmartArt graphics, 273

    range names to formulas, 108–109, 112–113

    rows of numbers, 109

    text to shapes, 267

    workbook footers, 164–165

    workbook headers, 162–163

    worksheet graphics. *See* graphics

aligning text within cells, 49, 72–75

alphanumeric values, filling ranges with, 30–31

analyzing data. *See* data analysis

Apply Names feature, 113

applying

    conditional formats to ranges, 84–85

    font effects, 68–69

    number formats, 80–81

    picture effects, 277

    picture styles, 276

    PivotTable filters, 216–217

    styles to ranges, 86–87

    table styles, 199

    workbook themes, 160–161

area chart, 247

arithmetic formulas, 101

array formula, 227

assigning names to ranges, 61

AutoComplete, troubleshooting, 15

Autofill feature, 30–31

AutoFit feature, 89, 91

AutoSum formulas, building, 110–111

AVERAGE() function, 4, 105

B

backgrounds

    adding color to ranges, 78–79

    picture, 271

bar chart, 247

benefits, of range names, 52–53

borders, adding to ranges, 94–95

box & whisker chart, 247

break-even analysis, 233